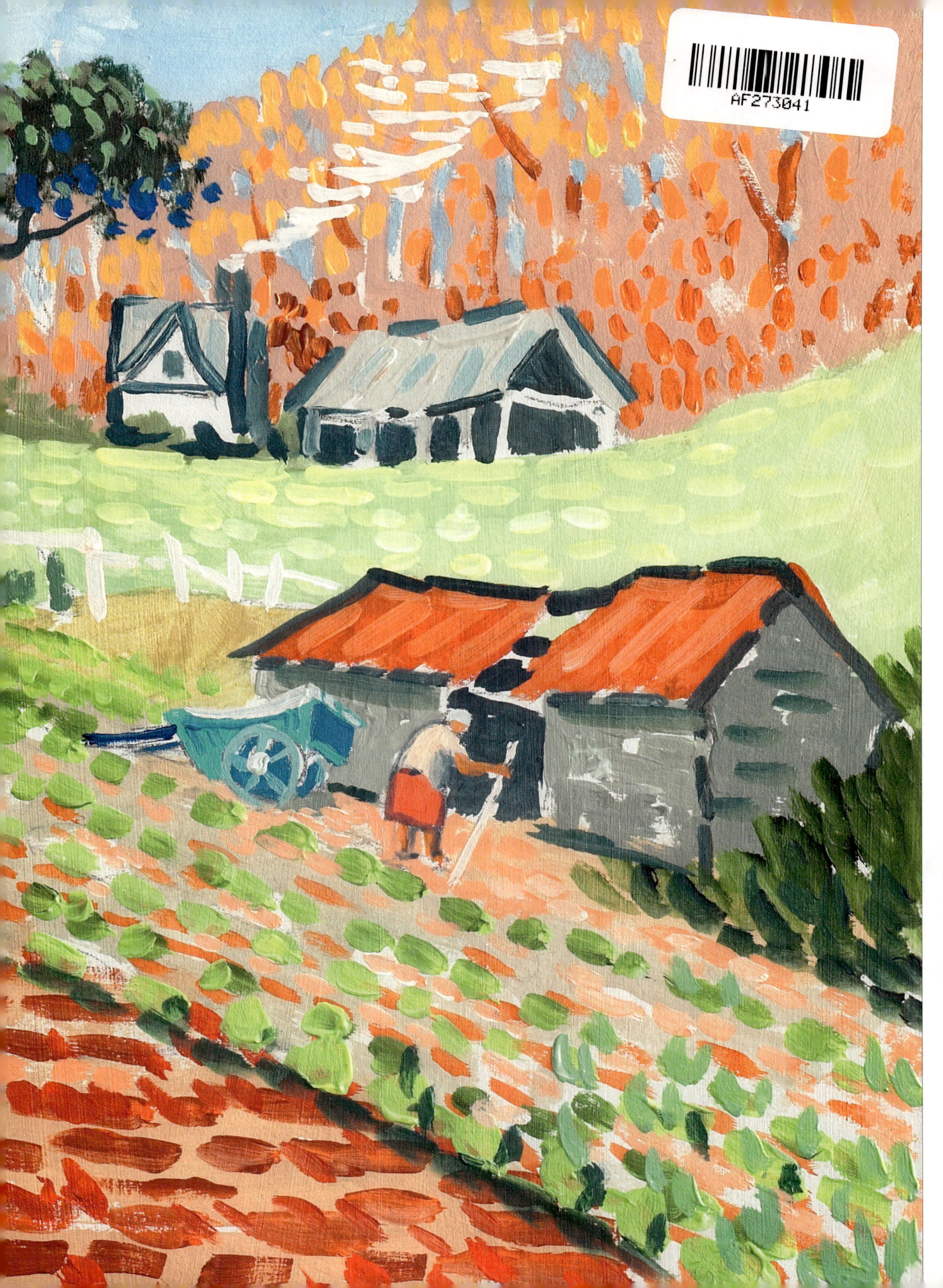

Index

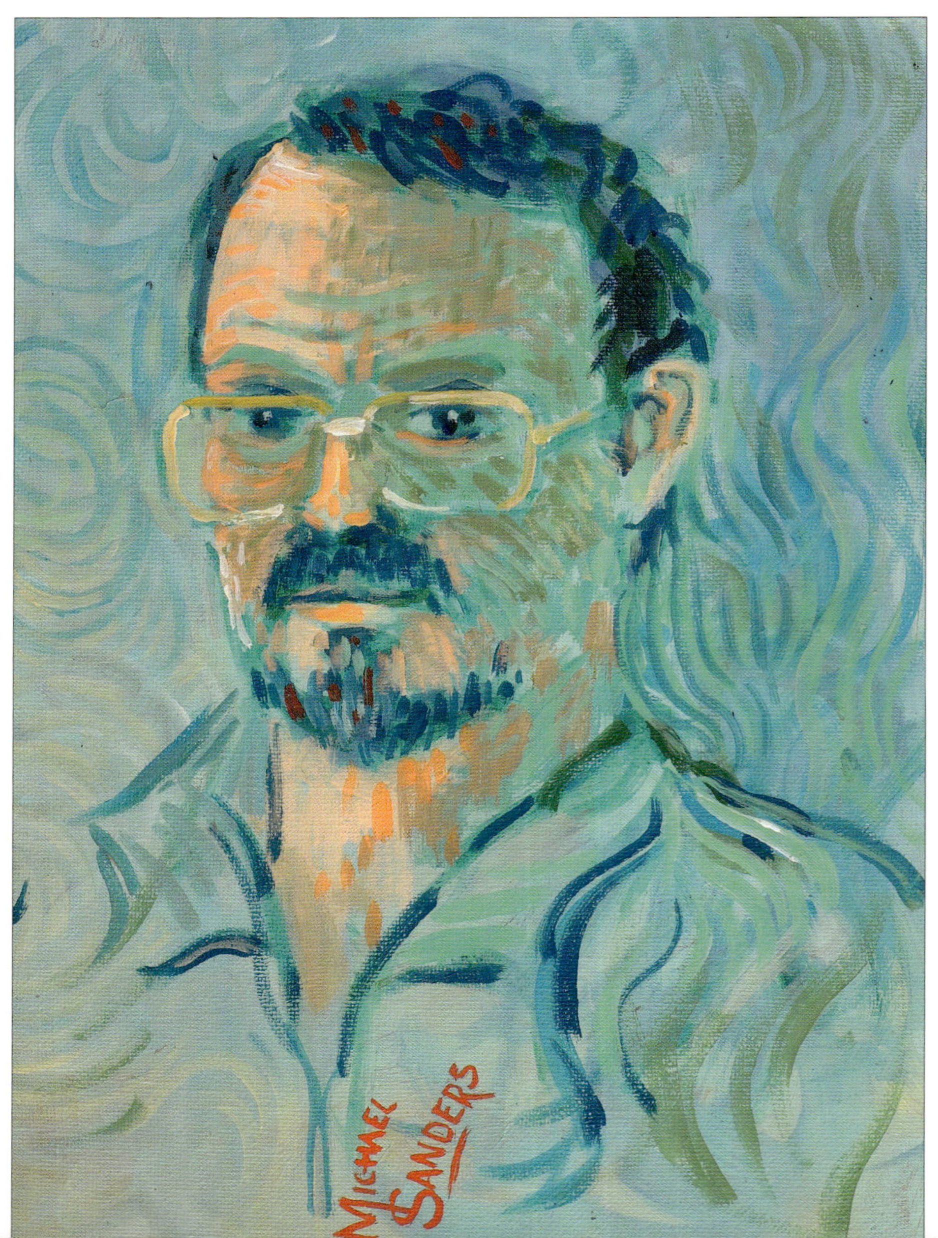

Self Portrait

210 x 290mm (8¼ x 11³⁄₈in)

Van Gogh painted many self portraits, and I have painted my image using a similar range of colours and swirling background shapes as the one shown on page 7. For this, he chose a lilac jacket and waistcoat which 'had faded somewhat', to make himself look more presentable; I wore a green and blue stripy shirt to fit in with the background. The swirls are possibly meant to denote the movement of foliage, blown by the strong wind of the Mistral. If you want to try a self portrait, it is easier if you work from a photograph, rather than a mirror.

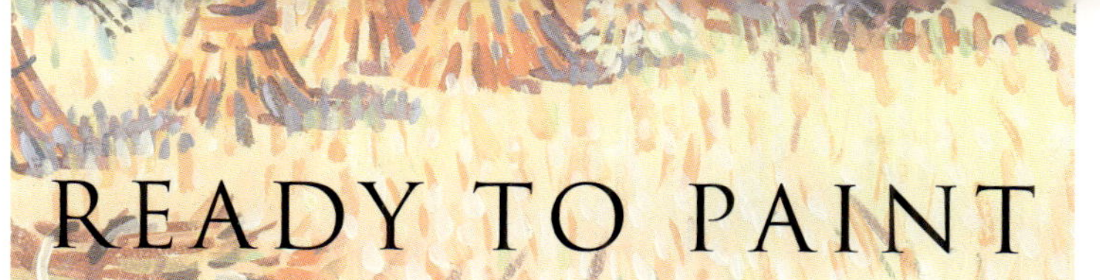

Van Gogh in Acrylics

Michael Sanders

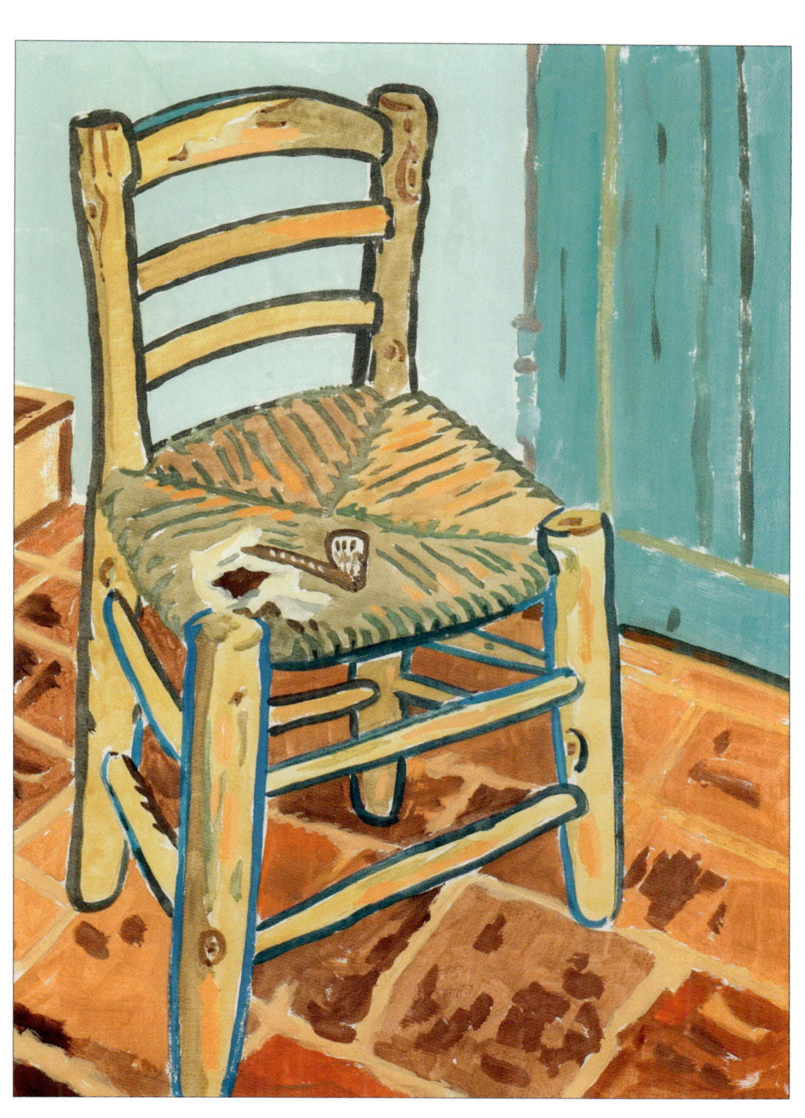

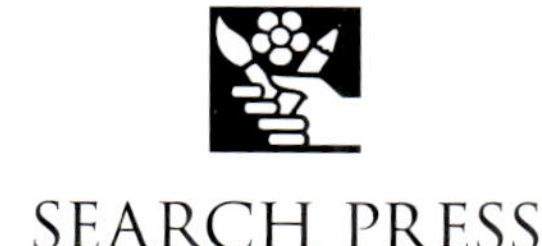

SEARCH PRESS

First published in Great Britain 2010

Search Press Limited
Wellwood, North Farm Road,
Tunbridge Wells, Kent TN2 3DR

Text copyright © Michael Sanders 2010

Photographs by Roddy Paine Photographic Studios

Photographs and design copyright © Search Press Ltd 2010

ISBN: 978-1-84448-454-6

The Publishers and author can accept no responsibility for any
consequences arising from the information, advice or instructions given
in this publication.

Readers are permitted to reproduce any of the tracings or paintings
in this book for their personal use, or for the purposes of selling
for charity, free of charge and without the prior permission of the
Publishers. Any use of the tracings or paintings for commercial
purposes is not permitted without the prior permission of
the Publishers.

Suppliers
If you have any difficulty obtaining any of the materials and equipment
mentioned in this book, please visit the Search Press website:
www.searchpress.com

Publisher's note
All the step-by-step photographs in this book feature the author,
Michael Sanders, demonstrating acrylic painting. No models have
been used.

**Please note: when removing the perforated sheets of tracing paper
from the book, score them first, then carefully pull out each sheet.**

Printed in China

Dedication
I would like to dedicate this book to you, the artist.
That's what you are, because, whenever you pick up
a brush in order to put some colours on a surface to
make a pleasing image, you become, by definition,
an artist. Enjoy this book, have fun doing the step-by-
step projects, and I hope it inspires you to carry on
painting. There's plenty of room in this world for more
artists; glad you could join us!

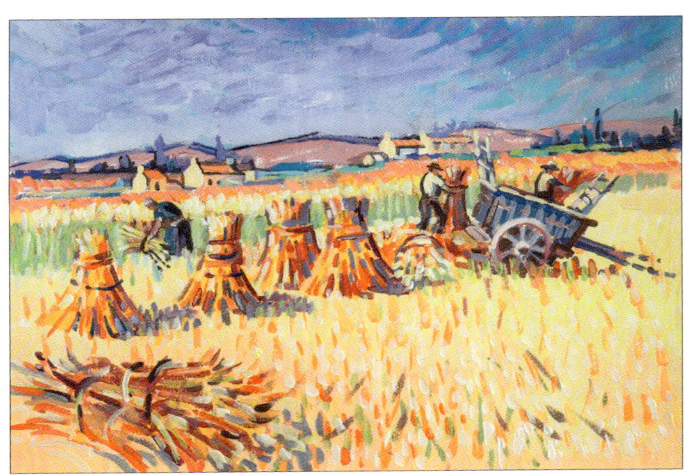

Acknowledgements
Thanks to all at Search Press for giving me the
opportunity to get involved in this exciting project.
Thanks especially to Roz, Sophie, Juan and Gavin.

Page 1

Chair With Pipe

295 x 418mm (11⅝ x 16½in)

*This version of Van Gogh's 1888 original appears as a step-by-step
demonstration on pages 22–29.*

Above

Harvest Scene

423 x 300mm (16⅝ x 11¾)

*This composition of my own includes several motifs that inspired
Van Gogh. Figures labouring in the sun, with strong orange and red strokes
placed among sheaves of wheat, create a hot feel. This is set against cooler
background hills.*

Contents

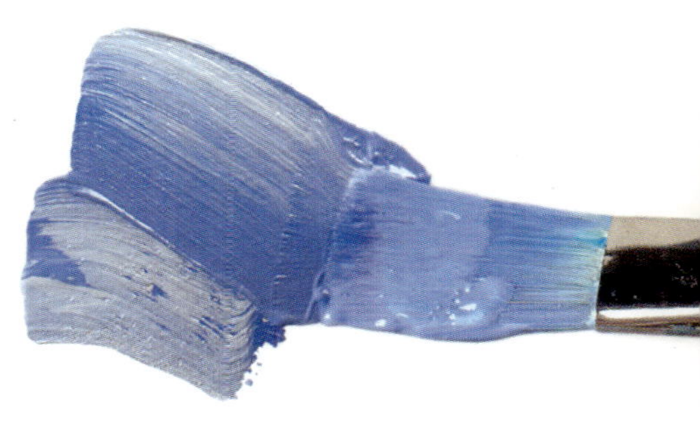

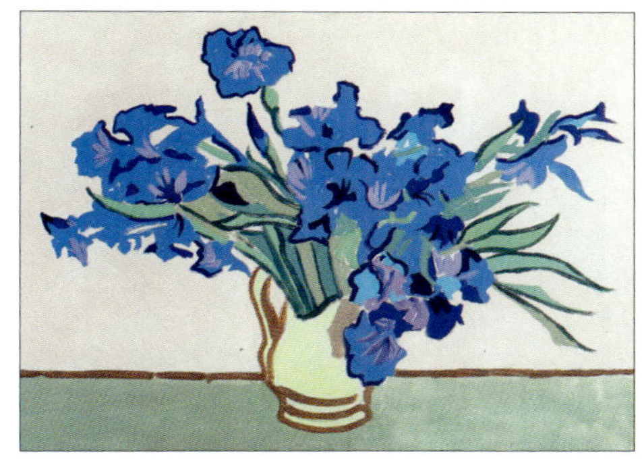

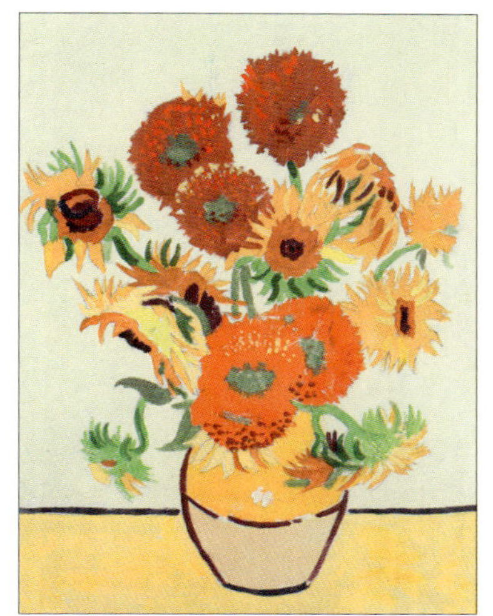

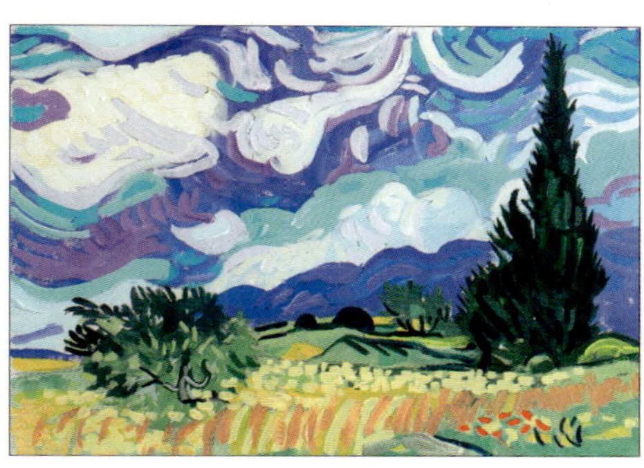

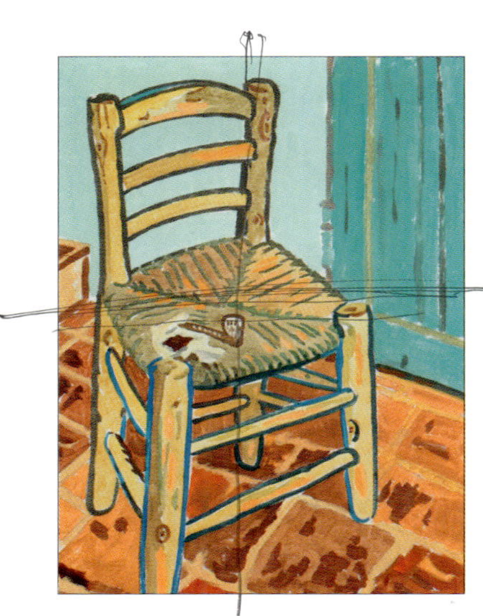

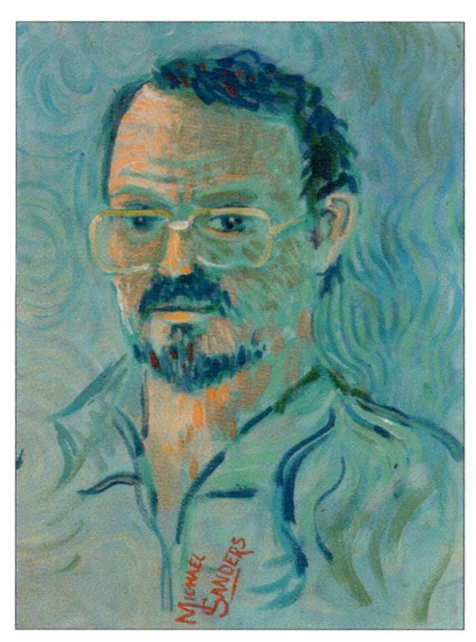

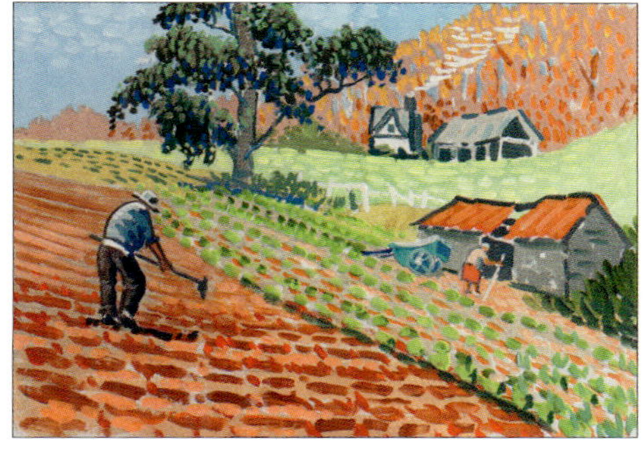

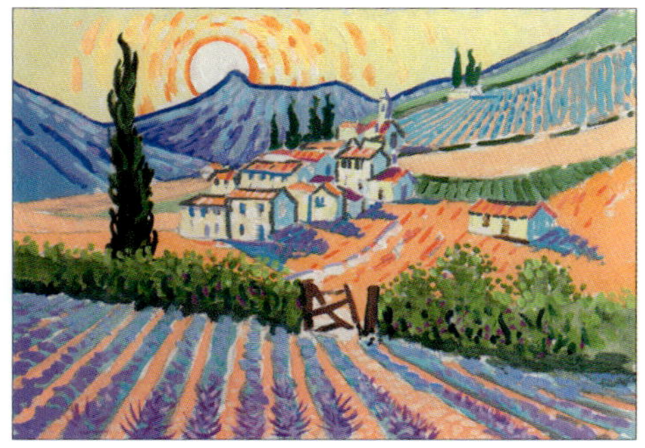

Introduction

The traditional way to become a painter has always been to spend some time studying the works of the old masters and to make copies of some of them. This book gives you the chance to do just that! I have made it easier for you by making detailed tracings, so you can leave out the drawing stage and get a feel for the direction of brush strokes, even if you have never tried painting like this before.

I was very excited by the chance to do this book. Vincent Van Gogh was an inspiration for me from the time I first became interested in art; his work, although over 100 years old, remains vibrant and modern looking. I have painted my own versions of some of the paintings, and also some of my own images using Van Gogh's style. Using acrylic paint instead of oils means that the work dries more quickly and the paint is not smelly or difficult to use.

We are going to paint some of Van Gogh's best-loved works of art, and, as you follow the steps, you will begin to develop an idea of how the direction of a brush stroke or the choice of a colour makes a difference, and how the artist's 'look' can be achieved.

Bear in mind that acrylics dry quite quickly, so make sure that you have a couple of jars of water handy; one to dip into if you want to dilute the paint, another to put the brushes into so they do not dry out. Never leave a brush with paint in it for very long; your brush could be ruined if the paint dries. The other thing to remember is that acrylic paint dries slightly darker. Allow for this by mixing colours so that they are slightly paler than shown in this book; (usually, using a little more white, or yellow).

While researching the colours for these paintings, I had three books showing the same image and each portrayed it in different colours! So, if you find that your colours are slightly different to mine, do not worry. The only person who could accurately describe the mixing of the colours in these paintings would have been Vincent himself.

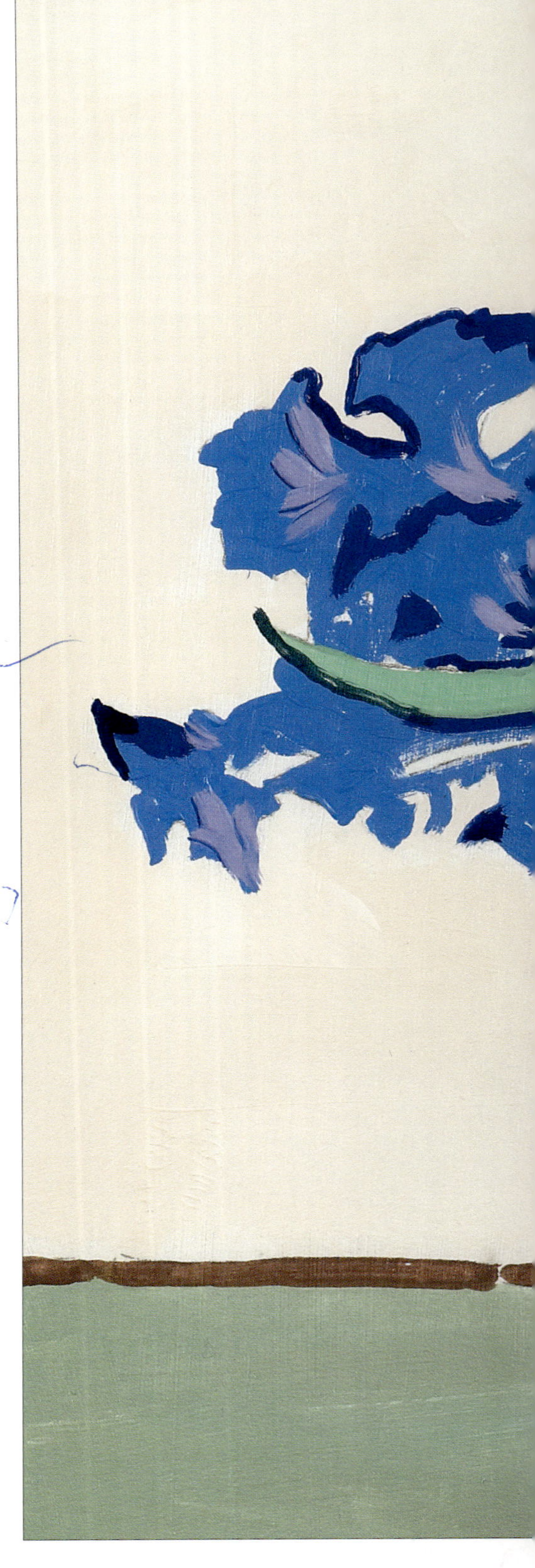

Vase With Irises
295 x 418mm (11⅝ x 16½in)

Van Gogh painted several versions of the painting, and this is my version of one of them. Since painting this, I have discovered that the background was originally a pale pink, but has faded to the neutral cream tone we see today. Several of the versions had white or yellow jugs, and a line across near the bottom to define the edge of a table, or to serve as a stabilising influence. Van Gogh was interested in oriental art and design, and this influence is echoed in the strong, sinuous shapes of the leaves; an element also found in the Art Nouveau decorative style of the period.

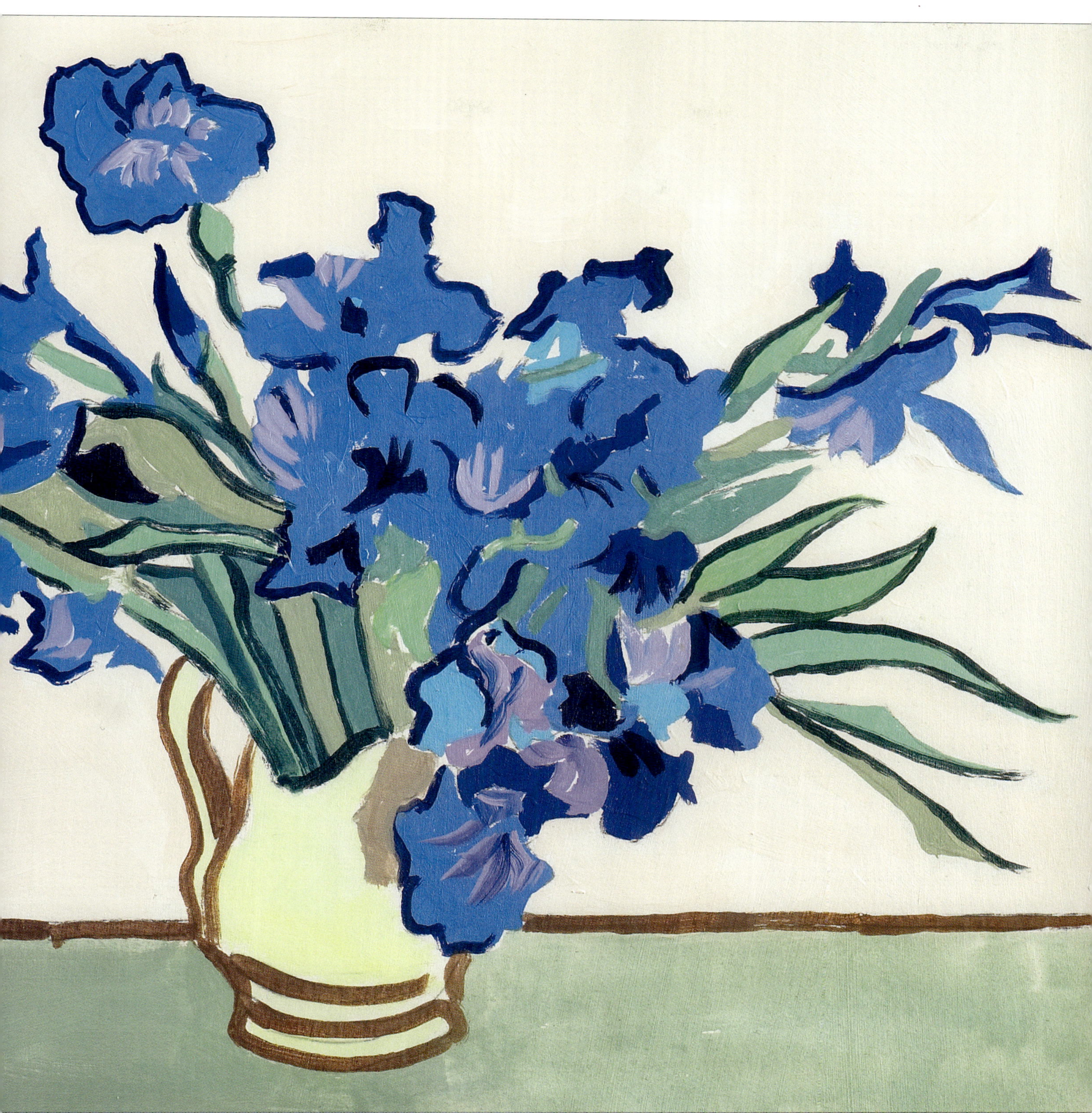

TRACING
1

Van Gogh

Vincent Van Gogh (1853–1890) is one of the world's most famous and collectable artists. In addition to producing some of the most iconic and memorable images ever painted, he almost single-handedly became responsible for the modern-day image of the struggling artist; the tortured genius. Amazingly, although his artistic endeavour spanned less than ten years, he produced a body of work that remains one of the most popular, exhilarating and enduring in all of art. The vibrant, vigorous brush strokes describing luminous fields of corn, labourers in the countryside, swirling clouds with cypress trees, and intense sunflowers will be familiar to almost everyone with even the slightest interest in art. It is even more extraordinary when you realise that many of these wonderful paintings were done while the artist was in a hospital or asylum.

A native of the Netherlands and the son of a pastor, Vincent's road to becoming an artist was fraught and circuitous. His life before becoming a full-time painter included several years as an apprentice art dealer in the Hague, London and Paris; studying theology; assisting a Methodist minister in Isleworth, near London, England; and working as a lay preacher in the impoverished coal mining area of Borinage, Belgium. The drab colours of the mines found their way into his early work, and living among poverty and deprivation, and sketching his surroundings, influenced his later images of peasants toiling.

His move to Paris in 1886 brought him into contact with many influential and avant-garde artists, including impressionists such as Pissarro, Gauguin, and Toulouse-Lautrec. It was this intense, two-year period that transformed Van Gogh from a mainly traditional artist into an avant-garde experimenter. During this time, he completed over two hundred canvases, including almost thirty self portraits. His palette changed from the earthy, dark tones of his earlier work to vibrant and light colours; intense oranges, reds and greens were applied with a vigorous passion.

It was, however, the 'other kind of light' of Provence in southern France that was to inspire him to produce work at a breathtaking rate. He was at Arles for a mere fifteen months (1888–1889), but there he painted his best work: over 200 paintings, most of them out of doors, and more than 100 watercolours and sketches. He also wrote over 200 letters, mostly to his brother and supporter, Theo. In his own words, he was 'In a constant state of feverish work'. He seems to have laboured in the fields in the Provençal heat until the point of exhaustion, identifying himself with the harvest and the toiling peasants he was portraying. Pushing the boundaries both of acceptable subjects and his own technique, he went on to produce images of night scenes, including the famous *Night Café*. Other famous iconic images from this period include a series of sunflowers, painted from fresh flowers at one sitting, 'before they fade'.

The bright vibrancy of these paintings belies a troubled mind, however. No one knows quite what happened on that night just before Christmas 1888 in Arles. All we know now for sure is that Van Gogh used a cut-throat razor to sever part of his ear. He was found the following day by police who broke into the house he had been sharing with the artist Gauguin. He was in bed, weakened and delirious, and was taken to hospital. This may or may not have marked the start of his mental decline, but, in the weeks following, even in considerable pain, he continued to paint.

Following a petition from neighbours, he was taken to an asylum, where he continued to paint feverishly. Works from this period include *Starry Night*, which he thought was unsuccessful and too abstract, and the cypress tree series, with swirling strokes of dark green and bright yellow cornfields, set against wavy clouds. Several more 'attacks' followed, leaving him dejected and disillusioned, but still continuing to paint.

In 1890 Van Gogh was living in Auvers, north of Paris, in the care of Dr Gachet, an amateur painter with a wide circle of friends including the artists Cézanne, Monet and Renoir and other notable creative people. Working fast and spontaneously, Van Gogh was to produce about seventy paintings here, in the two months before his death. During the harvest time he again produced studies of landscapes, with corn stacked in rows, and atmospheric skies, but now the human presence was minimal. Paintings from this period, weeks before his death, convey Vincent's love of nature, but his loneliness is dramatically conveyed by the emptiness of the panoramas. Not a soul appears to inhabit these last brooding landscapes. Whether the dark and dramatic *Wheat Field With Crows* was in fact Van Gogh's last painting remains unclear. All we know for sure is, on the night of 27th July 1890, returning to his room he was seen to be in pain. A local doctor was called and Vincent informed him and Dr Gachet that he had shot himself in the chest. Gachet sent a message to Theo Van Gogh, who rushed out and was with Vincent when he died, on 29th July, 1890.

He was buried the following day, in a small cemetery at the edge of some fields. Theo, his brother and financial supporter, was dead by the following January. We have Theo's wife, Johanna, to thank for establishing Vincent Van Gogh's reputation, initially in the Netherlands, France and Germany, and eventually worldwide. Within fifteen years of his death, Vincent's paintings were already fetching high prices in the art market. More than this however, his work became an inspiration for the new avant-garde, and made movements such as expressionism and fauvism possible. Today, over 100 years since his death, standing in front of an original Van Gogh painting is an awe-inspiring experience. It is possible to feel the presence of genius like a force of nature, wonder at the fluidity of brush stroke and directness of line, and be moved. If you get the chance to visit a gallery and see any of his work for yourself, I urge you to do it. Prints and posters are fine, but the originals are extraordinary.

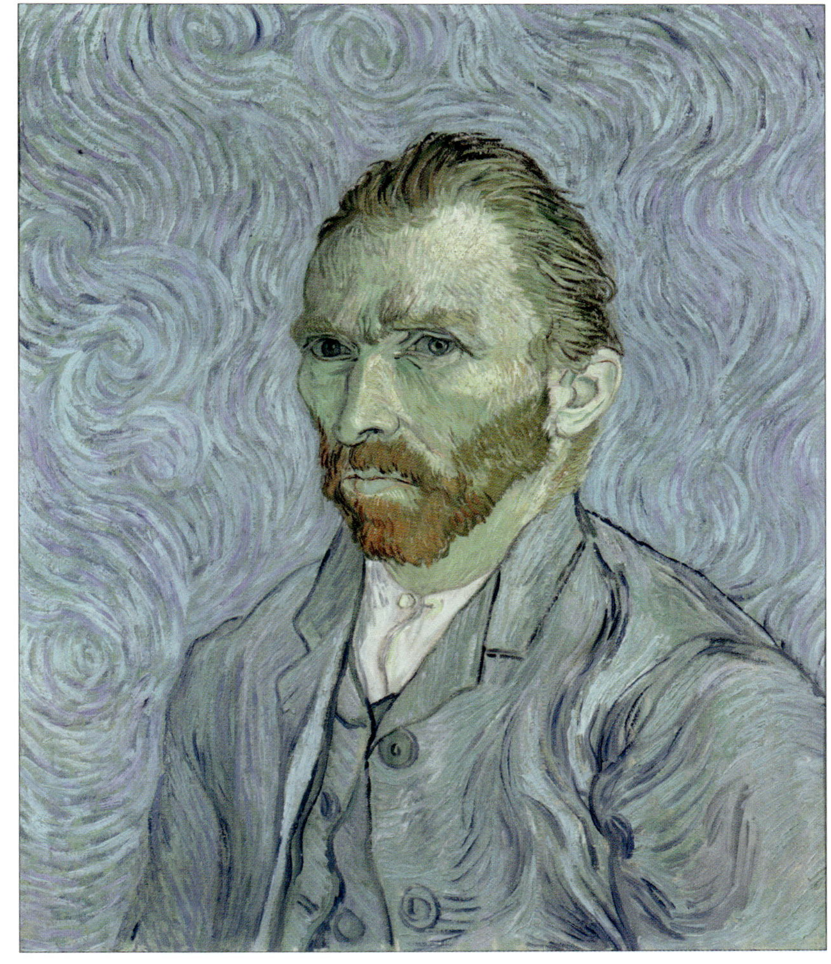

Self Portrait, 1889 (oil on canvas)

Musée d'Orsay, Paris, France, with thanks to Giraudon/ The Bridgeman Art Library.

This famous self portrait was done to show that Van Gogh's health was improving, after a spell in hospital at Saint Rémy. The swirling background colours imply shimmering leaves. These strokes are carried into the shape of the portrait. The stern look is a clue to Van Gogh's mental state at this time.

Materials

Paints

Van Gogh used oil paint for all his major work, but the drawback with using oils, if you are not used to painting, is that they are messy and slow drying. If you want to put a layer of paint on to another colour, for instance, the colours will often blend and become muddy. Acrylics are easier to use, and because they are quick drying, they can quickly be overpainted if you need to correct a mistake. Also, in acrylics, all of the dangerous toxic ingredients of 'old fashioned' oils have been replaced with safer pigments.

Acrylic paints are available from art shops, separately or in sets of colours. Avoid buying paints from market stalls or stationery shops; they are often inferior quality and you could be disappointed. Here are the colours that I have used to do the paintings; lemon yellow, cadmium yellow medium, cadmium yellow deep, Naples yellow, cadmium orange, cadmium red light, quinacridone magenta, dioxazine purple, phthalo blue (green shade), cerulean blue, phthalo green, sap green, burnt sienna, burnt umber and titanium white.

Acrylic paints in tubes.

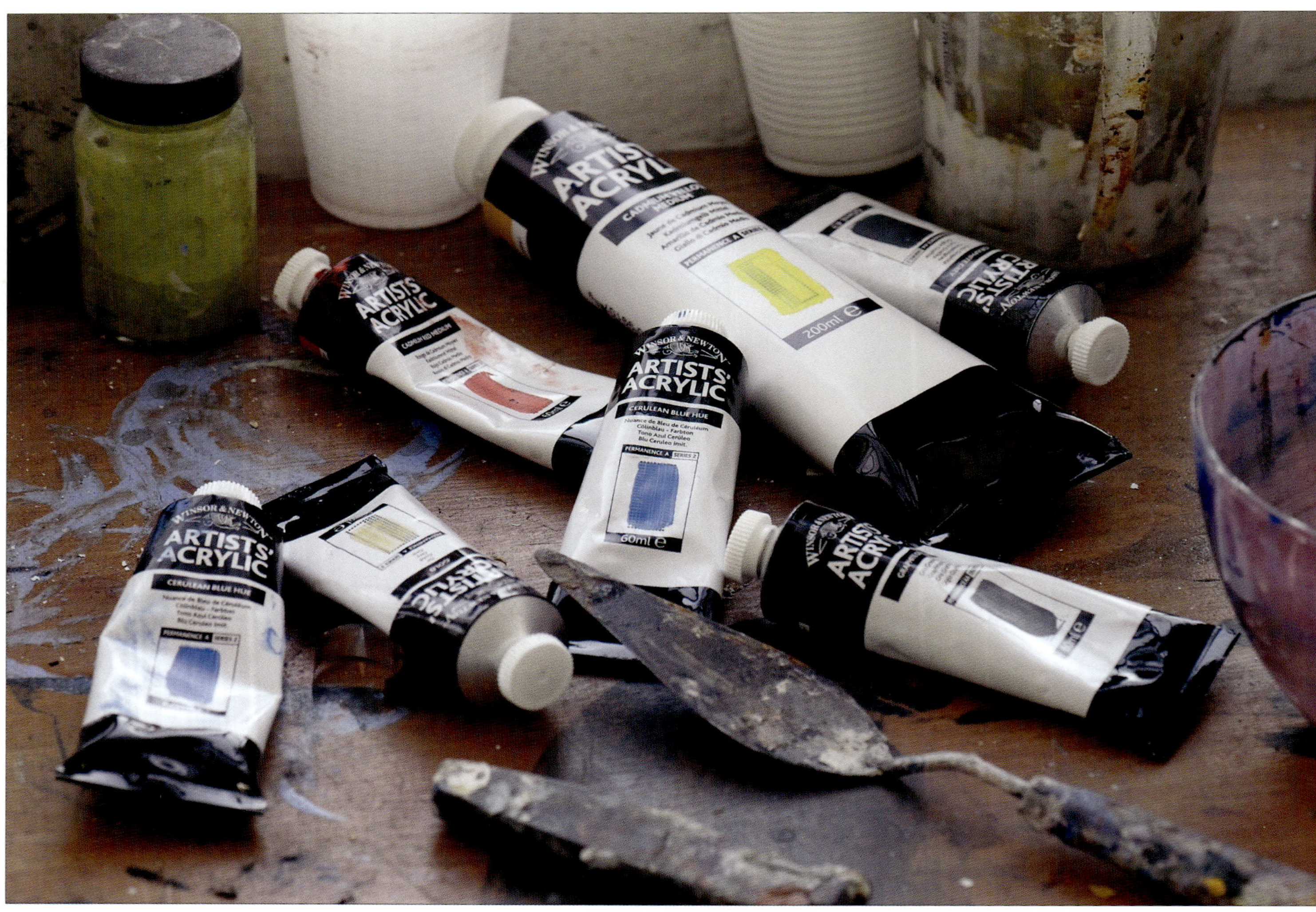

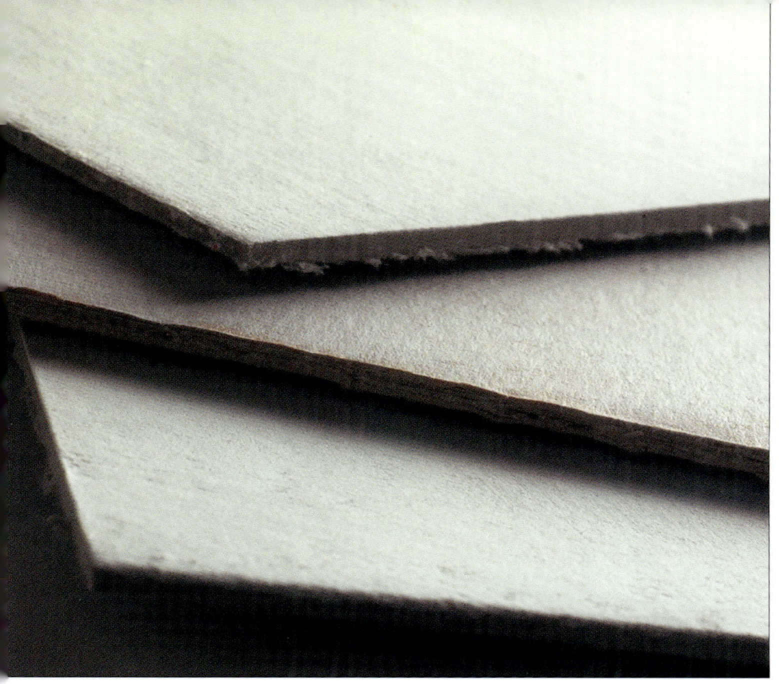

Surfaces

One of the benefits of using acrylic paint is that you can work on almost anything, as long as it is not greasy or shiny. The paintings in this book were done on thick cardboard known as grey board, available from art shops. This was primed before use with an acrylic primer called gesso. I used an old household paintbrush to give the boards two coats, allowing a few hours between for drying. After painting, you can cut the boards to size using a craft knife. Hardboard can also be used if lightly sanded and primed with gesso. If you want to get closer to the look of an oil painting, then you could use canvas boards. These are made from canvas glued on to a backing board, and come in a range of sizes, but are more expensive.

Brushes

Van Gogh was fond of applying thick layers of paint, a method known as 'impasto'. Lightweight hair brushes are not very good at picking paint up, so you need heavier, bristle ones. I have used synthetic bristle brushes, which last a long time if you look after them. Acrylic brushes are available in sets, from art shops, but make sure that they are stiff bristles and not soft hair, otherwise they will not give the desired effect. The shape of the brush is important, especially when emulating Van Gogh, because it is the brush that makes the defined stroke of colour. Flat brushes are used for most of the work, and a small round one for occasional detail. The ones I have used are; no. 18 flat, no. 12 flat, no. 6 flat and no. 2 round.

When using these brushes, the technique is to 'spoon' the paint up rather than 'dipping'. You will soon get used to it!

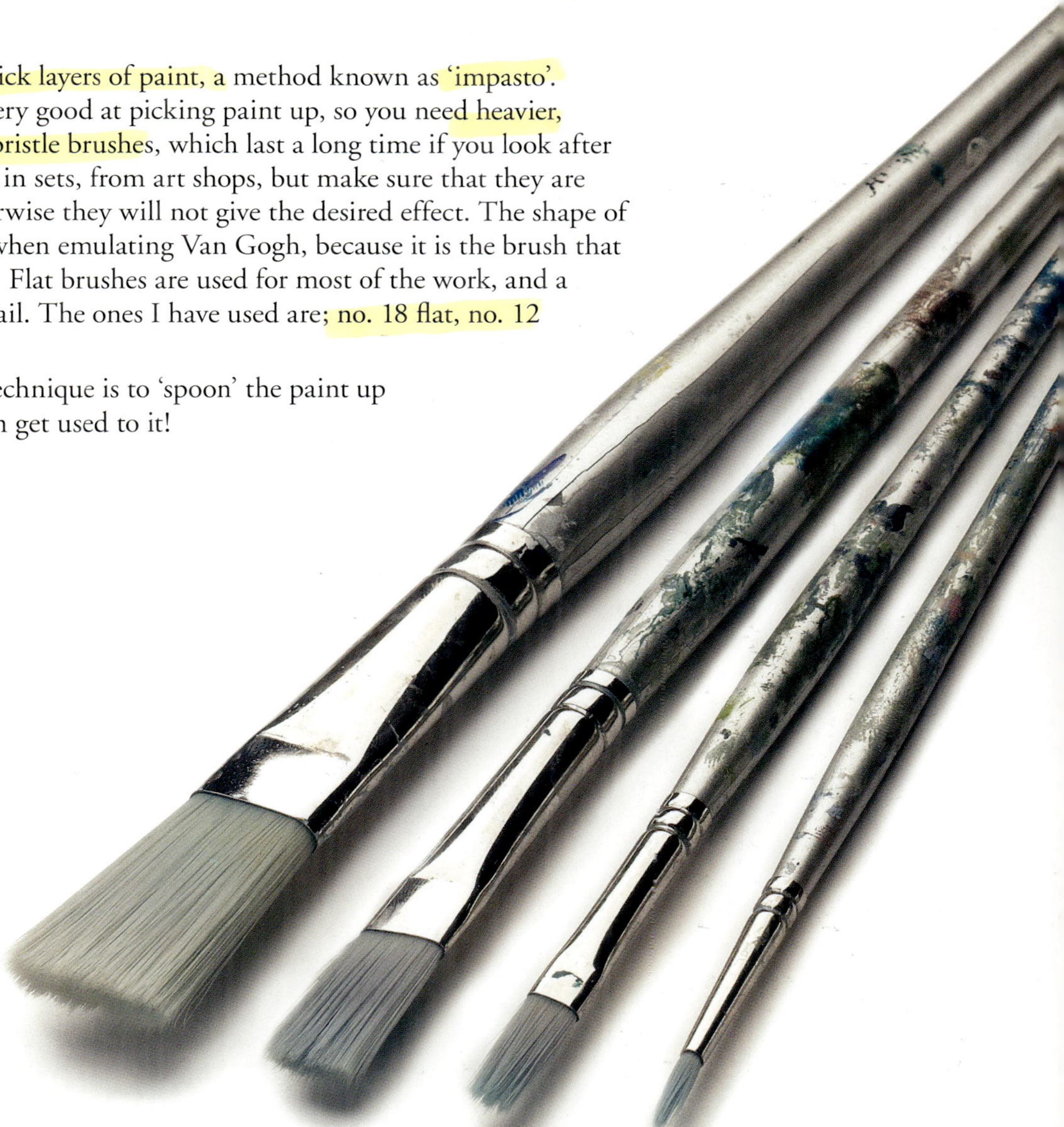

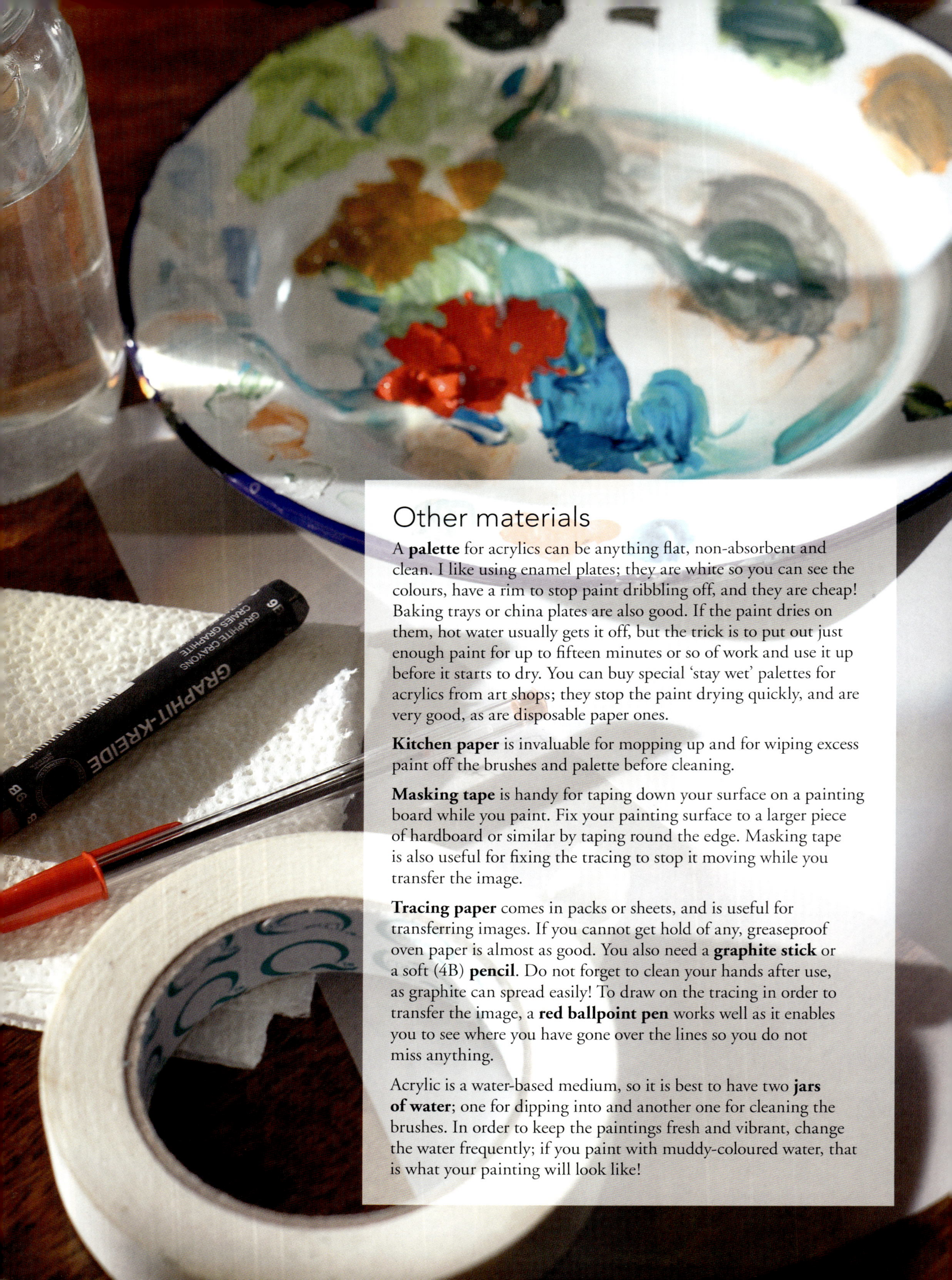

Other materials

A **palette** for acrylics can be anything flat, non-absorbent and clean. I like using enamel plates; they are white so you can see the colours, have a rim to stop paint dribbling off, and they are cheap! Baking trays or china plates are also good. If the paint dries on them, hot water usually gets it off, but the trick is to put out just enough paint for up to fifteen minutes or so of work and use it up before it starts to dry. You can buy special 'stay wet' palettes for acrylics from art shops; they stop the paint drying quickly, and are very good, as are disposable paper ones.

Kitchen paper is invaluable for mopping up and for wiping excess paint off the brushes and palette before cleaning.

Masking tape is handy for taping down your surface on a painting board while you paint. Fix your painting surface to a larger piece of hardboard or similar by taping round the edge. Masking tape is also useful for fixing the tracing to stop it moving while you transfer the image.

Tracing paper comes in packs or sheets, and is useful for transferring images. If you cannot get hold of any, greaseproof oven paper is almost as good. You also need a **graphite stick** or a soft (4B) **pencil**. Do not forget to clean your hands after use, as graphite can spread easily! To draw on the tracing in order to transfer the image, a **red ballpoint pen** works well as it enables you to see where you have gone over the lines so you do not miss anything.

Acrylic is a water-based medium, so it is best to have two **jars of water**; one for dipping into and another one for cleaning the brushes. In order to keep the paintings fresh and vibrant, change the water frequently; if you paint with muddy-coloured water, that is what your painting will look like!

Transferring the image

It could not be easier to pull out a tracing from the front of this book and transfer the image on to your painting surface.

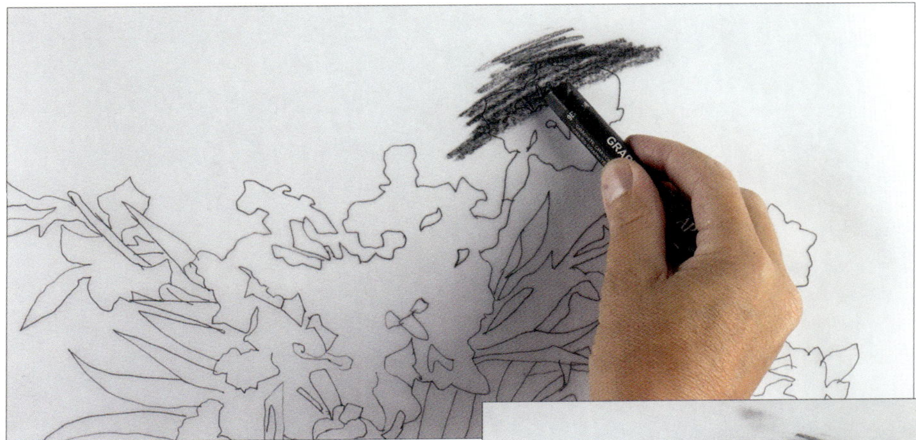

1 Scribble over the reverse of the tracing using a 4B pencil or a graphite stick, as shown here.

2 Turn the tracing right side up and tape it down with masking tape on your painting surface. Use a ballpoint pen to go over the lines of the tracing. I have used red ballpoint pen as this shows up better.

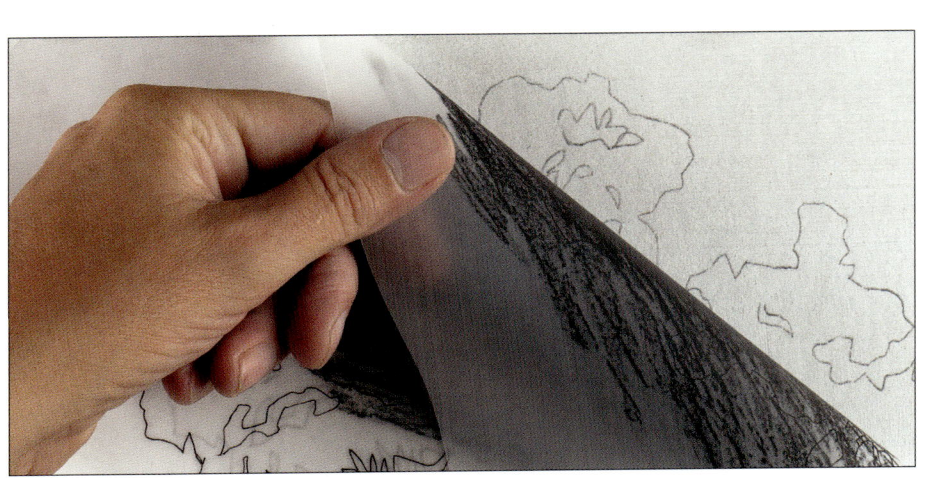

3 Lift up the tracing and you will see that the image has transferred to the painting surface.

Sunflowers

The series of sunflower paintings that Van Gogh did in Arles in August 1888 are instantly recognisable. Starting with small groups of three or four, he went on to paint images of twelve and eventually fifteen flowers. Each painting builds on the technique and use of colour from the last. The strong brush stroke is a huge part of the process, and, when you paint these, do not be too worried if your colours or shapes vary from the original. It is the expressive brush strokes that will make the painting work. The painting is full of vibrant reds, browns and oranges, in fact there are hardly any dull colours here at all. The line running across the painting background at the bottom appears in many of Van Gogh's flower studies; it serves to 'anchor' the image and links cleverly with the line around the vase. Vincent planned to use the sunflower paintings to brighten up the rooms of a house; your painting will achieve this too!

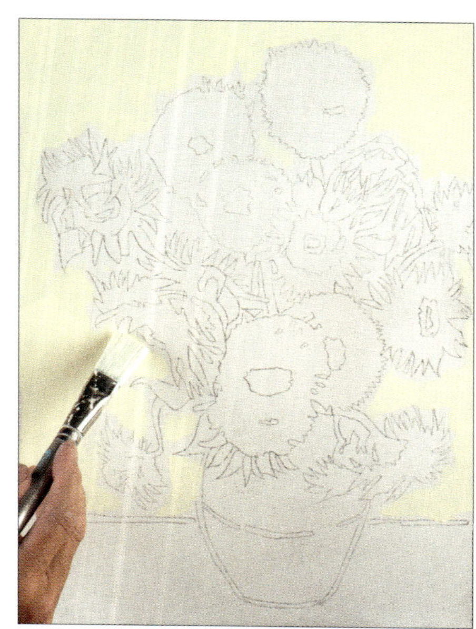

1 Take the no. 18 flat bristle brush and block in the background with a mixture of lemon yellow, burnt sienna and titanium white. The mix should be very slightly diluted with water, and it is good if the brush strokes appear streaky.

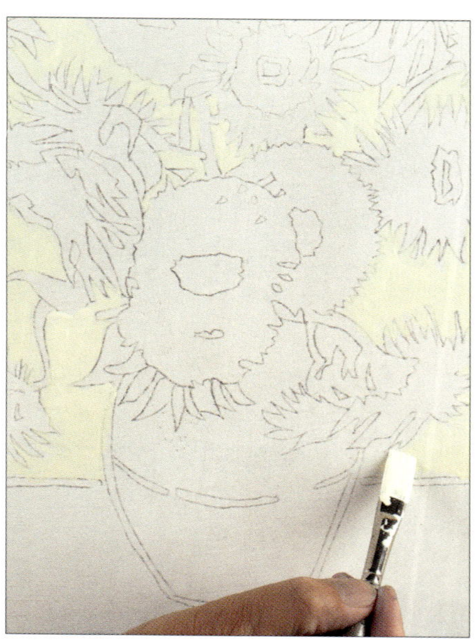

2 Change to the no. 12 flat bristle brush to paint the finer parts of the background.

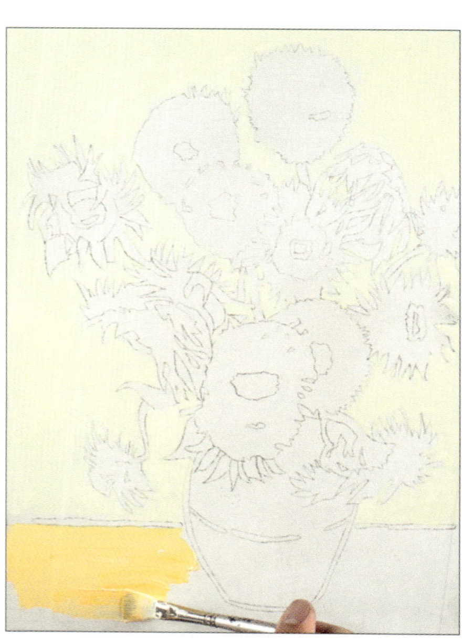

3 Add cadmium yellow deep to the first mix and paint the base on which the vase is standing.

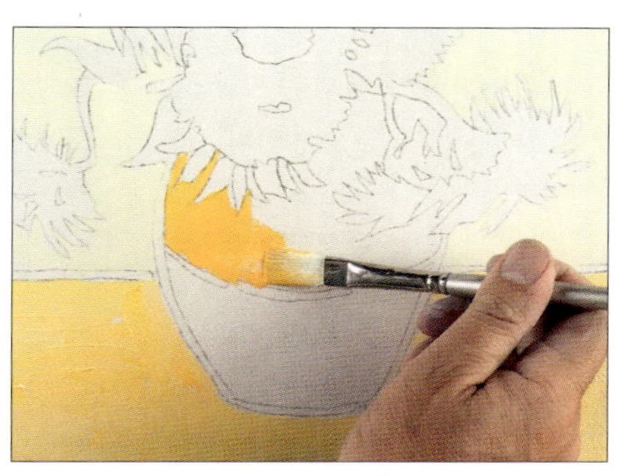

4 Add more cadmium yellow deep and a touch more burnt sienna and paint the top of the vase, still using the no. 12 flat.

5 Use the same mix to paint some of the sunflowers. Use the side of the brush and flick it out to create the petal shapes.

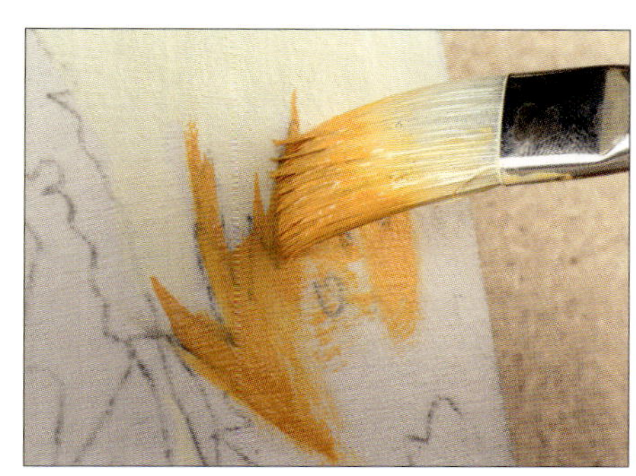

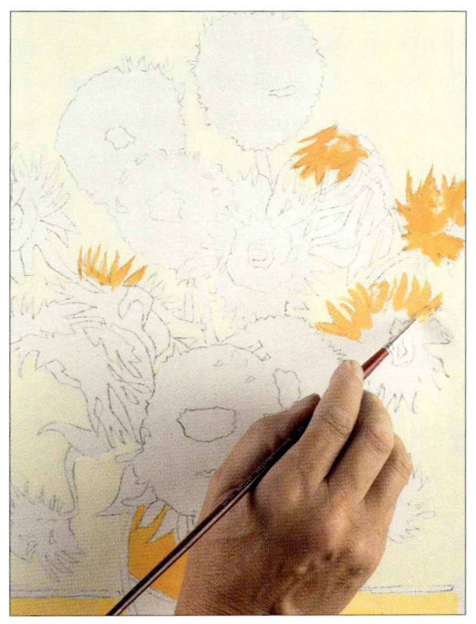

6 If you find the no. 12 brush too large, change to the no. 2 round bristle brush to paint the finer petals. Increase the pressure towards the flower centres.

7 Continue painting the yellow sunflowers, using the no. 12 flat or the no. 2 round as you prefer.

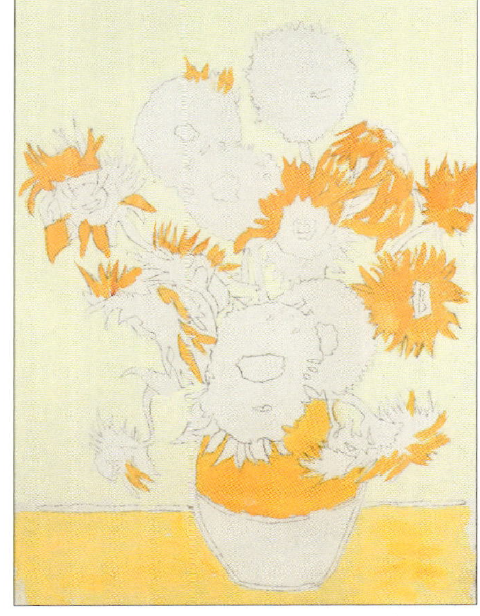

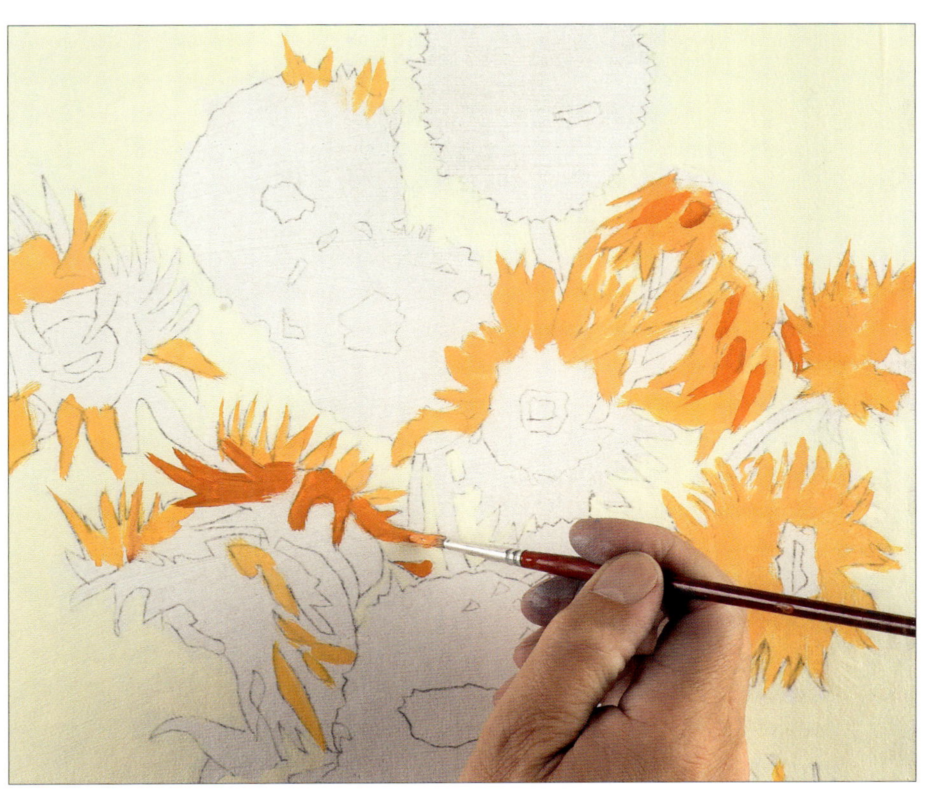

8 Mix cadmium orange with a touch of burnt sienna and dilute with a little water to paint the darker petals, using the no. 2 round brush.

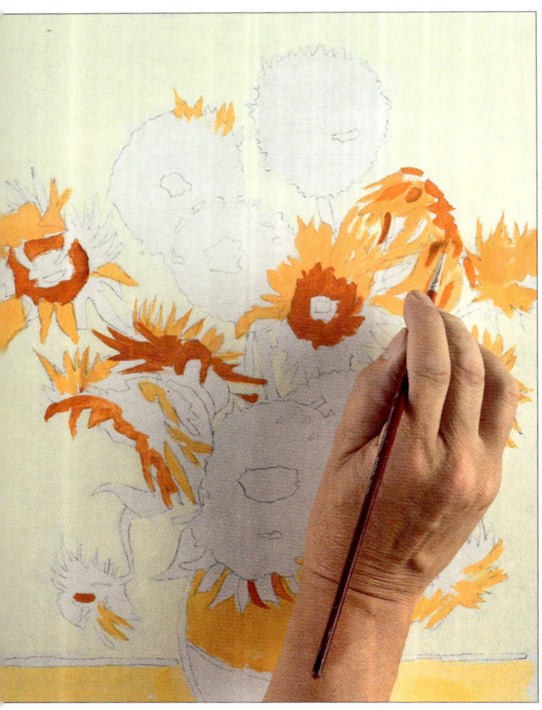

9 Continue adding flower details in this darker colour.

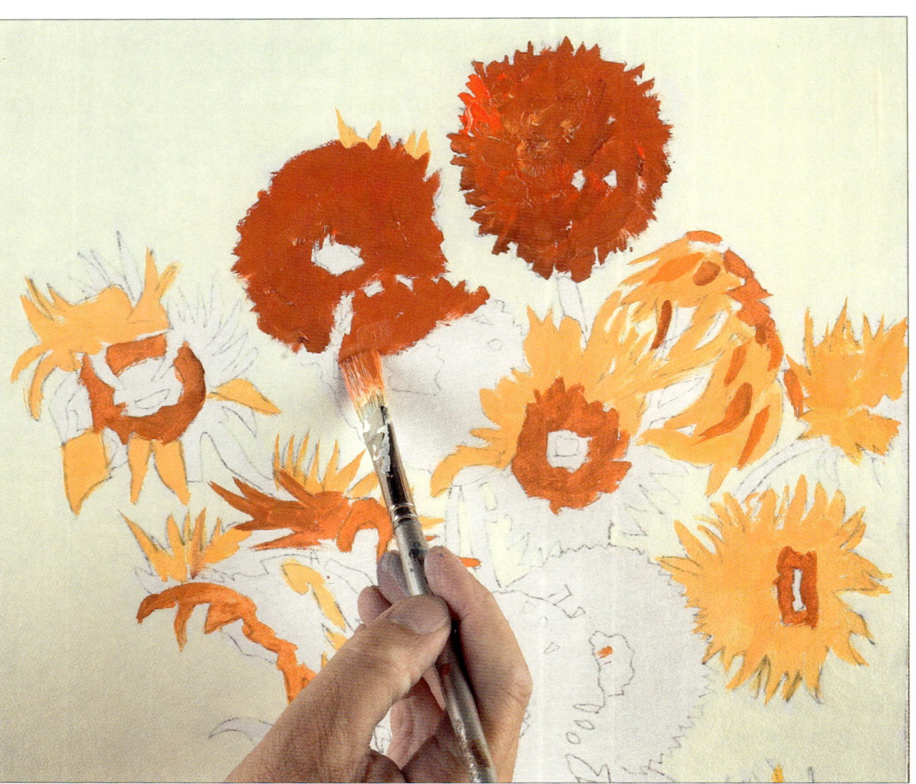

10 Mix burnt sienna with cadmium red light and a touch of white to paint the darker sunflowers. Dip one side of the brush in just cadmium red light to help achieve a streaked effect. Use thick paint with a stippling action to add texture to the darker flowers.

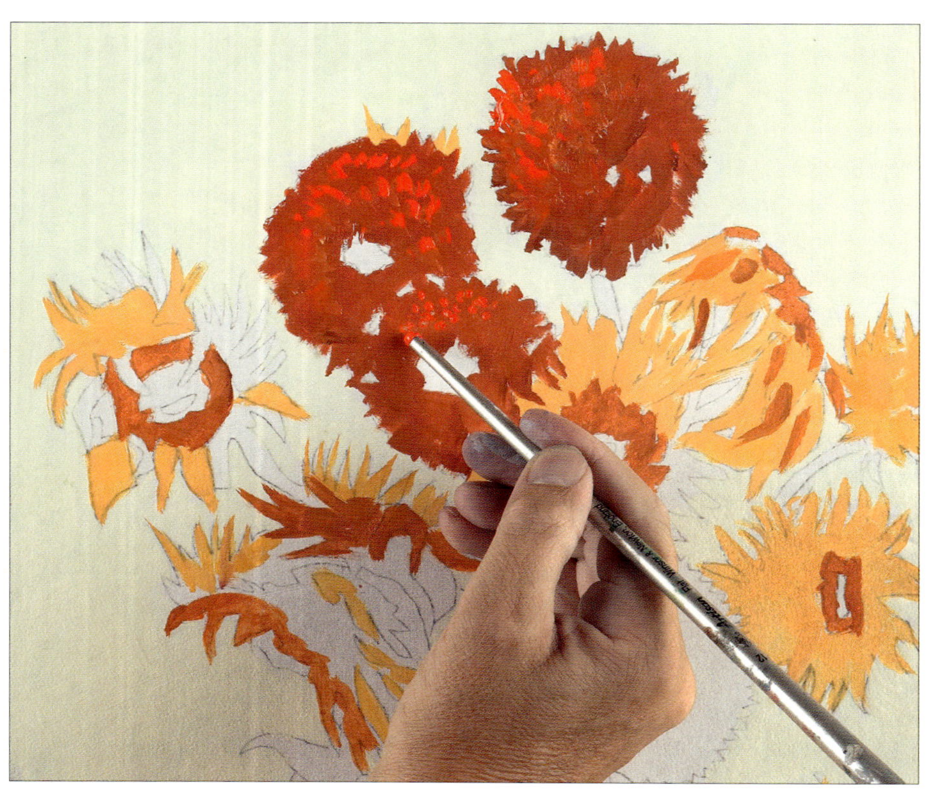

11 Pick up the same brown and a touch of cadmium red light on the handle end of the brush and stipple this on to the darker flowers for texture.

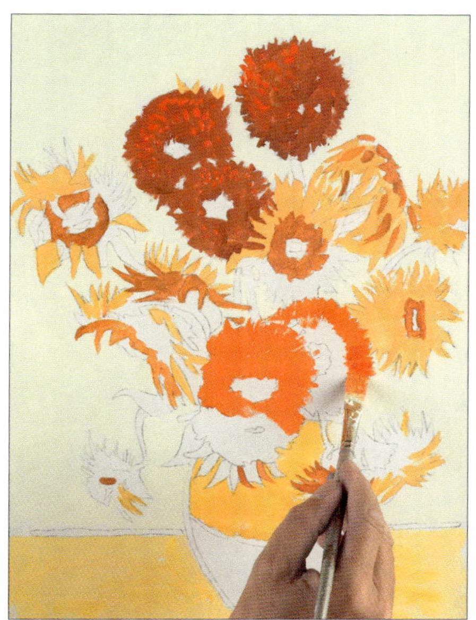

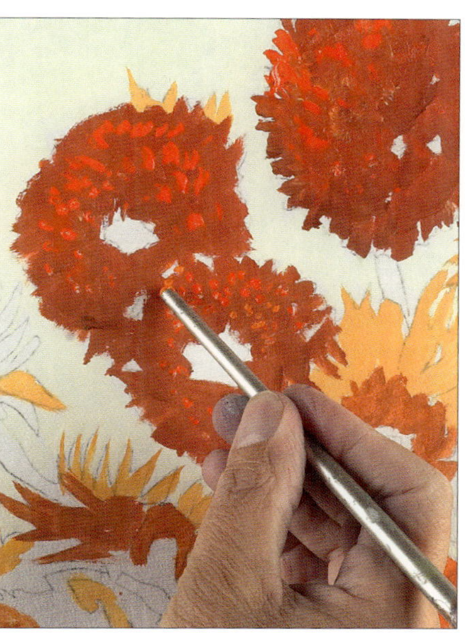

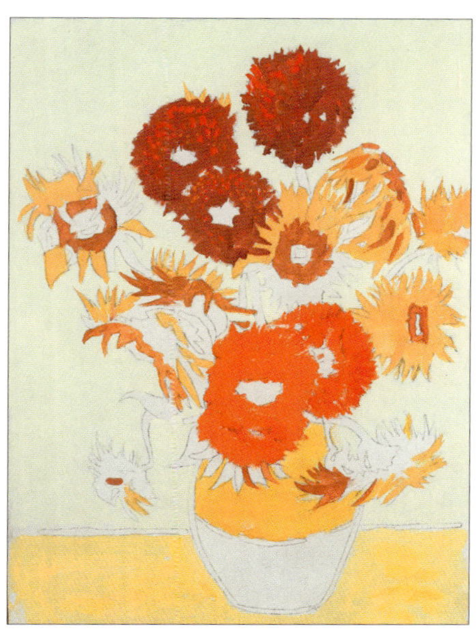

The painting so far.

12 Mix burnt sienna, cadmium yellow deep and cadmium orange to paint the orange flowers in the centre, using the no. 12 brush.

13 Use the brush handle again to stipple the same orange mix on to the darker sunflowers.

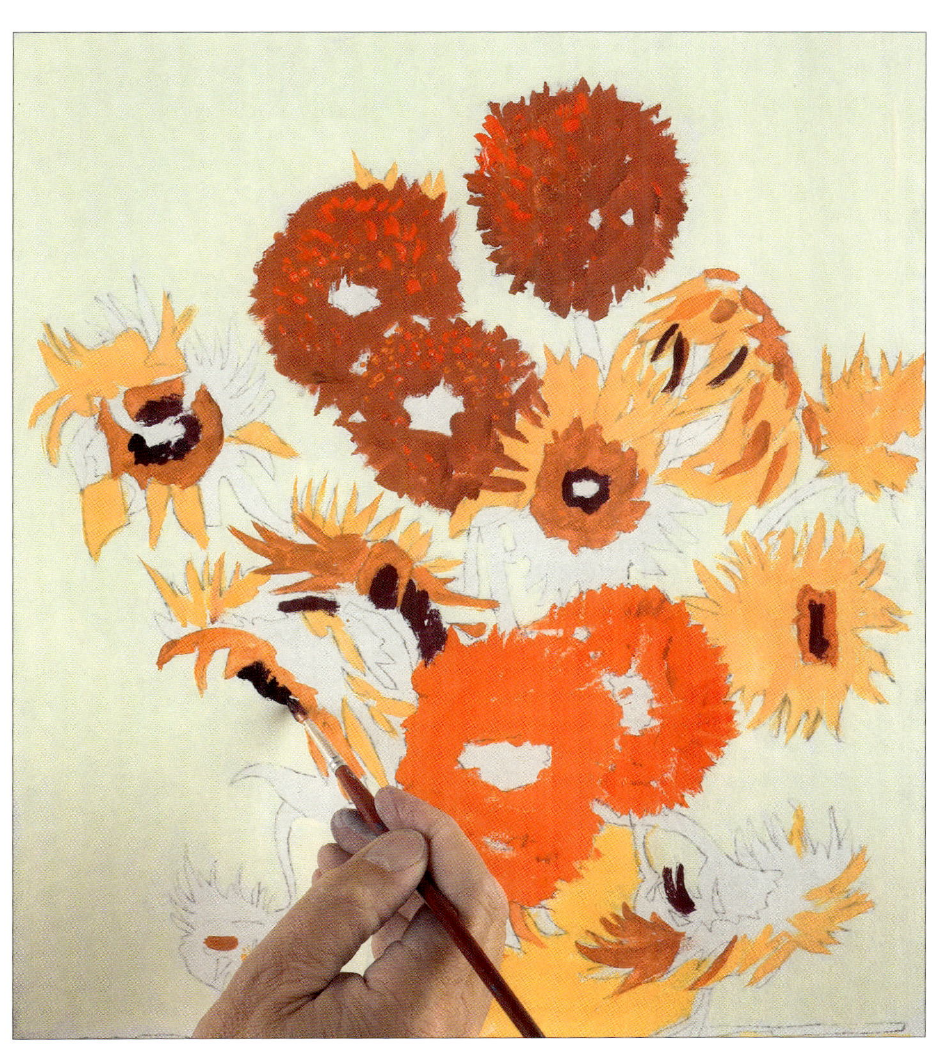

14 Use the no. 2 round brush and a mix of burnt sienna and a touch of dioxazine purple for the flower centres and darker parts. Paint with a stippling action.

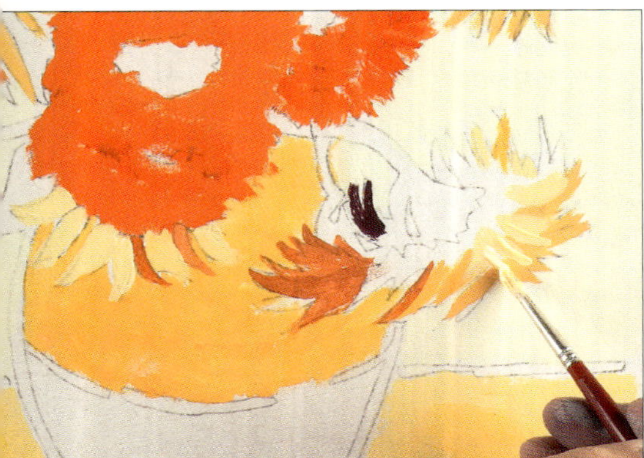

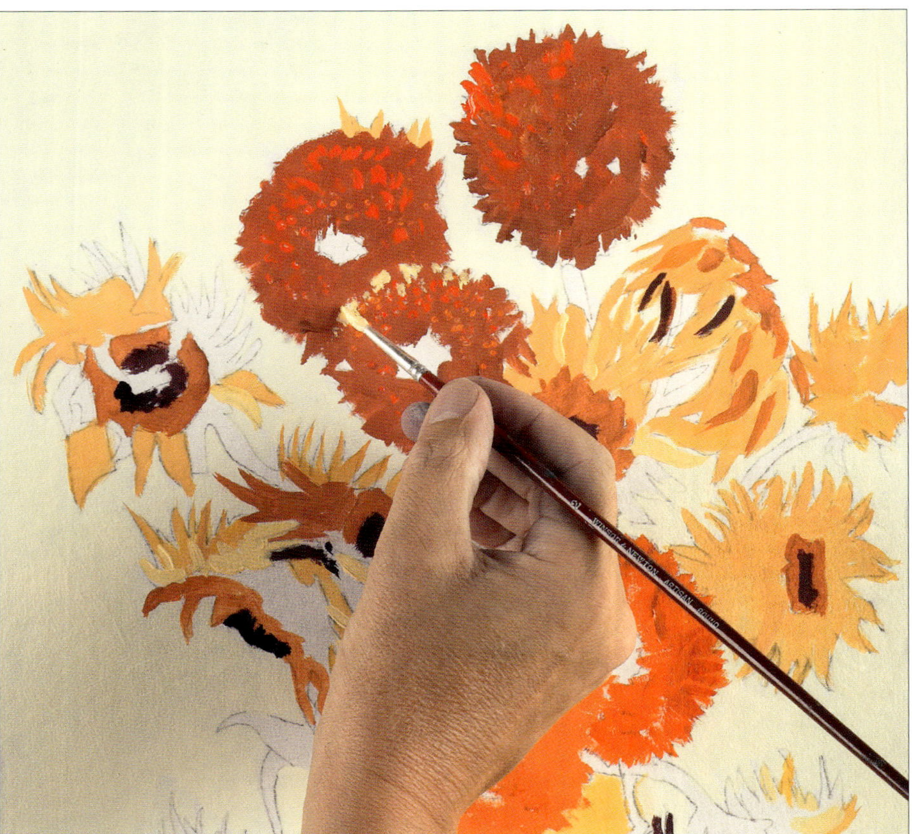

15 Mix cadmium yellow medium with titanium white to paint some of the petals at the bottom, near the vase. Aim for a streaky, impasto effect, by using thick paint and by picking up just yellow or white on one side. Continue in the same way over some of the other sunflowers' petals.

16 Stipple some of the same yellow shade at the top of the lower brown flower.

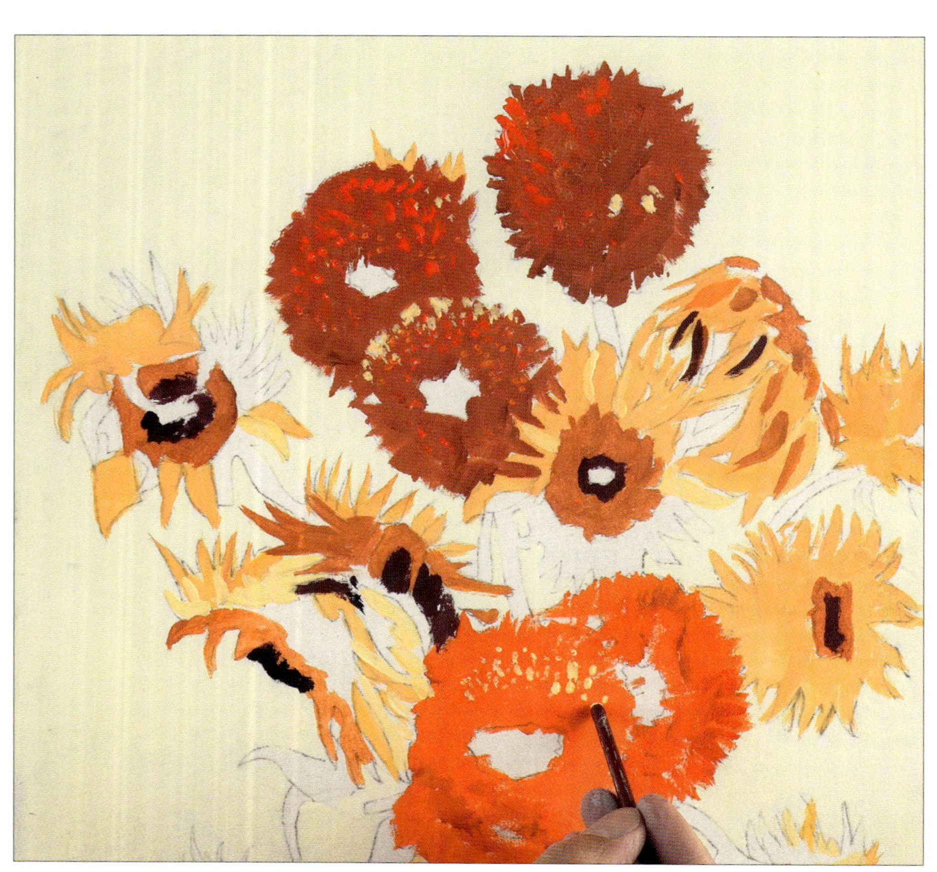

17 Use the end of a brush handle to stipple the same yellow on to the orange flowers.

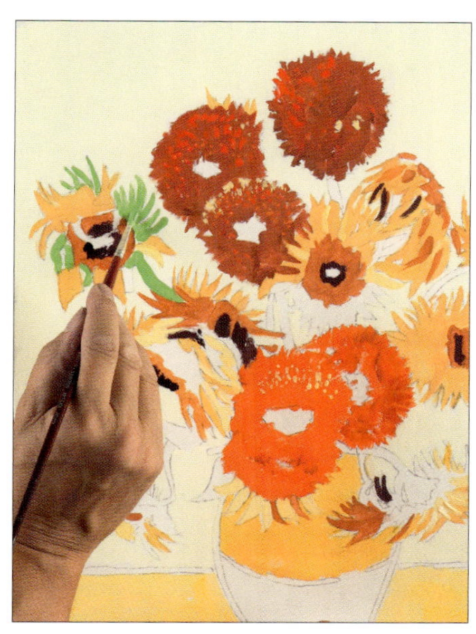

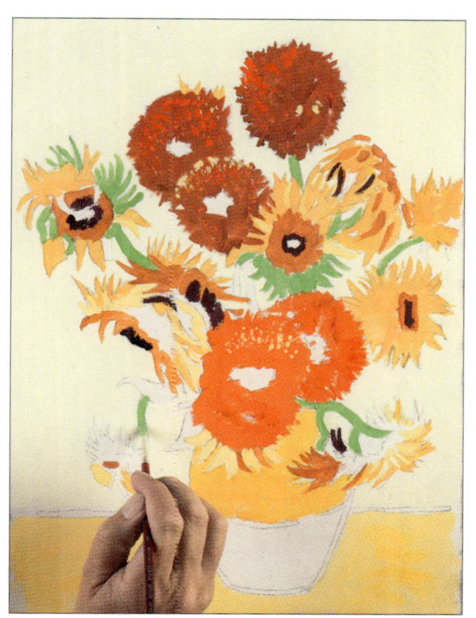

18 Mix a green from phthalo blue (green shade), lemon yellow and a touch of burnt sienna and titanium white. Use the no. 2 round brush to paint leaves, working from the outside in, and stalks.

19 Continue adding green in the same way. Do not try to be too neat and tidy.

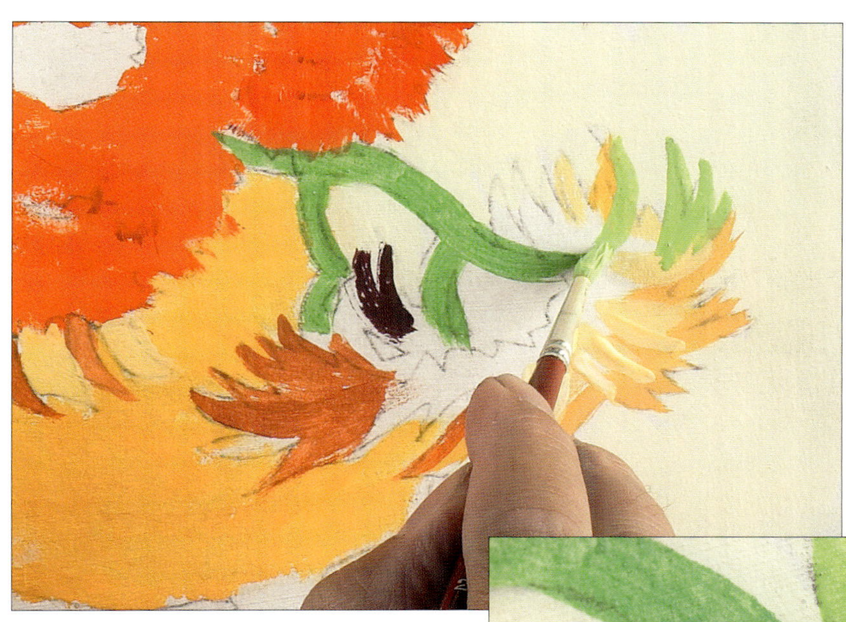

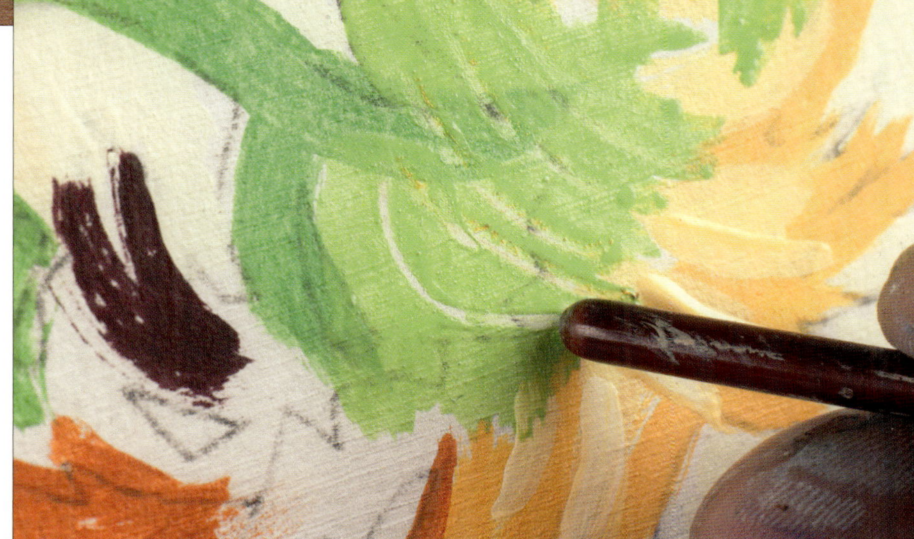

20 In places, paint the leaf first in the normal way, then scrape out texture with the sharpened handle end of a brush. This technique is known as sgraffito.

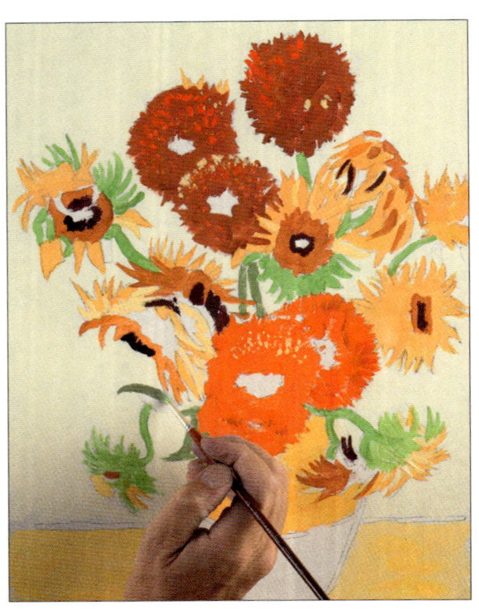

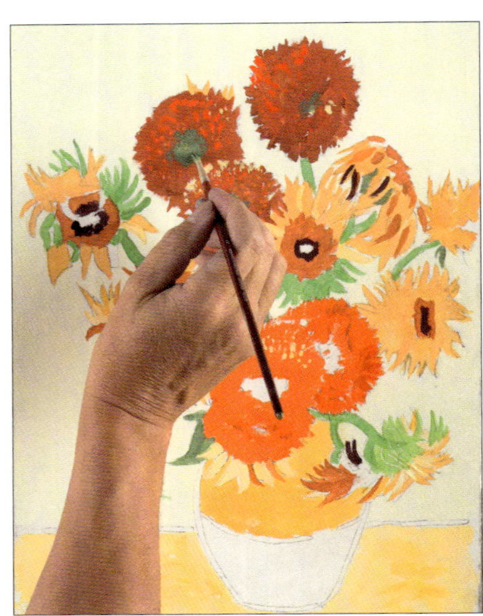

21 Add burnt sienna and phthalo blue (green shade) to darken the green and continue painting the leaves and stalks.

22 Paint green in some of the flower centres.

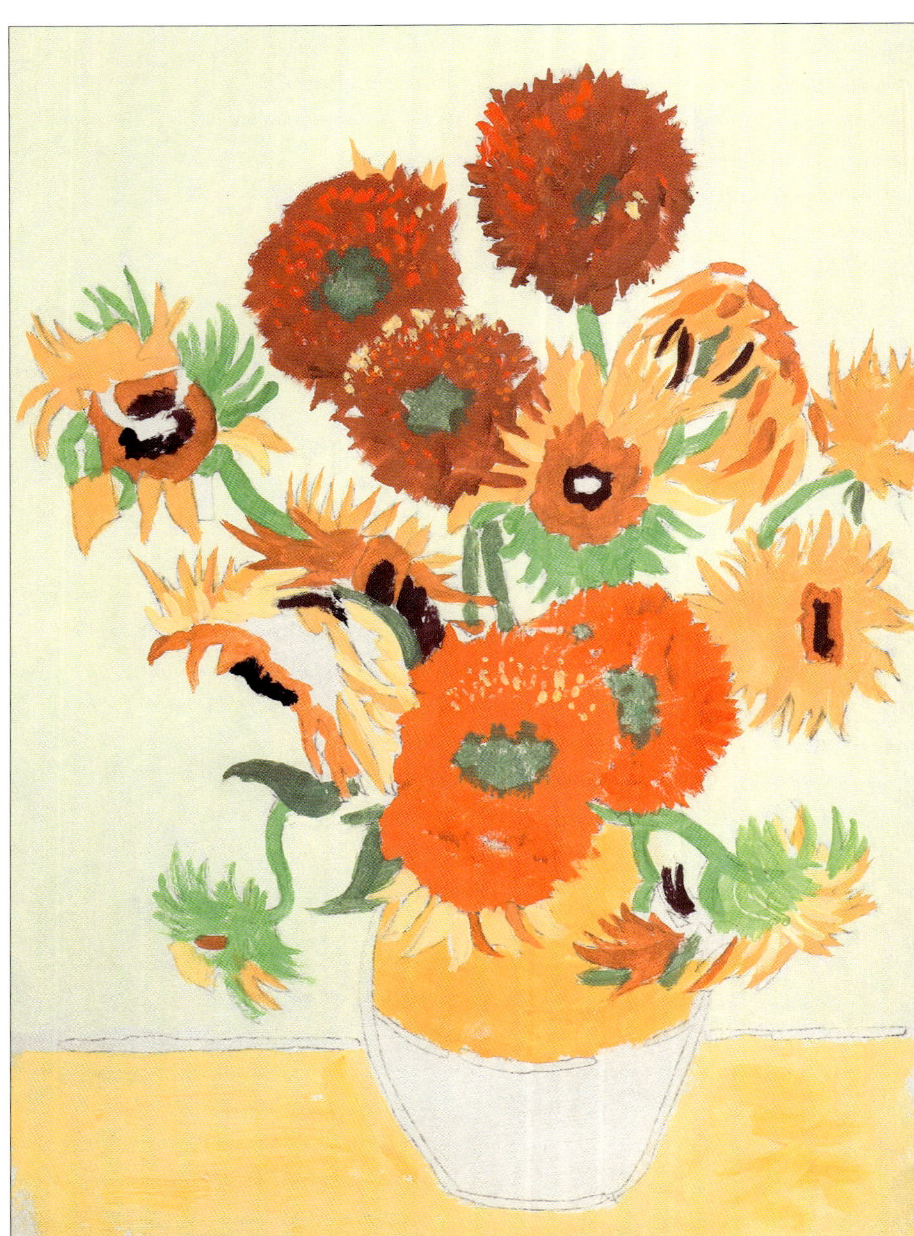

The painting so far.

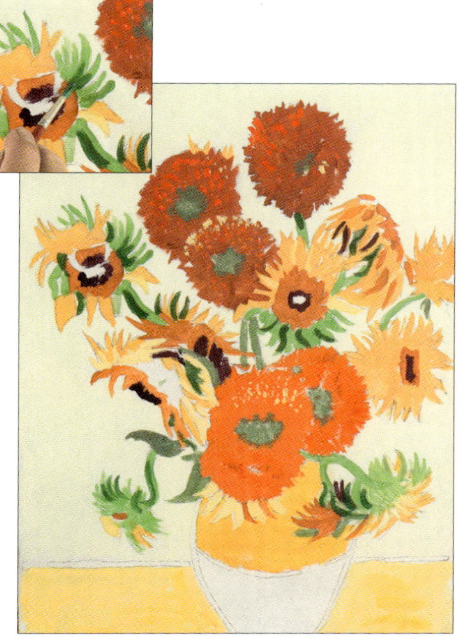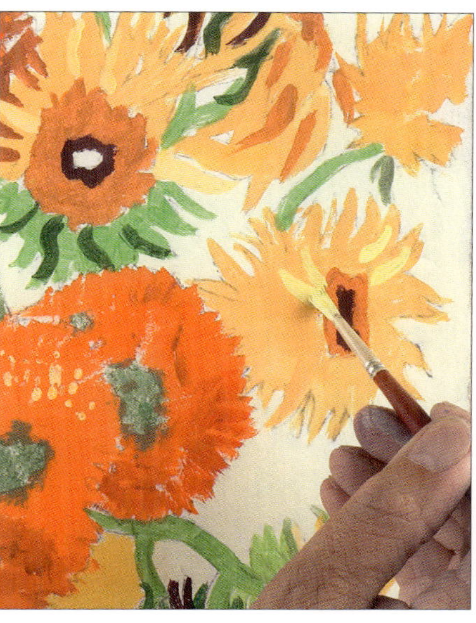

23 Mix phthalo blue (green shade), lemon yellow and burnt sienna to make a darker green and use the no. 2 round brush to paint wavy lines round the petals and on the stalks.

24 Paint cadmium yellow deep, lemon yellow and titanium white highlights on some of the petals using thick, textural lines and working towards the flower centres.

25 Mix cadmium red light, dioxazine purple and a touch of burnt sienna and paint the darks around the centres. Stipple the same colour at the bottom of the large flower heads.

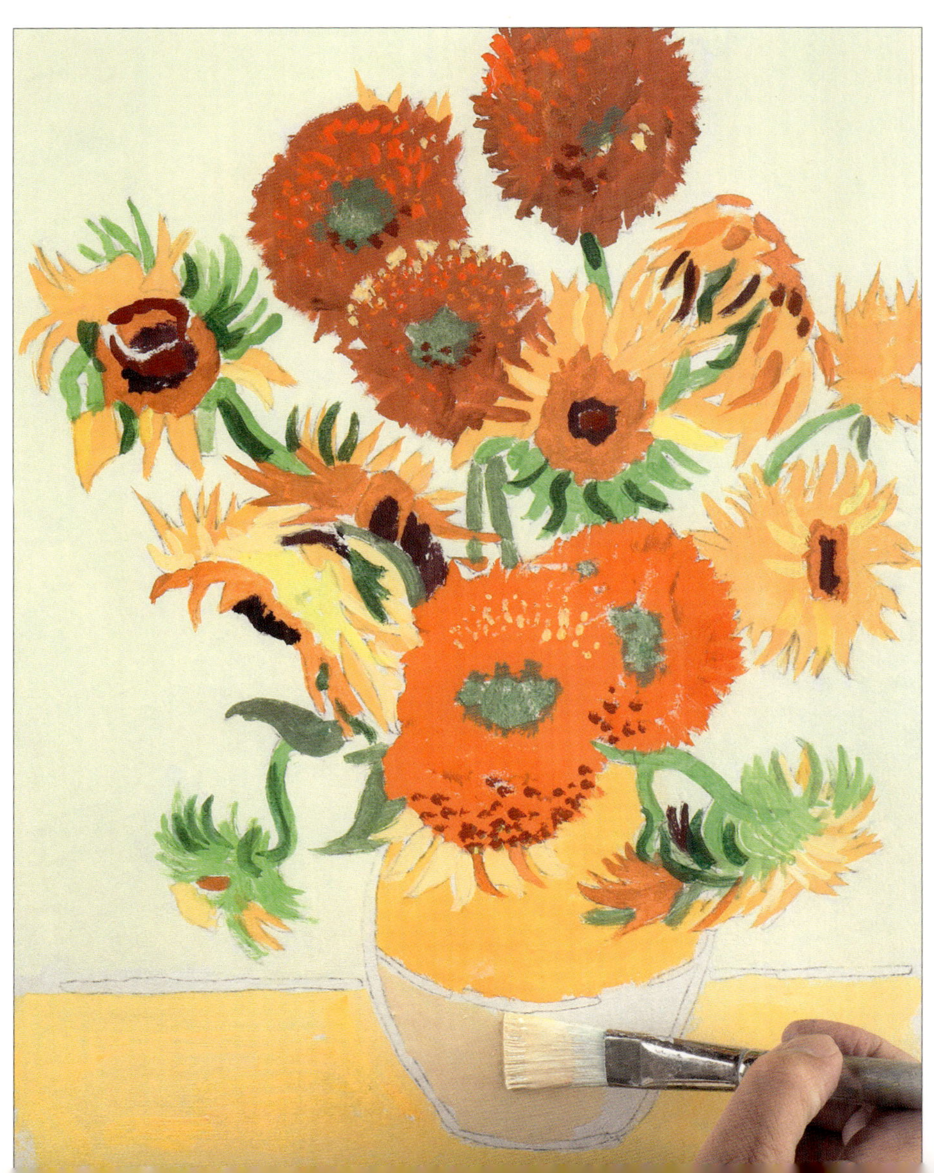

26 Mix white with a touch of burnt sienna and a touch of lemon yellow and use the no. 18 flat brush to paint the bottom of the vase.

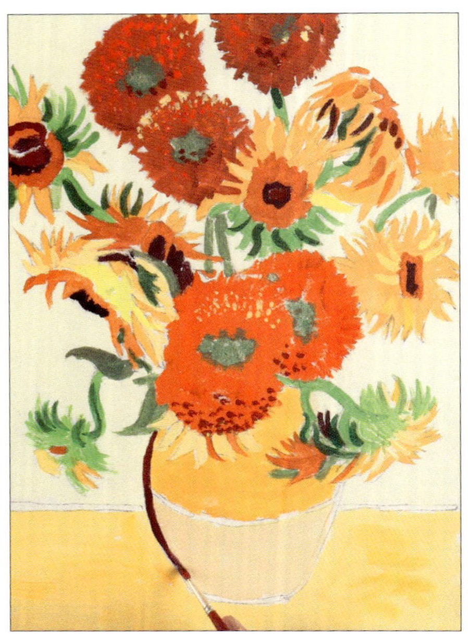

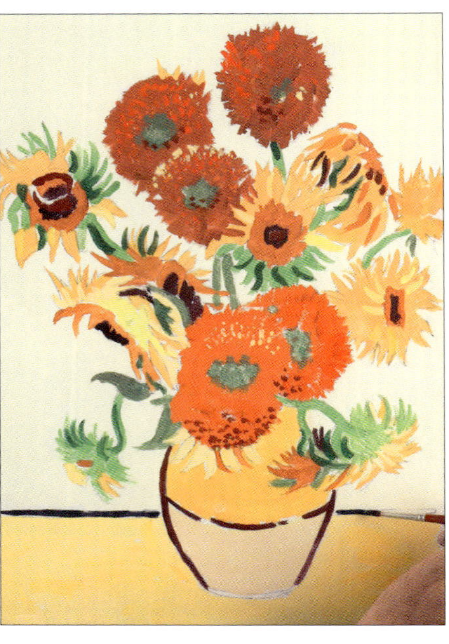

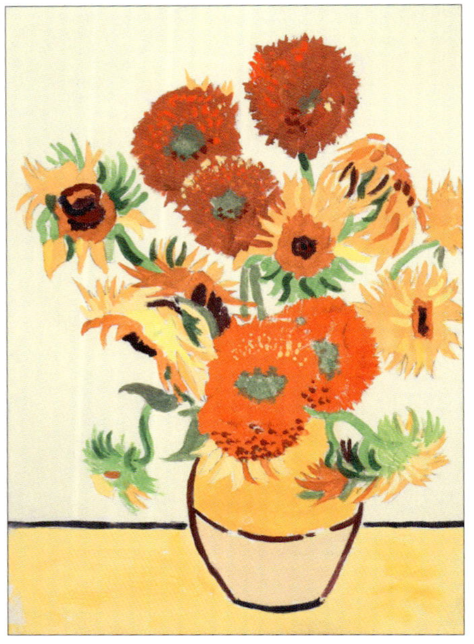

27 Paint a line around the vase using a mix of burnt sienna and dioxazine purple.

28 Add phthalo blue (green shade) to paint the horizon.

29 Paint the base of the vase with the same colour, and stipple this mix into the centres of some of the sunflowers.

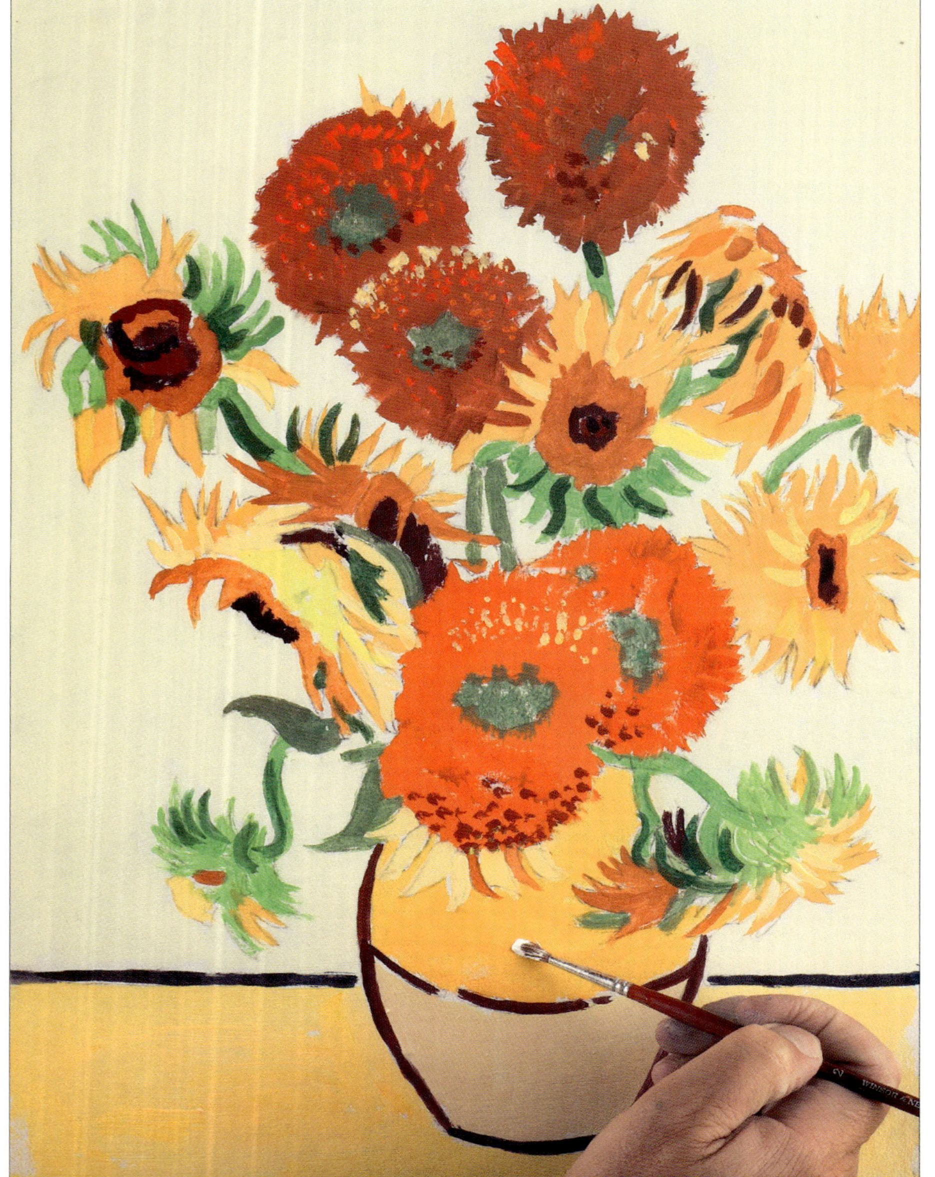

30 Add a shine on the vase with a touch of pure titanium white.

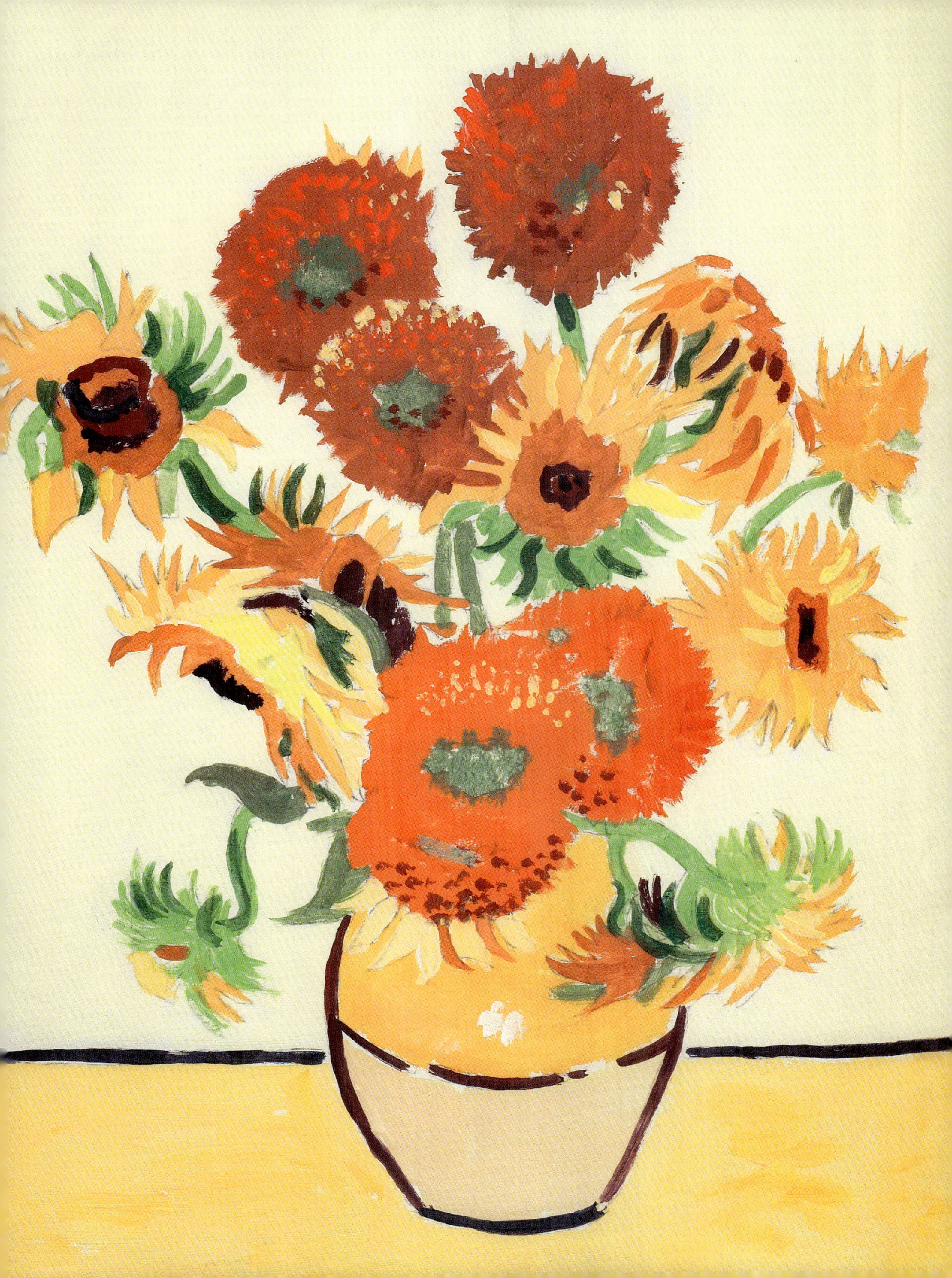

Chair With Pipe

A wonderful example of the everyday item becoming art in the hands of a master, this painting of Van Gogh's own chair was intended to be one of a pair. The other was *Gauguin's Chair*, painted in a darker range of colours, with some books on it. Vincent wanted these two paintings to portray a friendship; perhaps to be hung together to symbolise the harmony between the two artists, which existed only briefly. The use of dark colour around the outline of the chair seems to be a Gauguin influence. If you find it difficult painting the outlines, dilute the paint slightly. Aim for an irregular, textured look for the tiles; do not be too neat! The pipe and tobacco pouch lend a personal touch.

TRACING
3

You will need

Grey board primed with white gesso

Colours: titanium white, phthalo blue (green shade), Naples yellow, burnt sienna, burnt umber, cadmium orange, cadmium red light

Brushes: no. 18 flat bristle brush, no. 2 round bristle brush, no. 6 flat bristle brush, no. 12 flat bristle brush

Masking tape and board

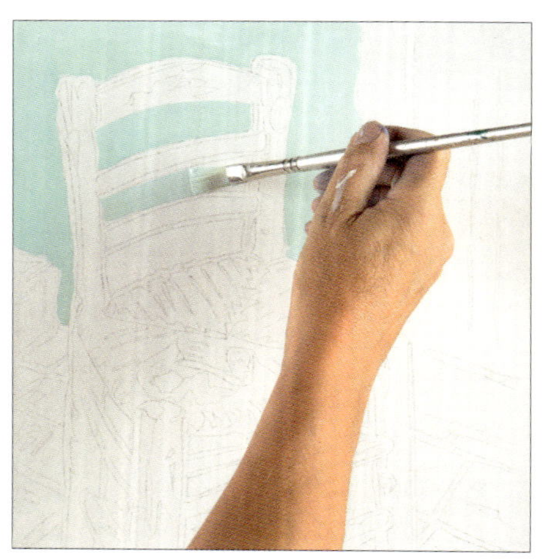

1 Make a pale mix of titanium white with a touch of phthalo blue and Naples yellow and use the no. 18 flat brush to block in the background. Add a touch more white on the right and more blue on the left to vary the colour.

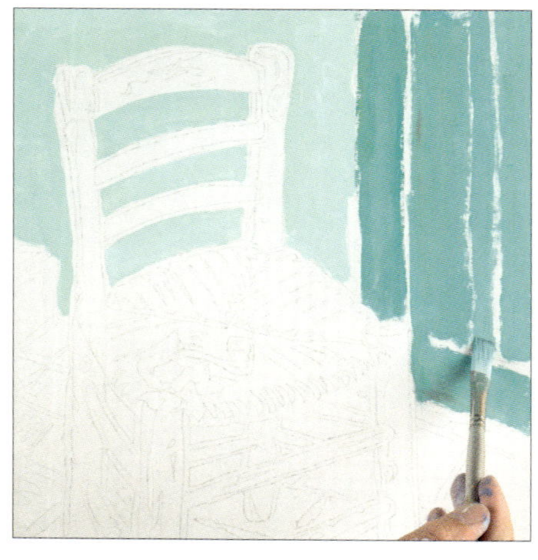

2 Mix phthalo blue, Naples yellow and a touch of burnt sienna to paint the door on the right. Keep the brush strokes loose and create a streaky look by dipping one corner of the brush in a paler mix of the same colours.

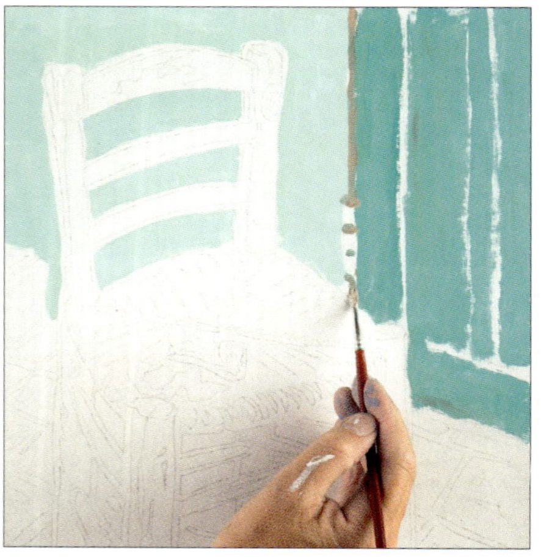

3 Mix burnt sienna with a little of the same blue mix to paint the dark lines of the hinges using a no. 2 round brush.

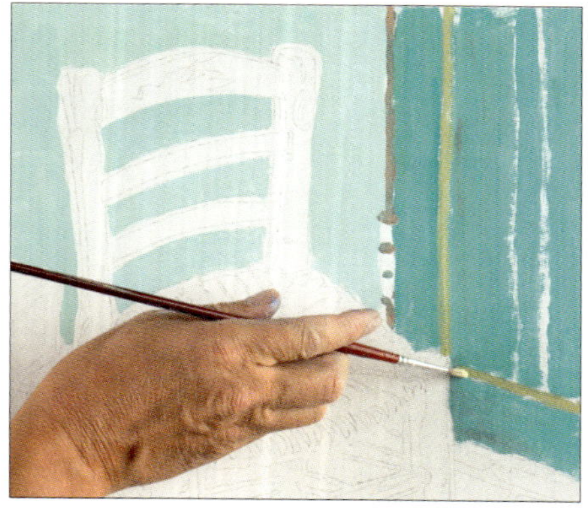

4 Add Naples yellow to the same mix to paint the lines on the door.

5 Return to the mix from step 3 to paint the line under the door. Allow to dry.

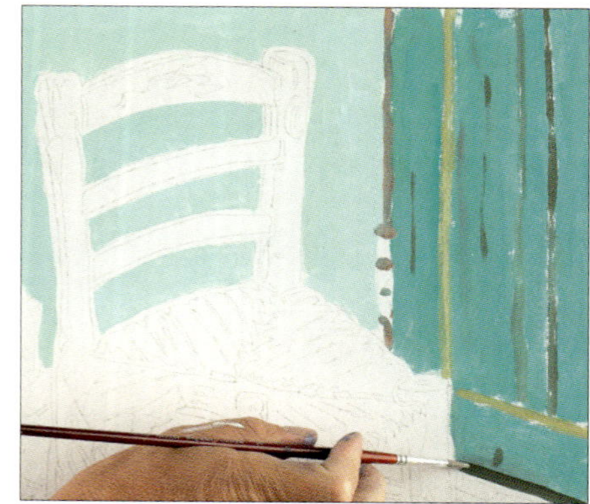

"

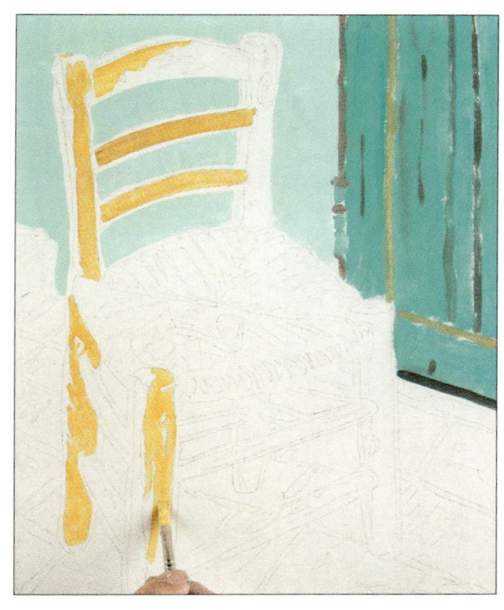

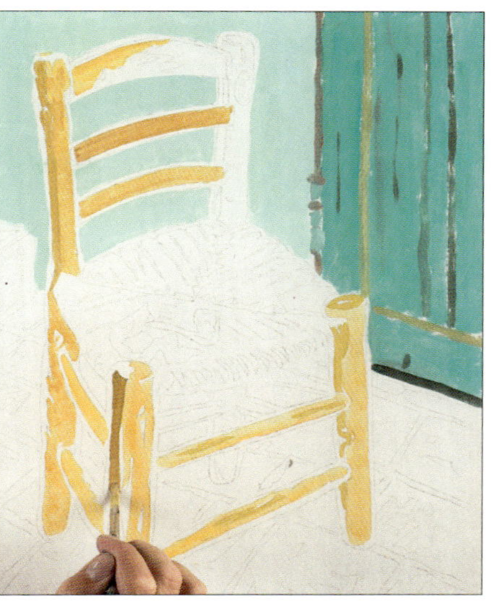

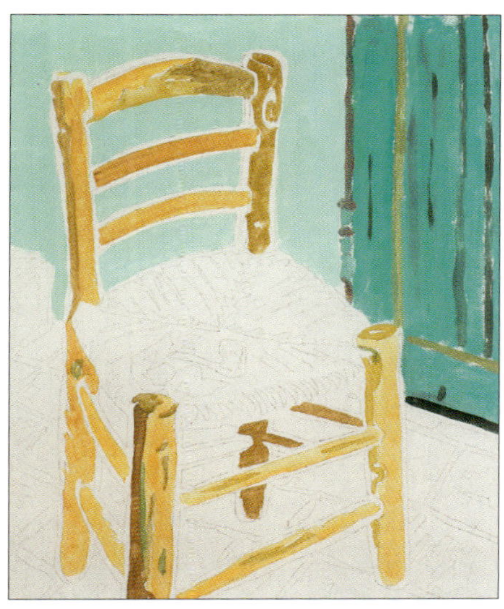

6 Use a no. 6 flat brush with Naples yellow and burnt umber to block in the chair. Add a little more burnt umber for the bars in the chair back.

7 Add a tiny touch of phthalo blue to darken the mix and continue painting the chair.

8 Continue painting the darker parts of the chair.

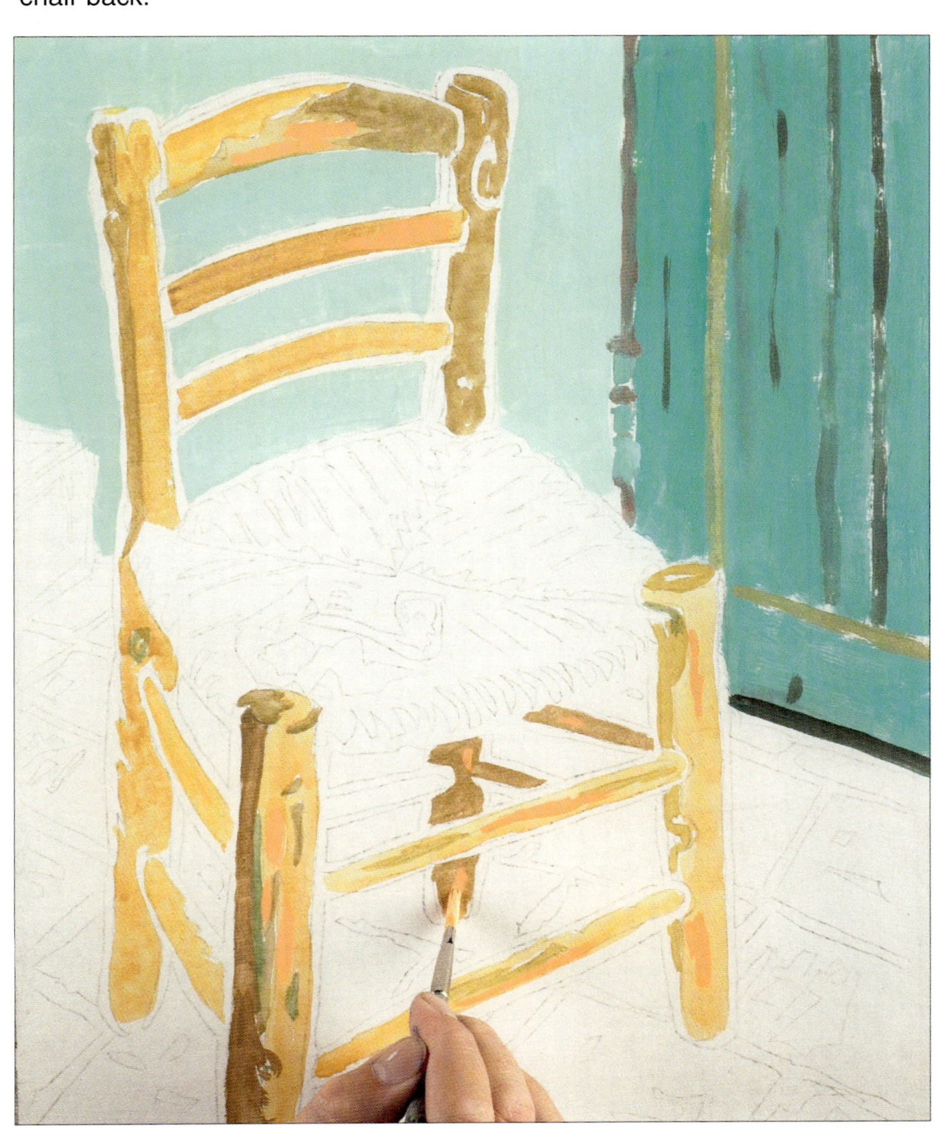

9 Mix cadmium orange with Naples yellow and white and brush on the warmer parts of the chair.

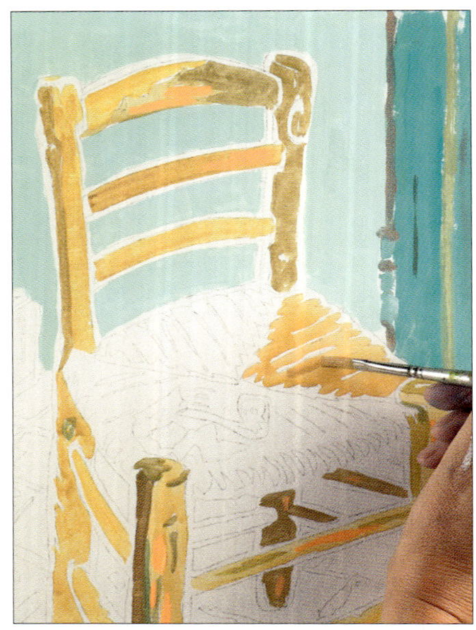

10 Add a tiny touch of burnt umber to the mix and begin to paint the seat of the chair.

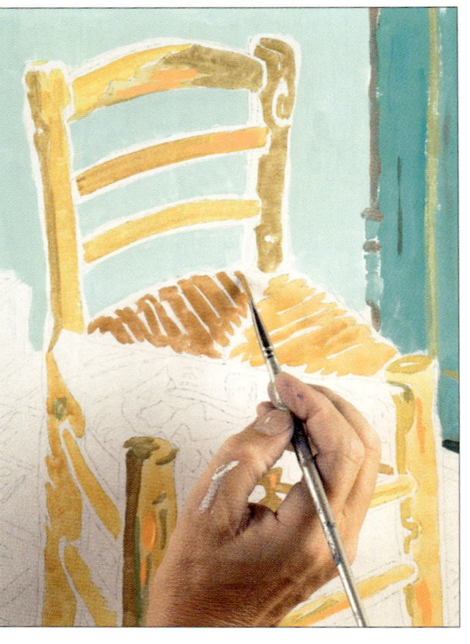

11 Add more burnt umber for a darker version, and paint the back of the seat.

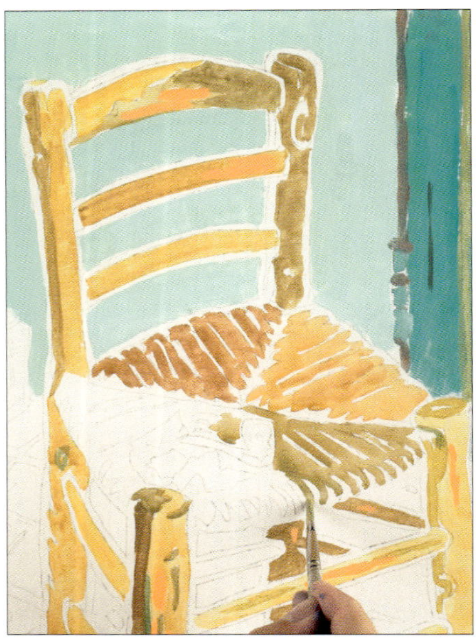

12 Add a little phthalo blue to the mix and paint the front of the seat. Carefully paint the curves at the front.

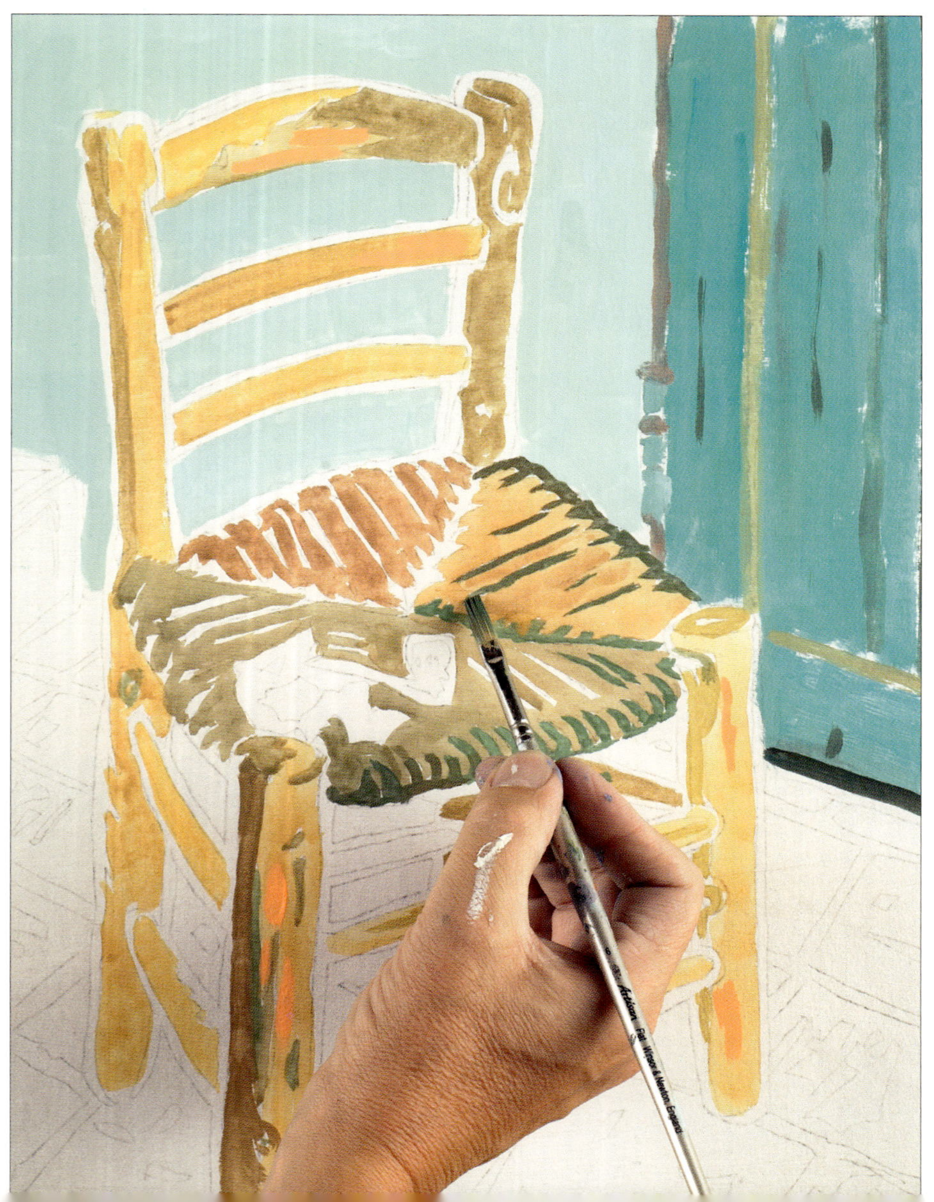

13 Continue painting the straw seat, painting carefully round the pipe and tobacco pouch. Mix Naples yellow, phthalo blue and white to create a bluey-green and paint the shadows in the straw.

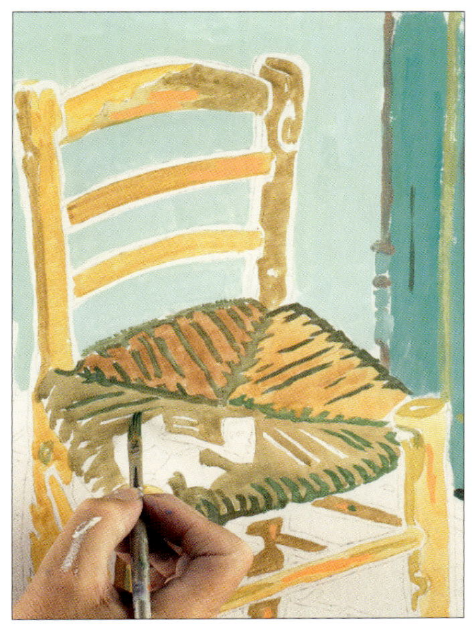

14 Add a little burnt sienna to the mix and continue painting shadows.

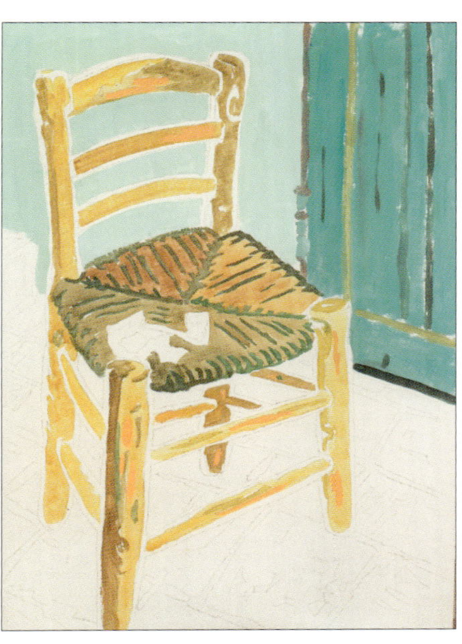

The painting so far.

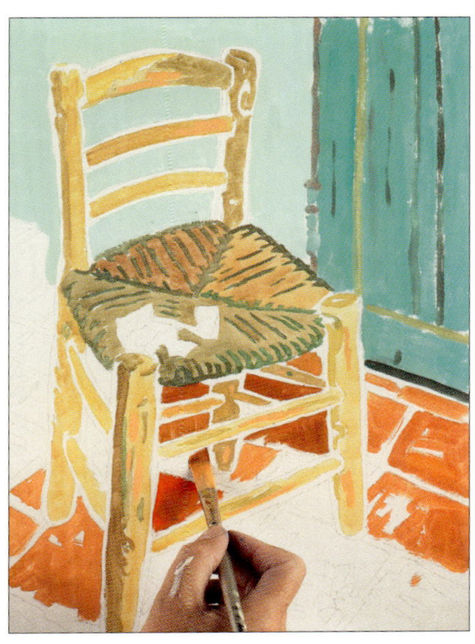

15 Begin to block in the tiles using a no. 12 flat brush and a mix of burnt sienna, cadmium red light and Naples yellow.

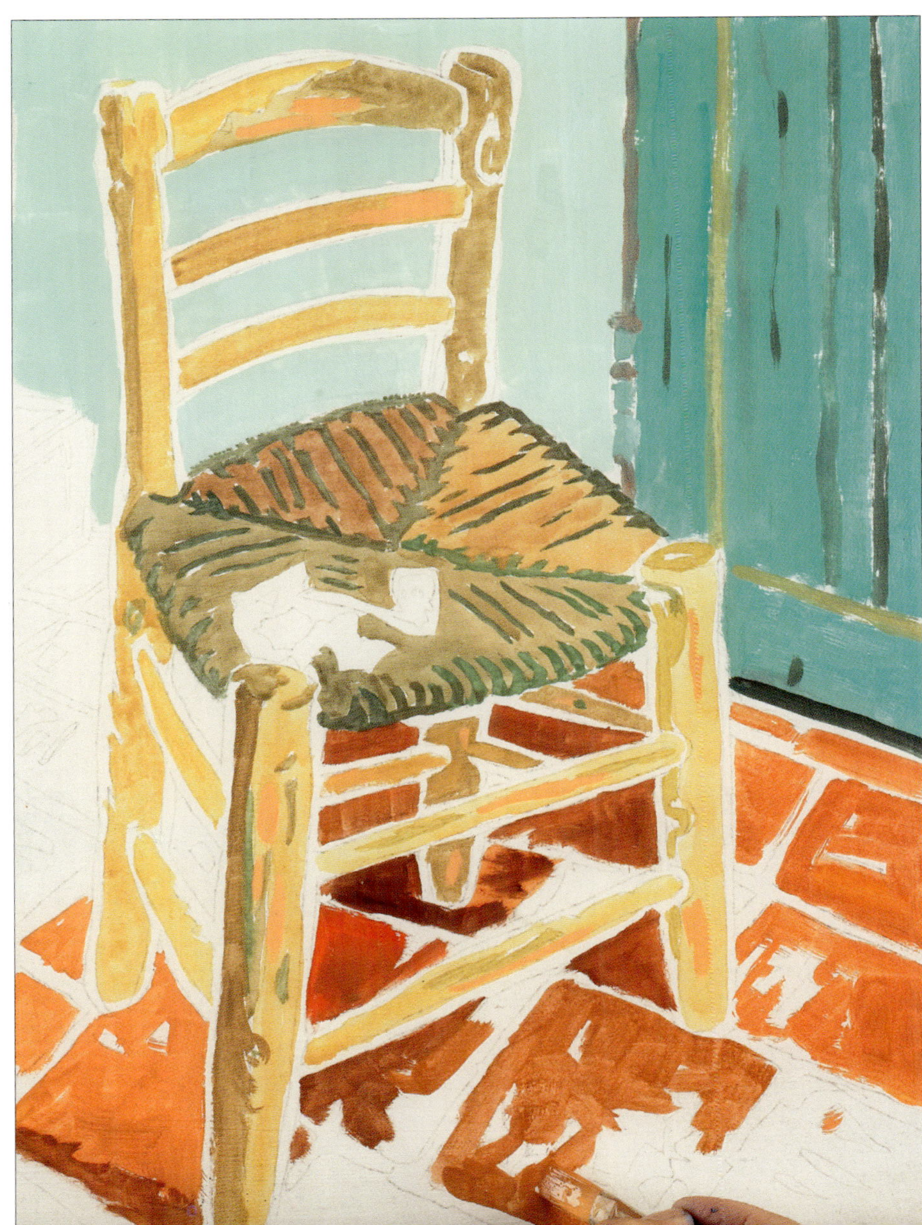

16 Add burnt umber to the mix and paint some of the darker tiles.

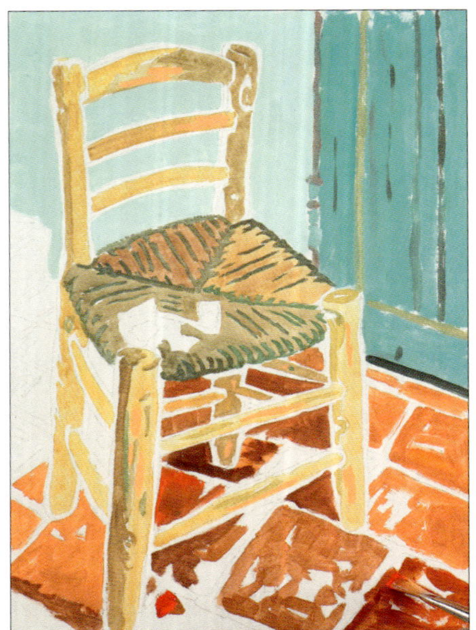

17 Add more burnt sienna and cadmium red light for some redder tiles.

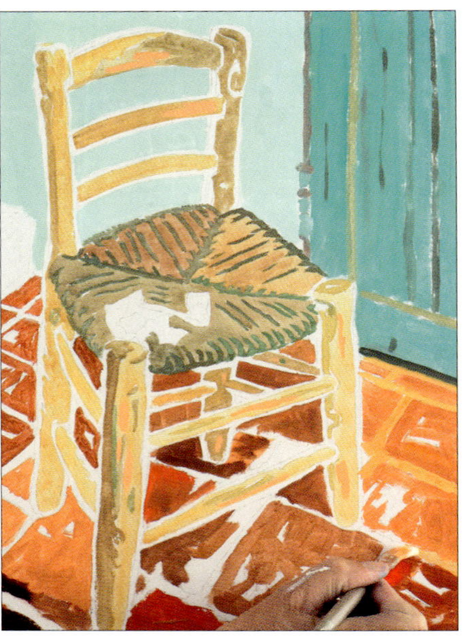

18 Paint between the tiles with a mix of Naples yellow and a little white, using loose brush strokes.

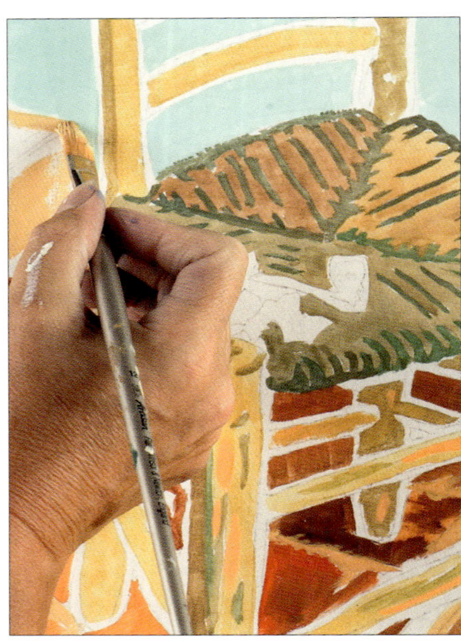

19 Paint the box in the background using the same colour.

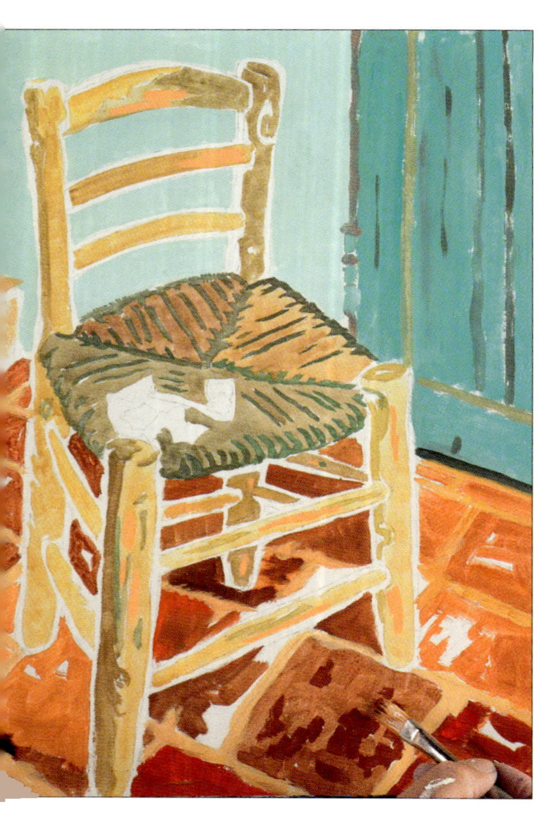

20 Make textural marks on the tiles with burnt umber and coarse brush strokes.

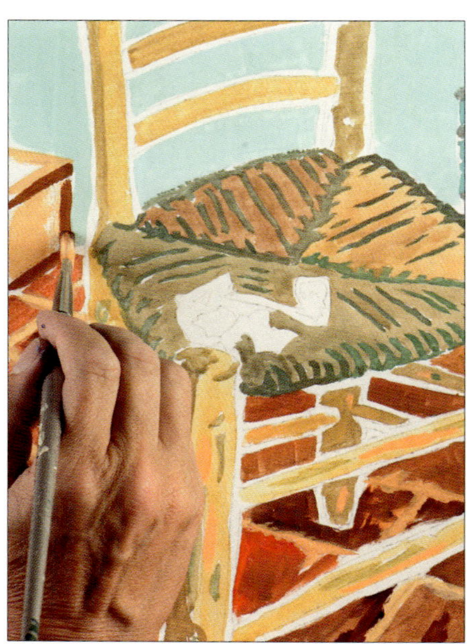

21 Add dark lines on the box in the background with burnt umber.

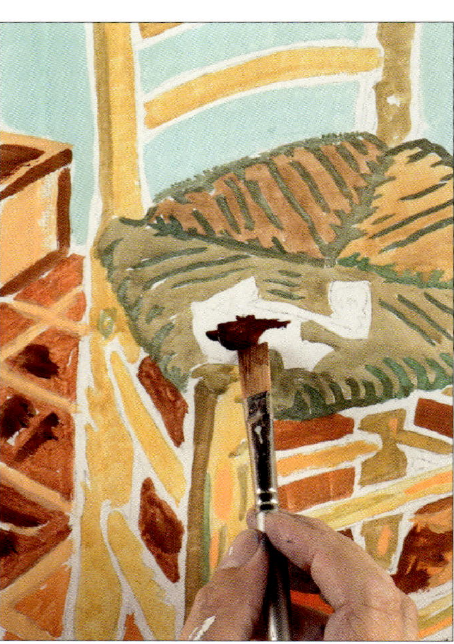

22 Paint the tobacco on the chair with the same colour.

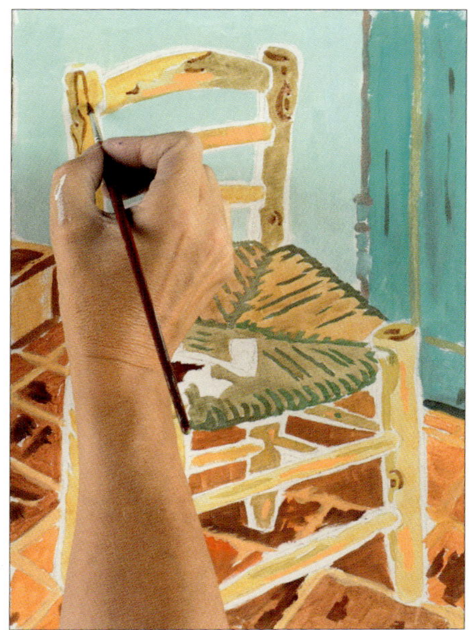

23 Change to the no. 2 round brush and paint the knot holes in the chair with burnt umber.

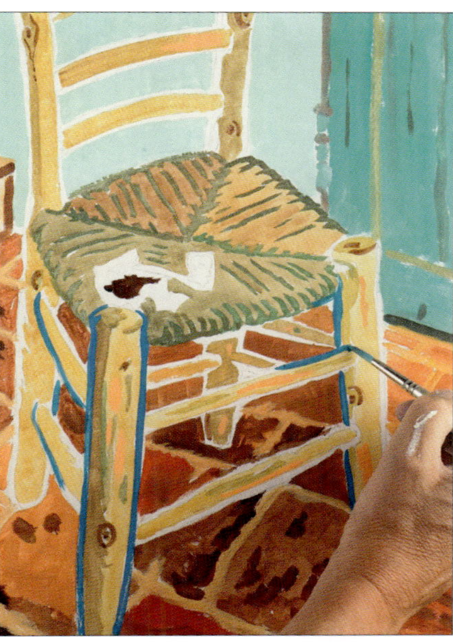

24 Mix phthalo blue with a touch of white and begin to paint the outline of the chair.

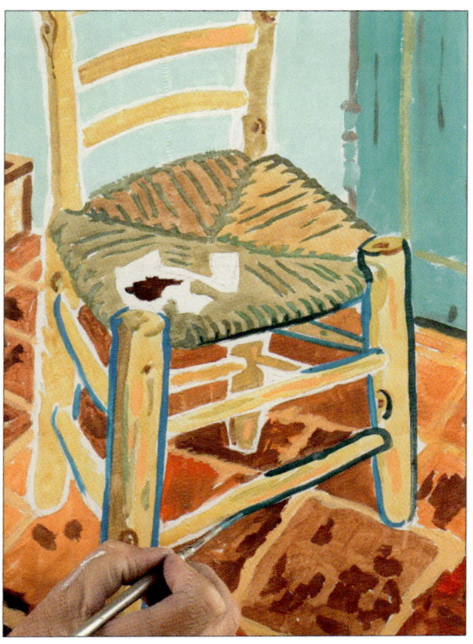

25 Add burnt umber to the blue mix to darken it and paint darker touches in the outline and in some of the knots in the wood.

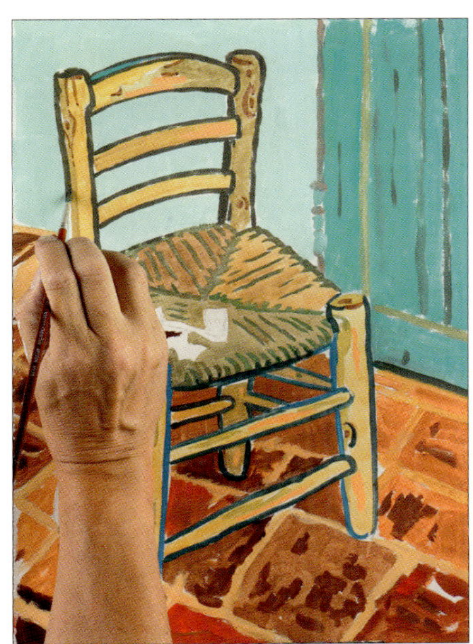

26 Paint a shadowed outline along the top of the chair with burnt umber and phthalo blue. Continue painting outlines around the chair back with the same mix.

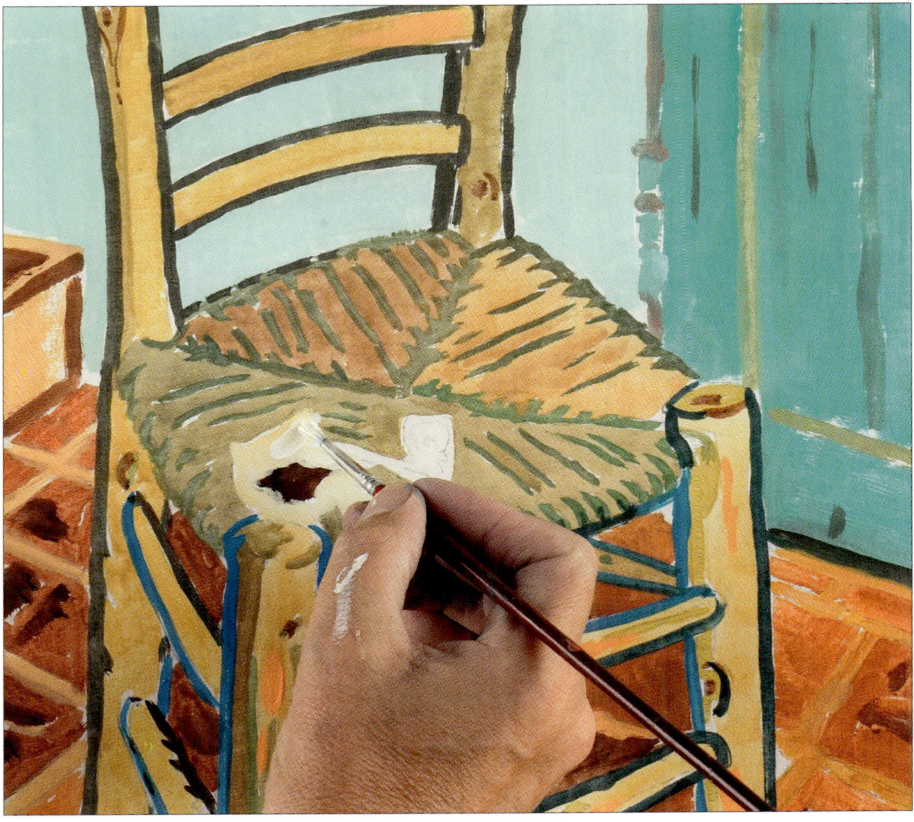

27 Mix white with a touch of Naples yellow and paint the tobacco pouch on the chair.

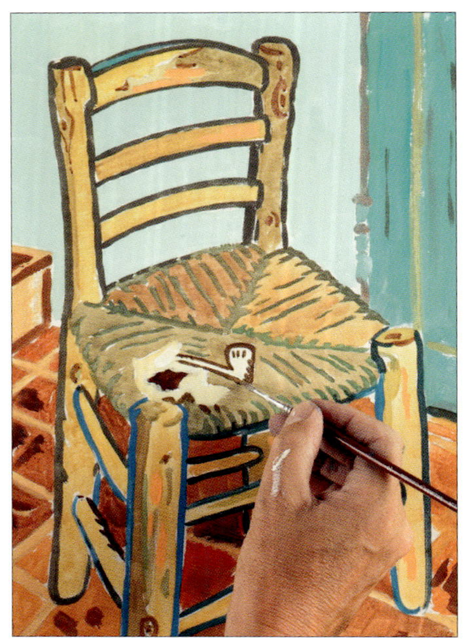

28 Paint the pipe in the same light colour, then outline it with diluted burnt umber.

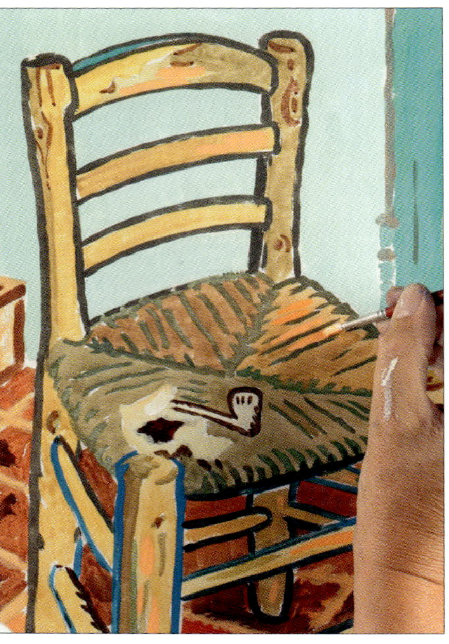

29 Mix white with cadmium orange to paint highlights in the straw of the chair seat.

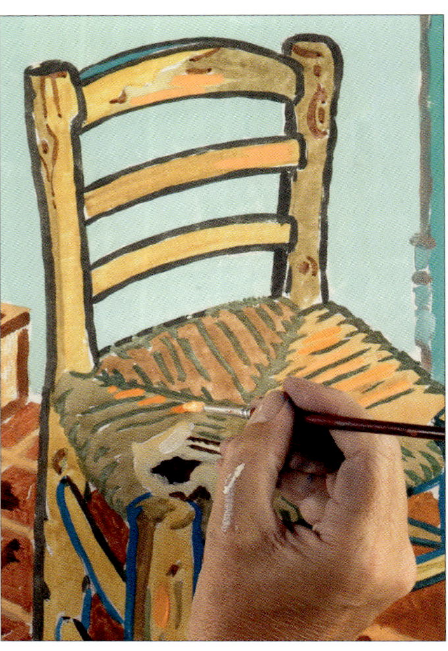

30 Continue painting highlights.

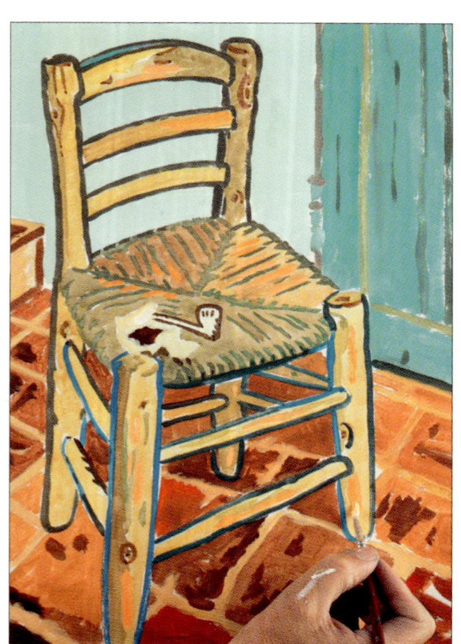

31 Add highlights to the rest of the chair in the same colour.

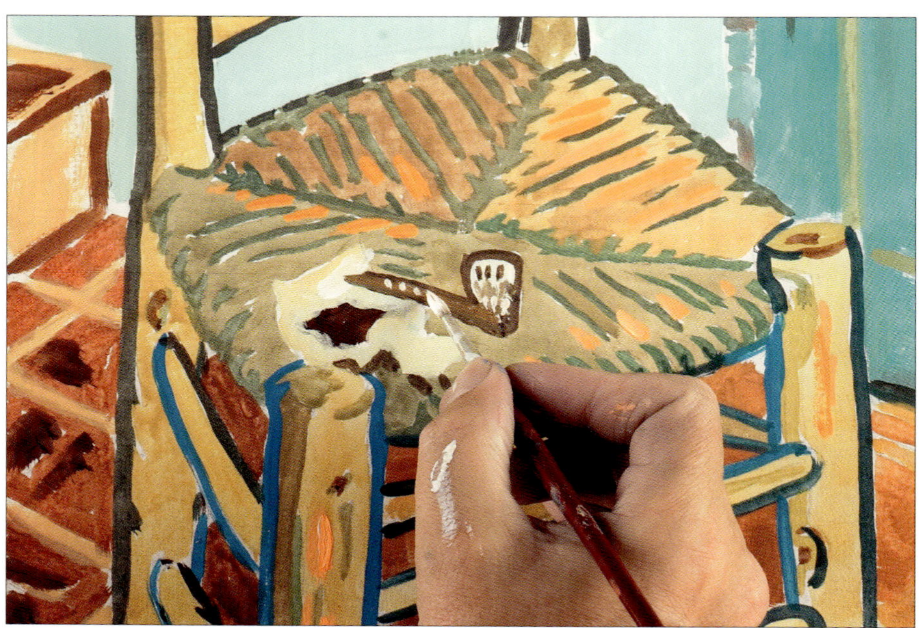

32 Finally, add detail to the pipe with a background mix of burnt umber, white and a touch of phthalo blue. Add dots of white with a touch of cadmium orange.

The finished painting, reduced in size.

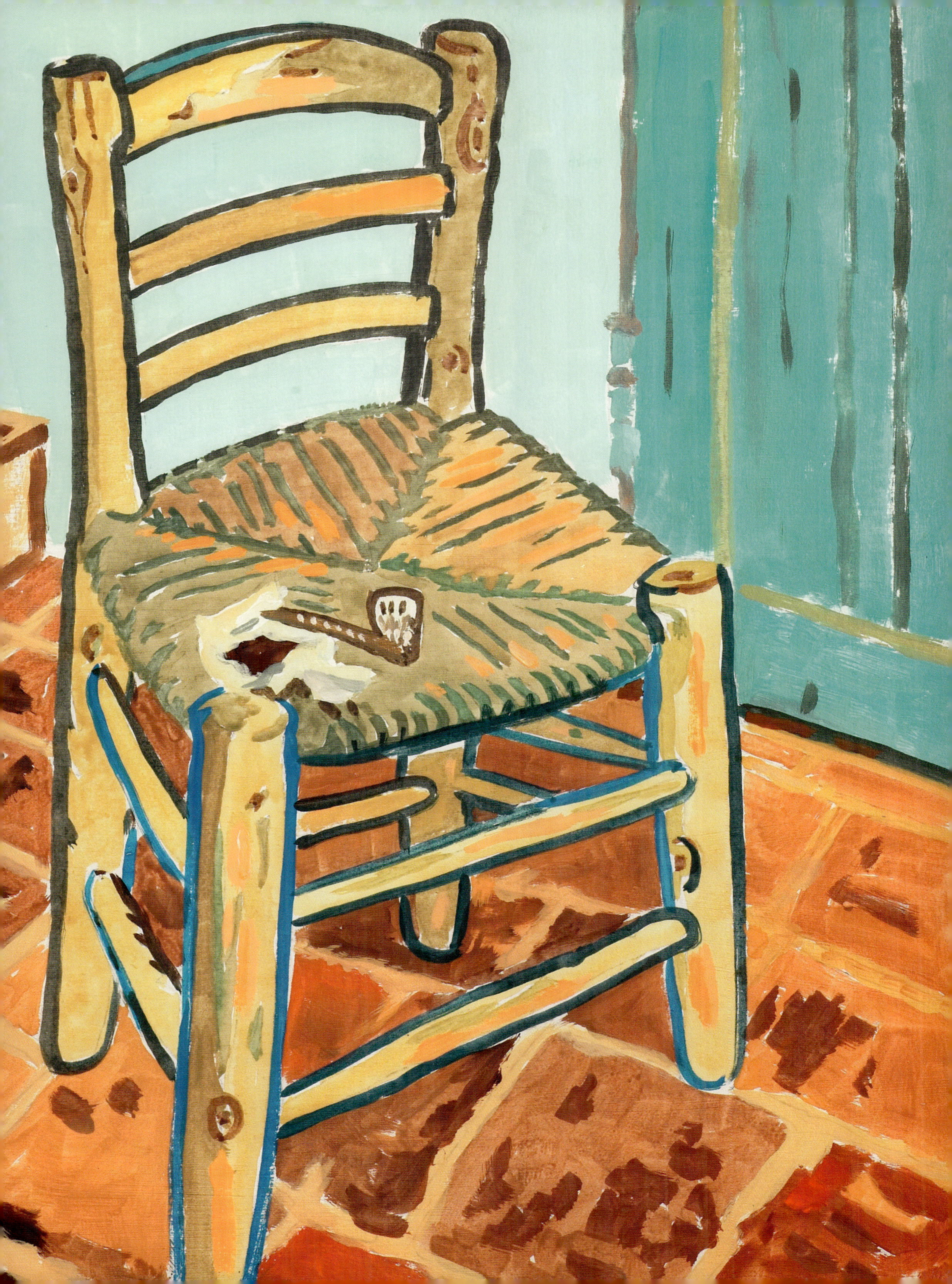

Wheat Field With Cypresses

The emphasis in this painting, which is one of a series, is the windy, swirling sky, captured with curved brush strokes, and the way these swirls are echoed in the cypress trees on the right. The effect is one of heat and movement, and the colours suggest the heat of Provence set against the blues and violets of the blustery sky. The stylised way that this image was painted suggests that it may have been painted from memory, evoking the experience, rather than from life.

Tip

For this project you need to transfer the tracing on to the painting surface in two stages. First, transfer the main shapes, marked with thicker lines. Then when the main colour has been blocked in, leave the painting to dry overnight and then transfer the rest of the tracing over the top. This is to prevent the opaque acrylic paints from obscuring the drawing during the painting process.

You will need

Grey board primed with white gesso

Colours: titanium white, phthalo blue (green shade), dioxazine purple, Naples yellow, lemon yellow, burnt umber, sap green, cadmium yellow deep, burnt sienna, cadmium red light

Brushes: no. 12 flat bristle brush, no. 6 flat bristle brush, no. 2 round bristle brush

Masking tape and board

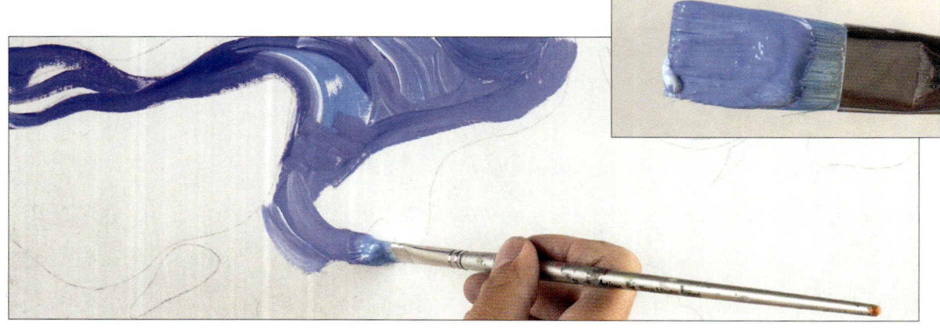

1 Transfer the main shapes from the tracing, marked with thicker lines. Mix titanium white, phthalo blue (green shade) and dioxazine purple. Also make a paler mix of the same colours with more white. Pick up the first mix with the no. 12 flat bristle brush, then dip one corner in the paler mix. Begin to paint the curves in the sky area, creating streaks as your brush is dipped in the two different shades.

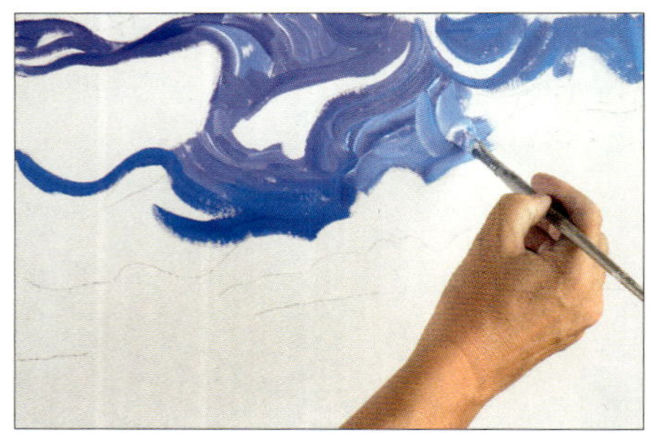

2 Do not worry about following the curves on the tracing too closely. The painting should have a spontaneous look, with plenty of texture. Continue to pick up slightly different shades of the white, blue and purple mix.

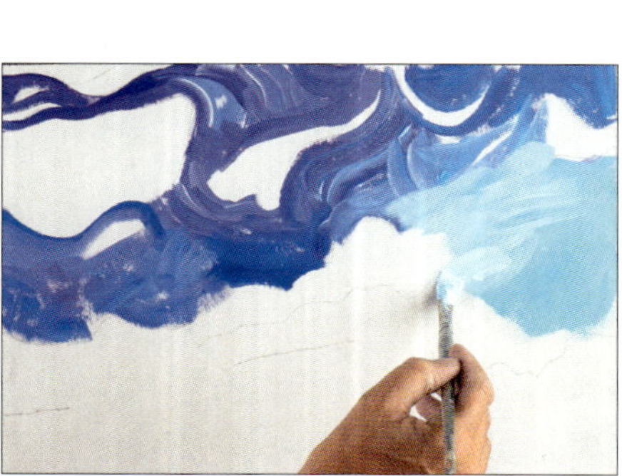

3 Paint a pale mix of white and phthalo blue over where the trees will be. Make the mix paler towards the left. The brush strokes should be allowed to show.

4 Block in the lighter shapes in the sky with a mix of white and Naples yellow.

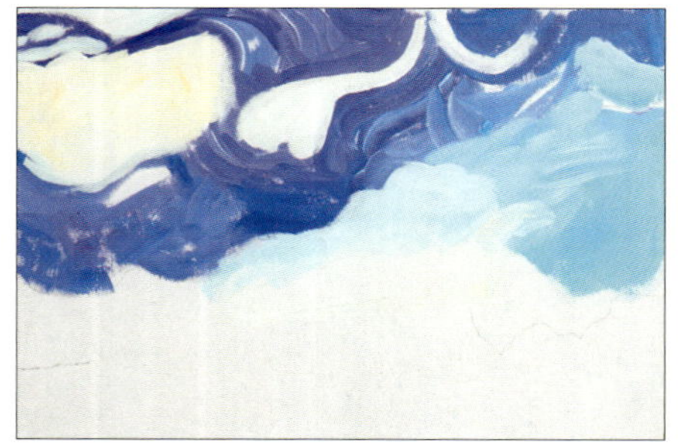

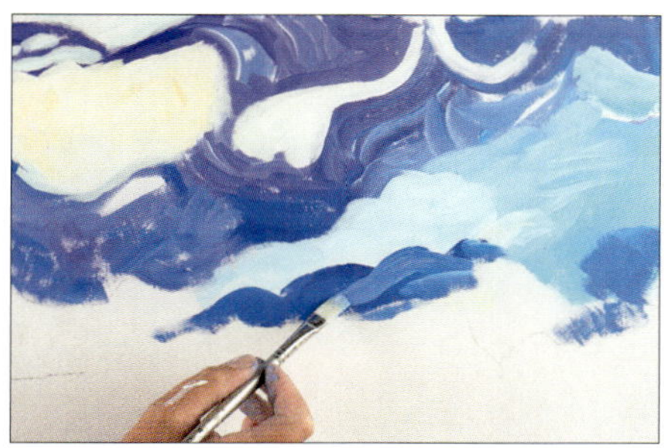

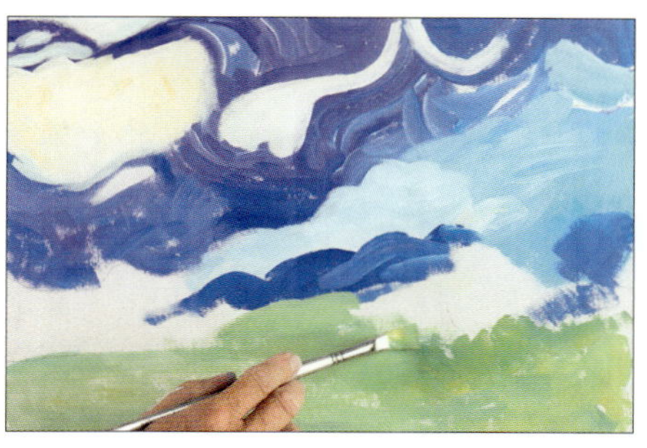

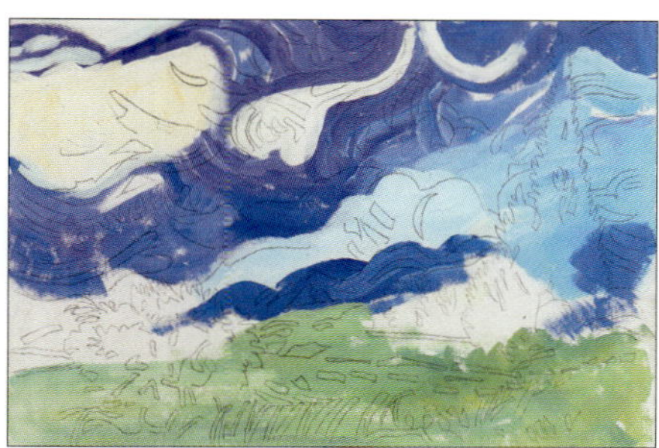

5 Mix phthalo blue and dioxazine purple to paint the distant mountains.

6 Mix lemon yellow with a tiny bit of phthalo blue and Naples yellow and paint green at the bottom, picking up different shades to create a streaky effect. Leave the painting to dry, preferably overnight.

7 When the painting is completely dry, transfer the second stage of the tracing, which is indicated with finer lines.

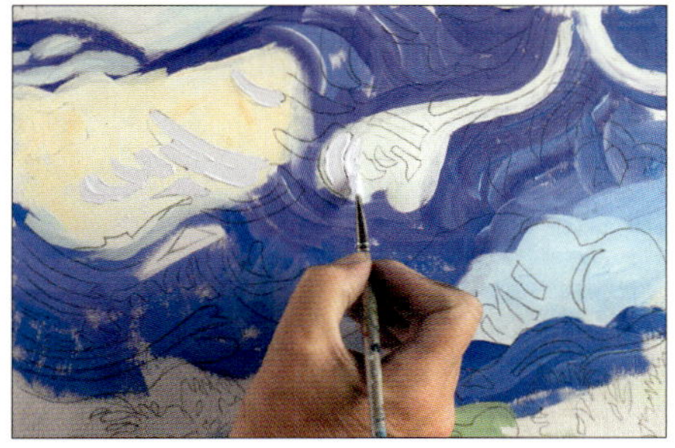

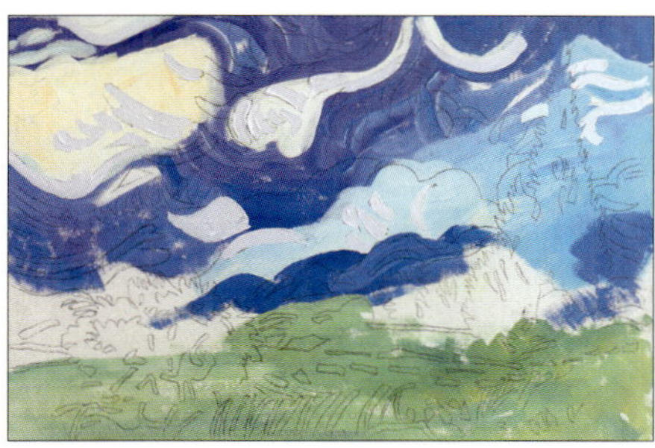

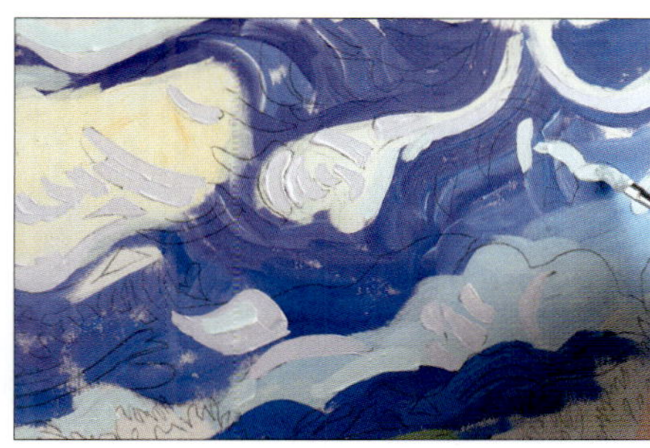

8 Mix dioxazine purple, titanium white and phthalo blue and use a no. 6 flat brush to paint touches of this in the sky. Do not worry if you go over the lines, as it should look spontaneous and should have a textured, impasto effect.

9 Finish painting these pale areas as shown.

10 Add a hint of phthalo blue to white and paint more brush strokes in the sky.

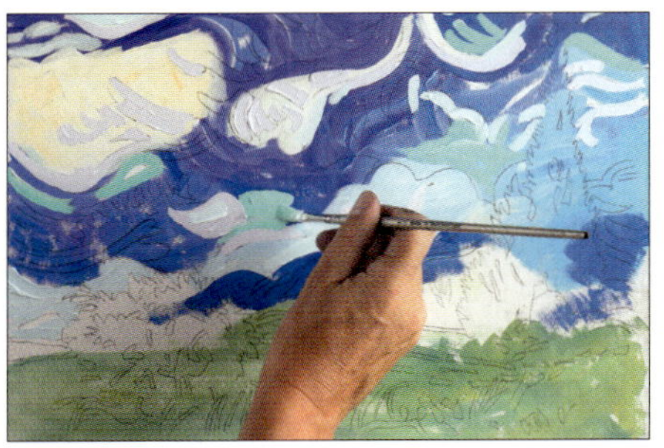

11 Add a little lemon yellow to the mix and paint more brush strokes in the sky with this turquoise.

12 With the brush loaded with the turquoise mix, dip the corner in white to create streaks.

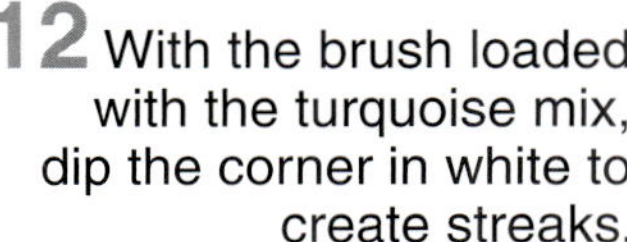

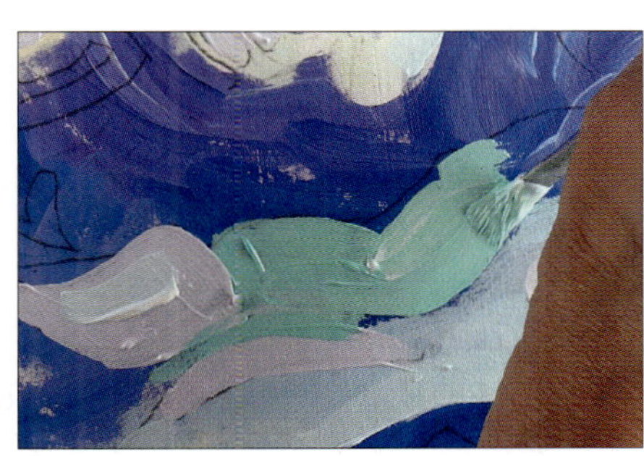

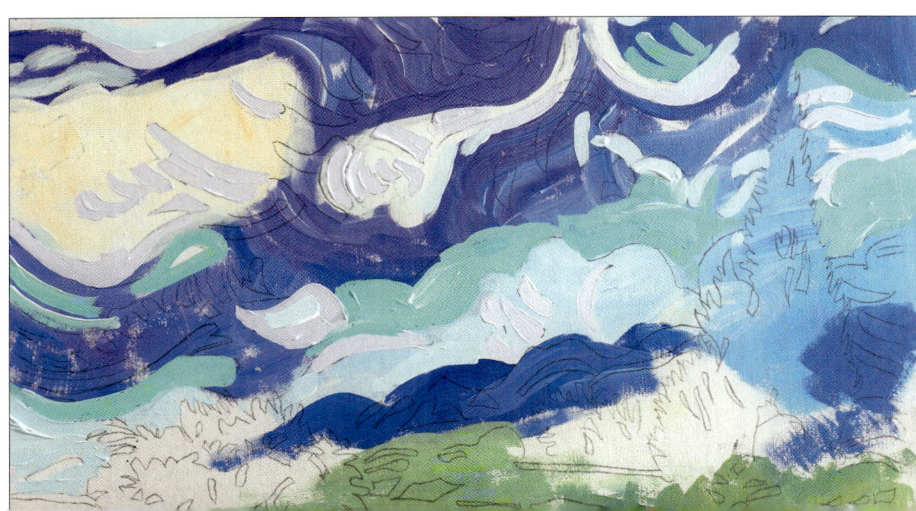

The sky area so far.

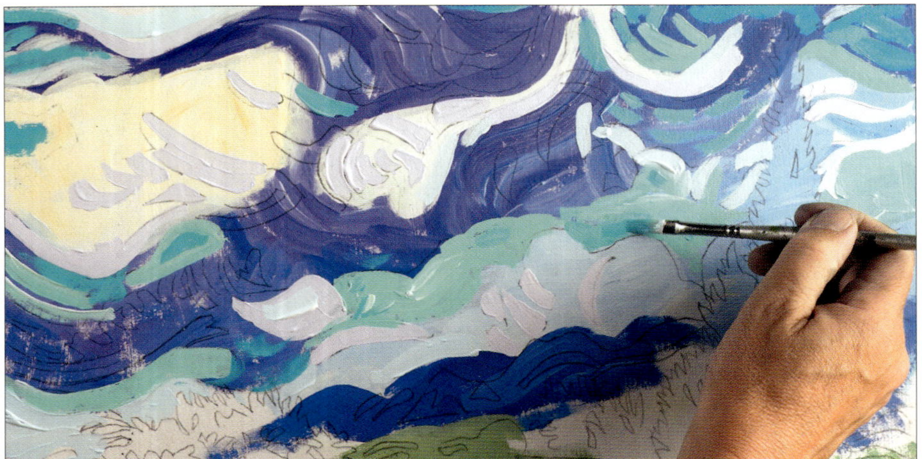

13 Add phthalo blue to the mix and add streaks to the sky, following the curves of the clouds.

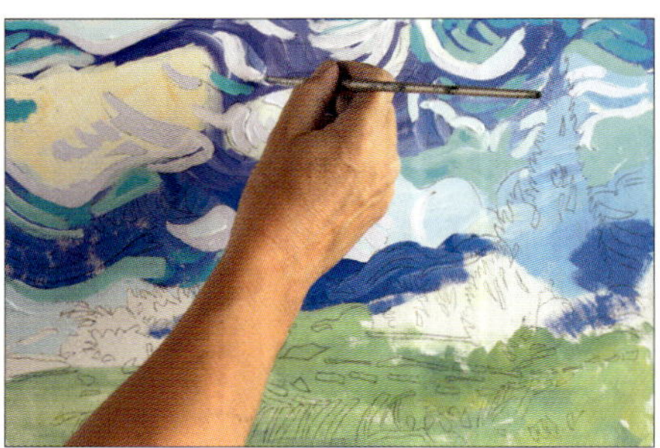

14 Mix white with a hint of dioxazine purple and work on the clouds.

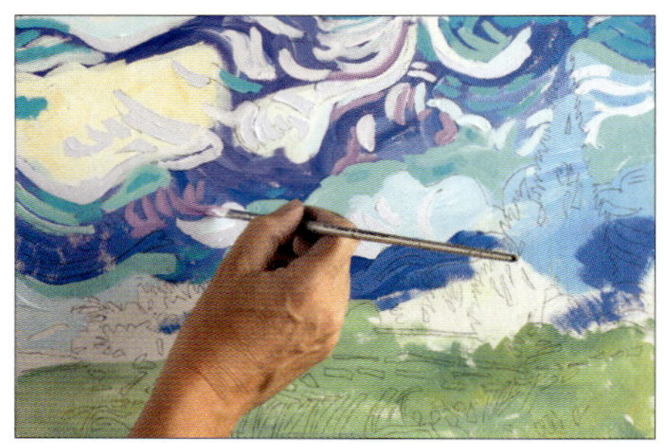

15 Add much more purple to the mix to paint touches round the edges of the clouds. These brush strokes should be streaky and textured.

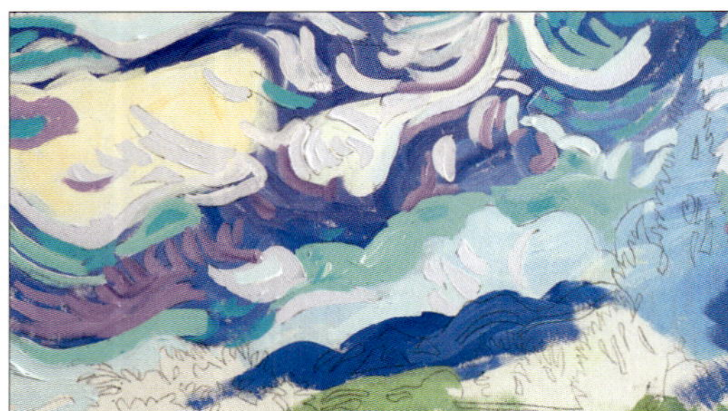

The sky area so far.

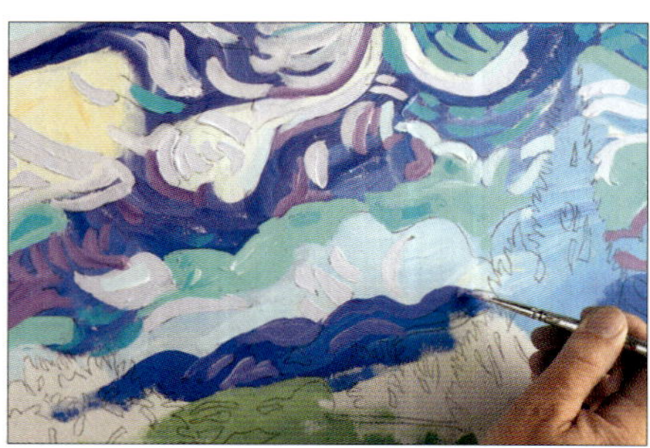

16 Add phthalo blue to the purple mix and paint brush strokes on the mountains. These should be lighter than the dark blue underpainting.

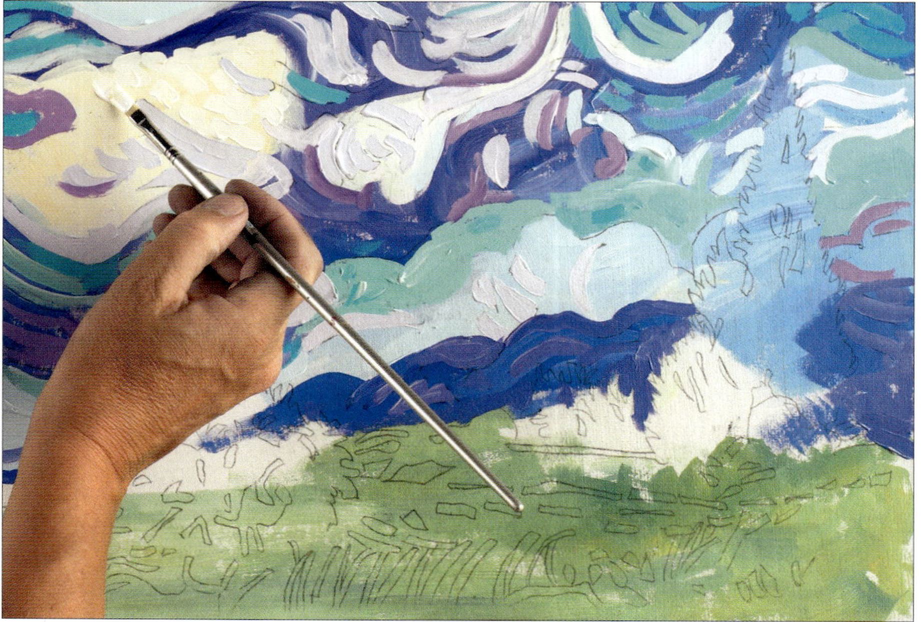

17 Mix white with a touch of Naples yellow to finish the clouds. Break up the flat colour with chunky texture. These marks are not in the tracing.

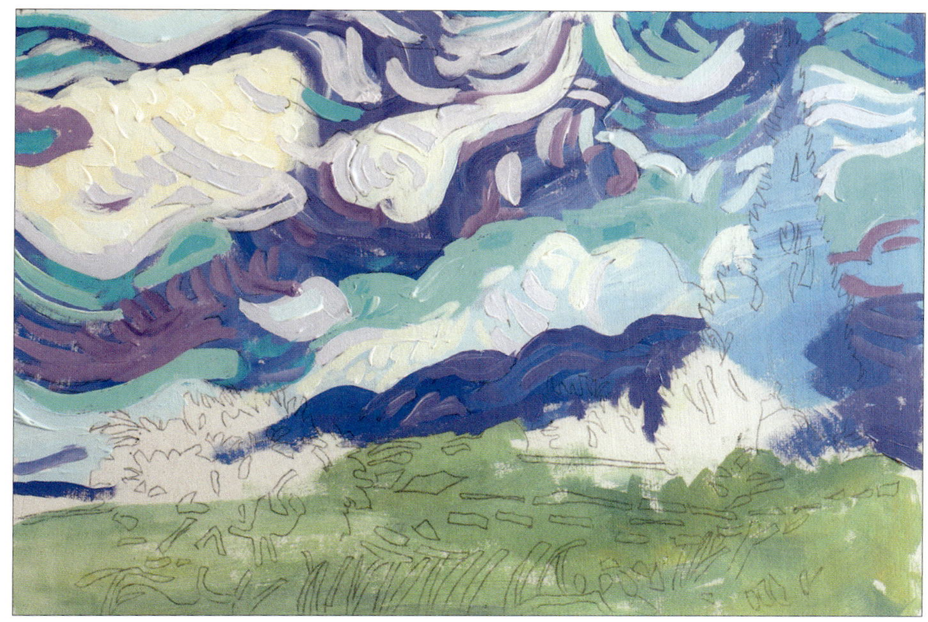

18 Add more cloud texture with the same mix, and some swirling lines at the edge of the distant mountains.

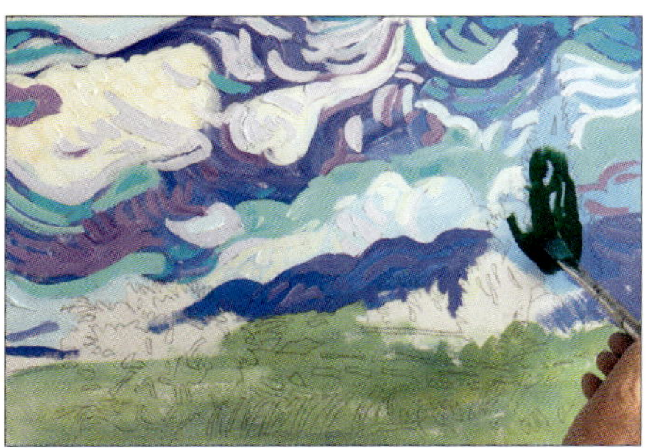

19 Begin painting the cypresses with phthalo blue with a touch of lemon yellow and burnt umber, using the no. 12 flat brush. Start with large, bold brush strokes.

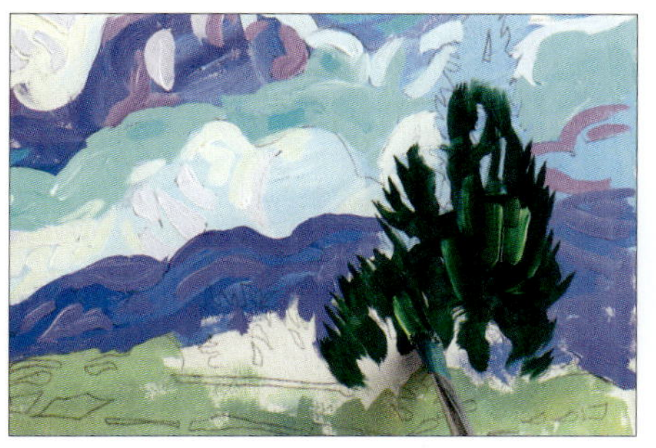

20 Dip the corner of the brush in lemon yellow to create streaky brush strokes as you paint on the dark green.

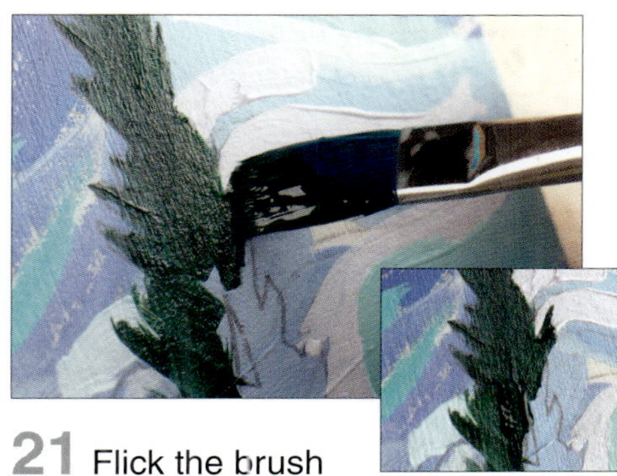

21 Flick the brush outwards to create the outer branches of the trees.

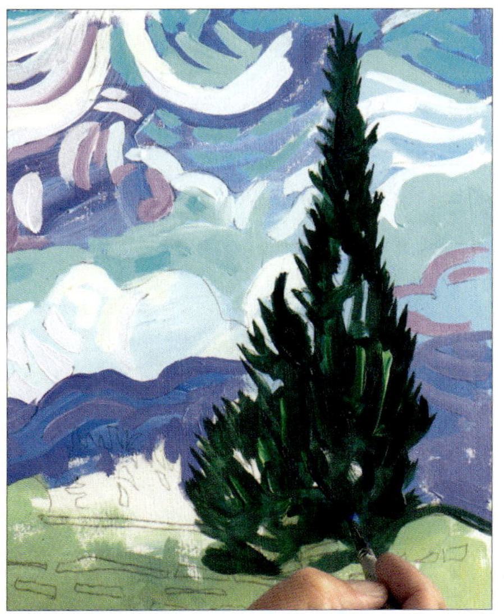

22 Mix burnt umber and phthalo blue and use the no. 6 flat brush to paint wavy lines going up the trees.

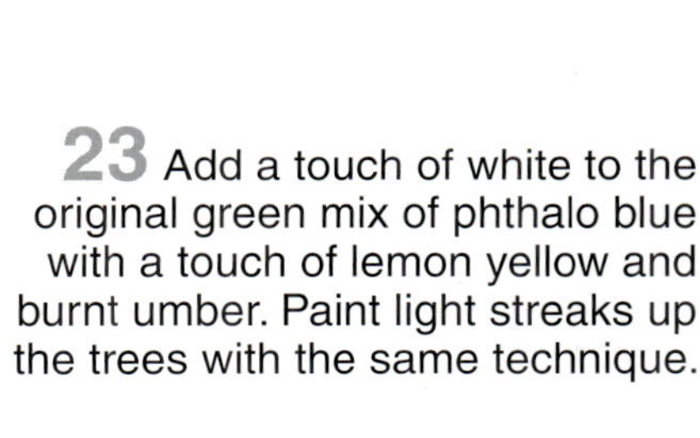

23 Add a touch of white to the original green mix of phthalo blue with a touch of lemon yellow and burnt umber. Paint light streaks up the trees with the same technique.

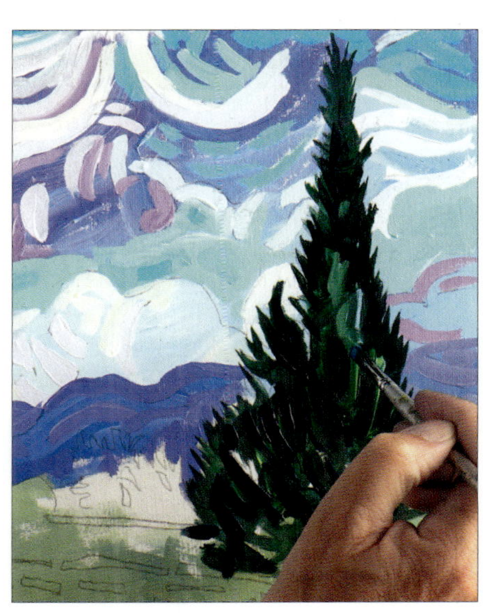

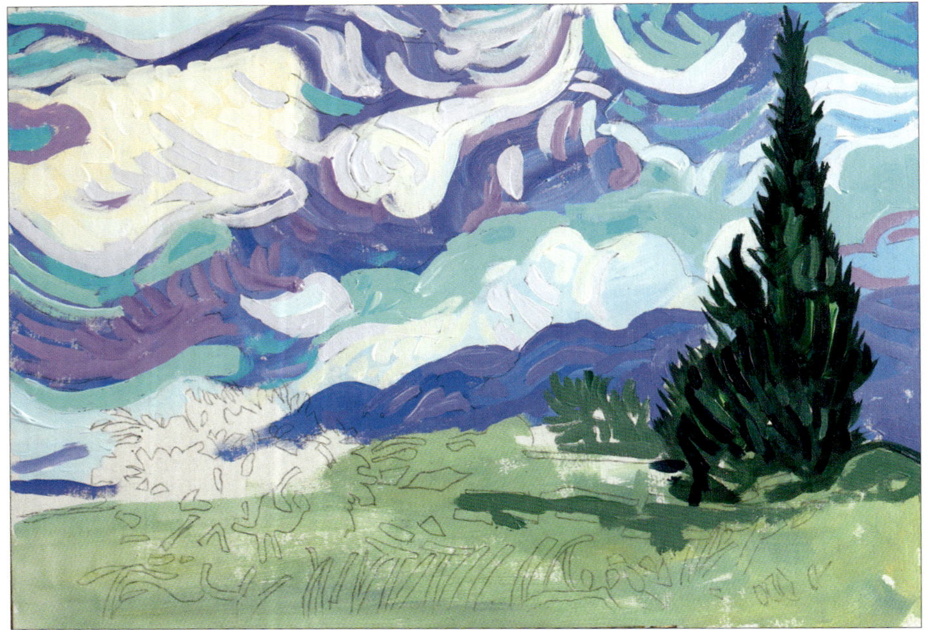

24 Use the same paler green to paint the small tree on the left and the cornfield below the main trees, leaving the background showing through.

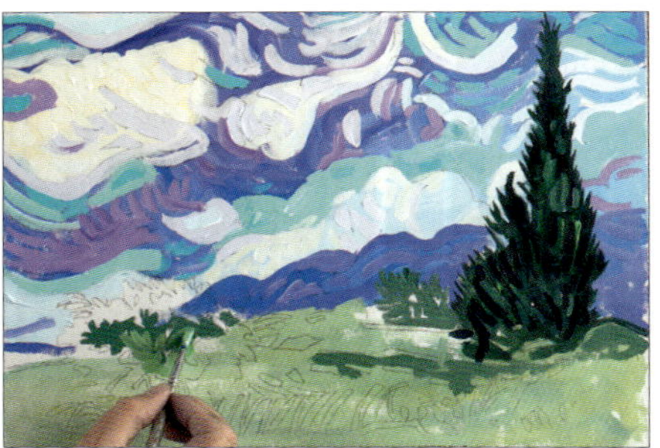 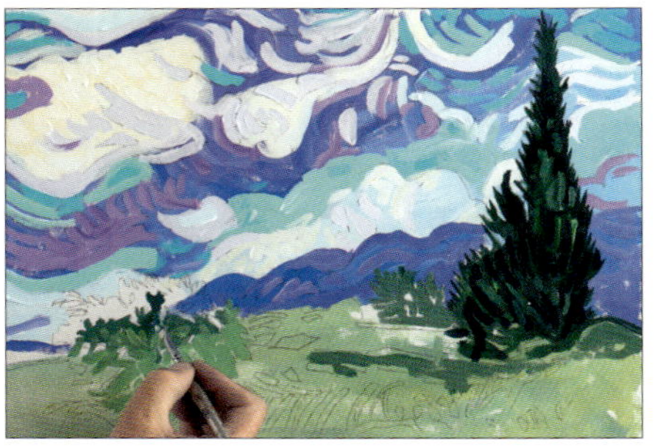 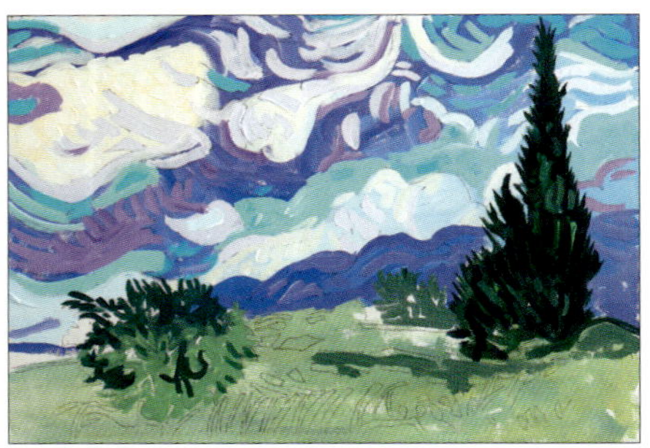

25 Use the same mix but dip the corner of the brush in pure lemon yellow to paint the bushes on the left.

26 Paint the top of the bushes with phthalo blue, lemon yellow and burnt umber.

27 Continue adding dark green to the bushes, working from the tracing but also adding short, stabbing brush strokes and little curves.

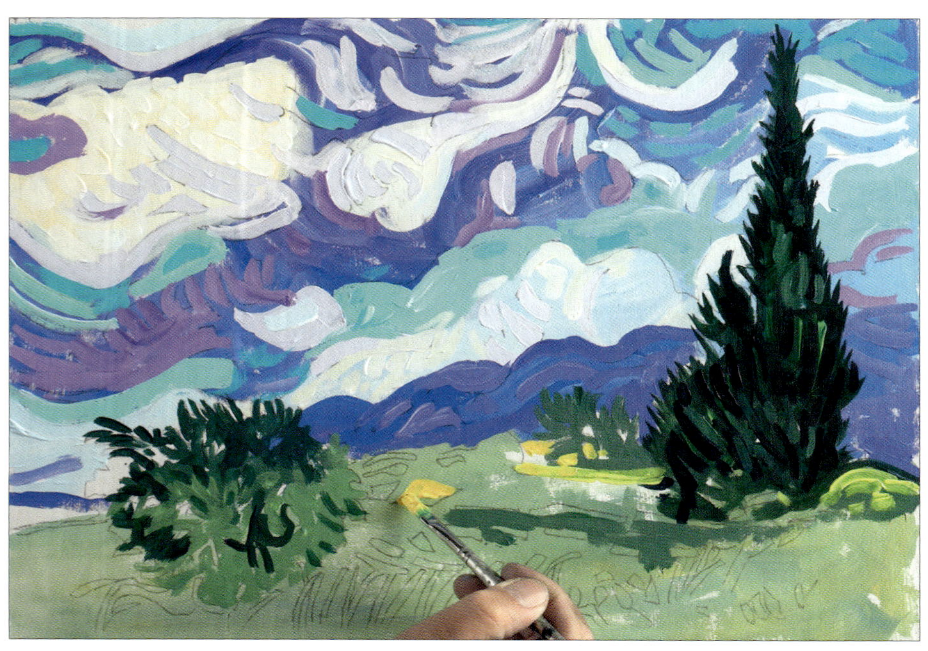

28 Paint the cornfield with a mix of lemon yellow and Naples yellow. Add a tiny touch of the previous green to create streaks.

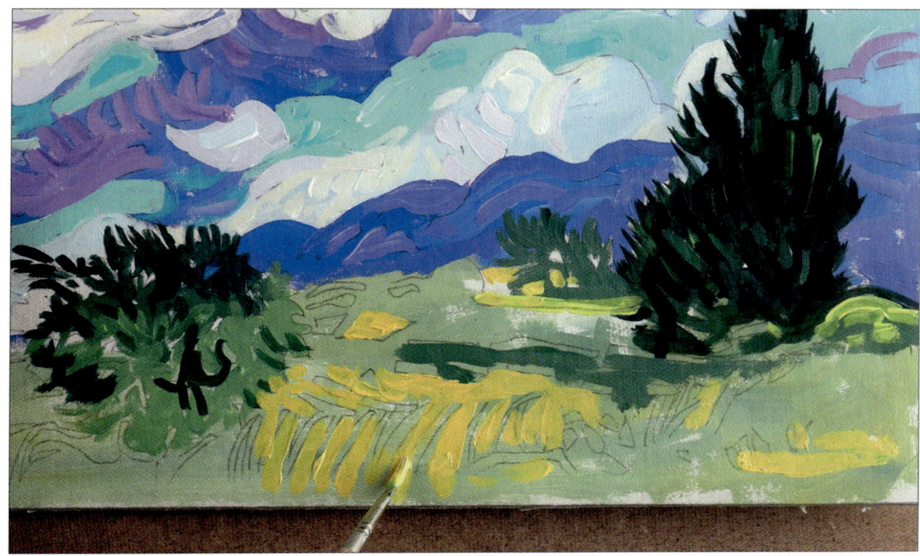

29 Paint vertical strokes, following the drawing and allowing the green to show thrcugh.

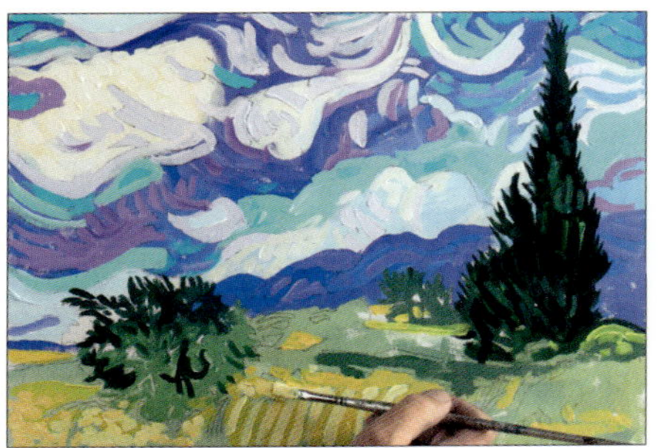

30 Add white to the mix and add paler streaks. Also paint dabs on the left, as in the clouds.

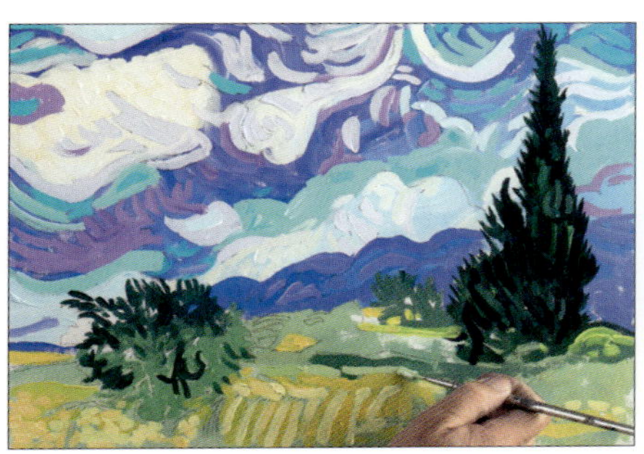

31 Mix sap green and lemon yellow to make a pale green, and paint this along the top of the corn colour in streaky brush strokes.

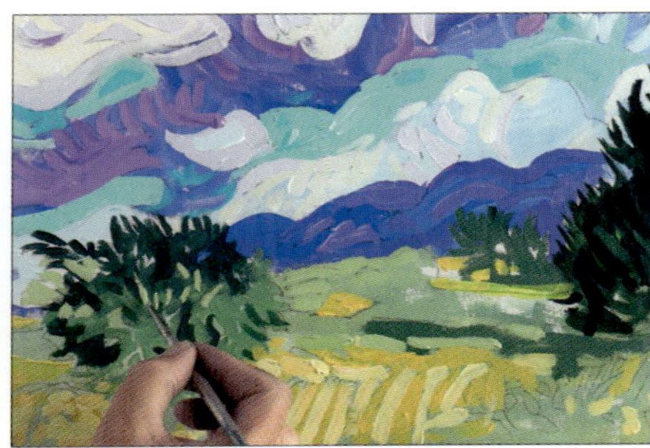

32 Paint stabbing strokes of the same bright green cn the left-hand bushes with the no. 2 round brush. Some are shown in the tracing, but you can add more of your own.

33 Mix white with cadmium yellow deep and a touch of burnt sienna to make a brownish yellow. Paint vertical lines in the foreground cornfield.

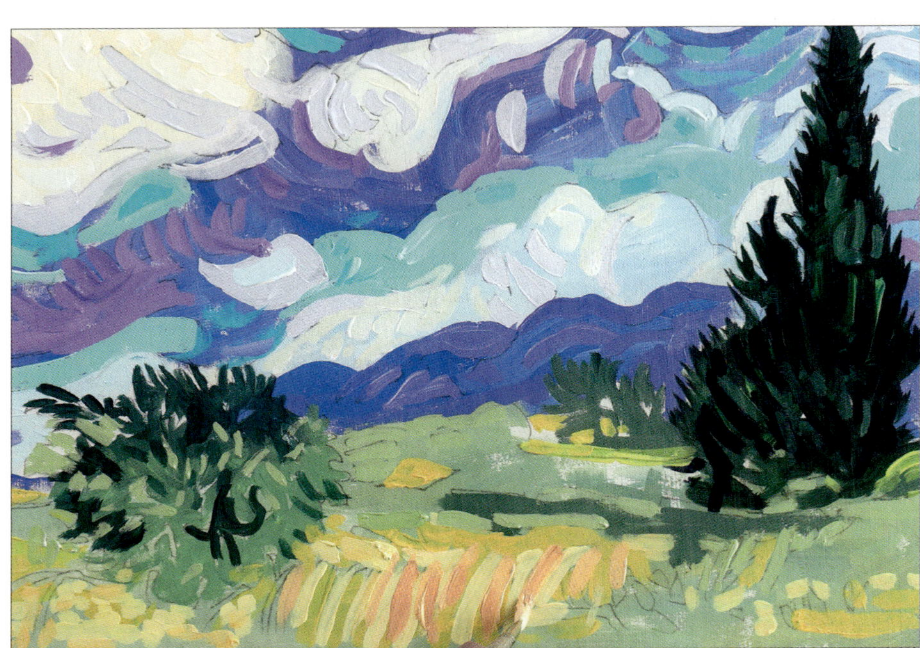

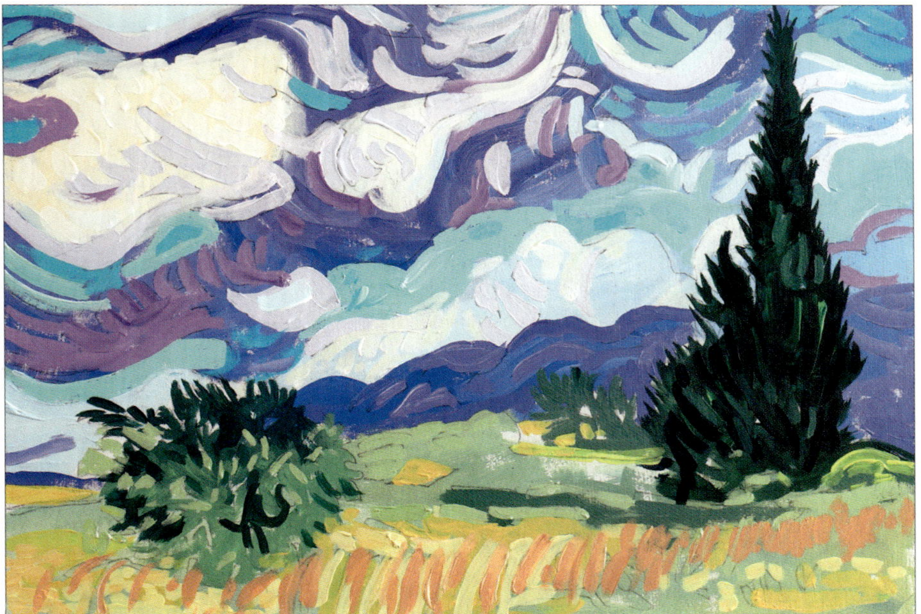

34 Continue the vertical lines in the cornfield to the right as shown.

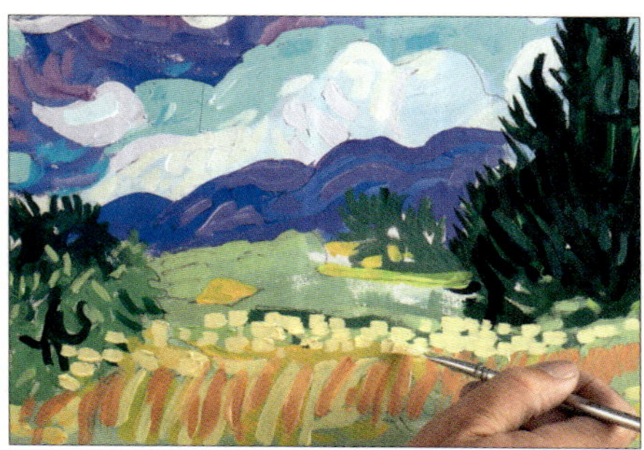

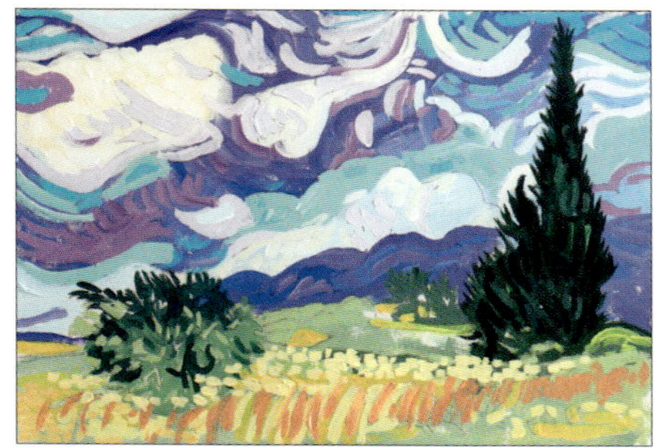

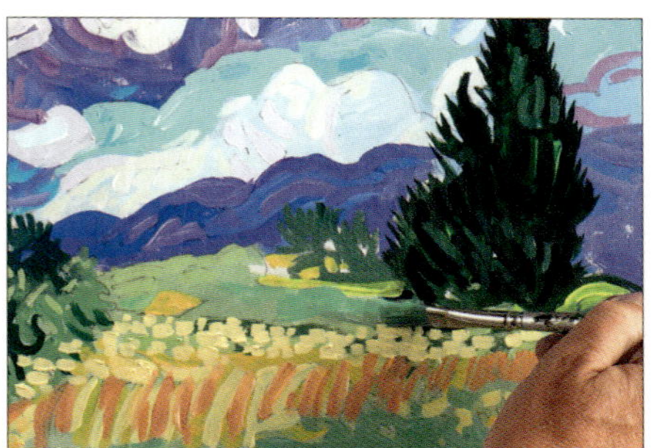

35 Use a mix of white, lemon yellow and cadmium yellow deep with the no. 6 flat brush to stab little brush strokes on top of the corn.

The painting so far.

36 Mix sap green and white and stipple paint on to the foreground, leaving some yellow showing through. Also paint under the cypresses with the same colour.

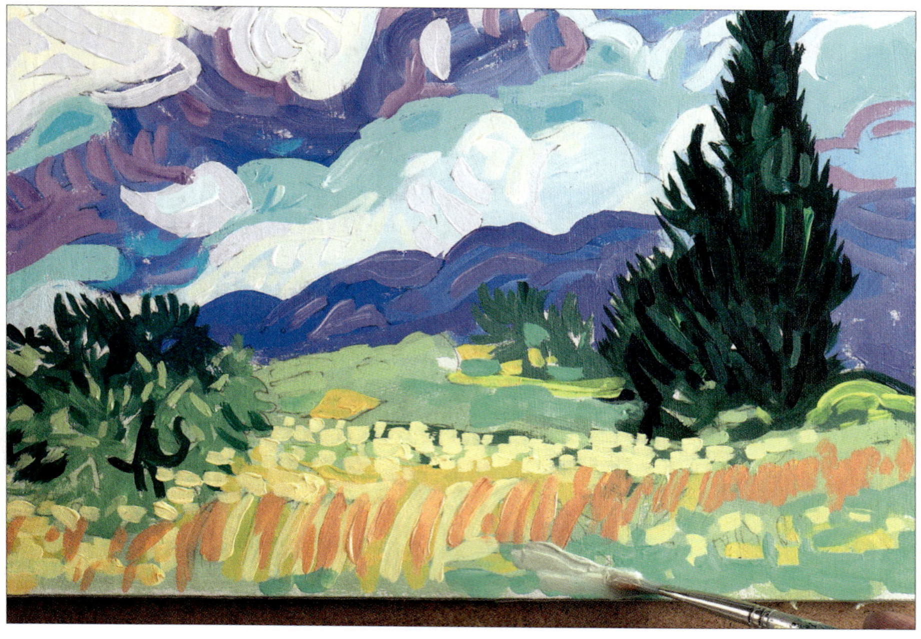

37 Make a pale grey to paint the stones in the foreground using burnt umber and phthalo blue with a little white.

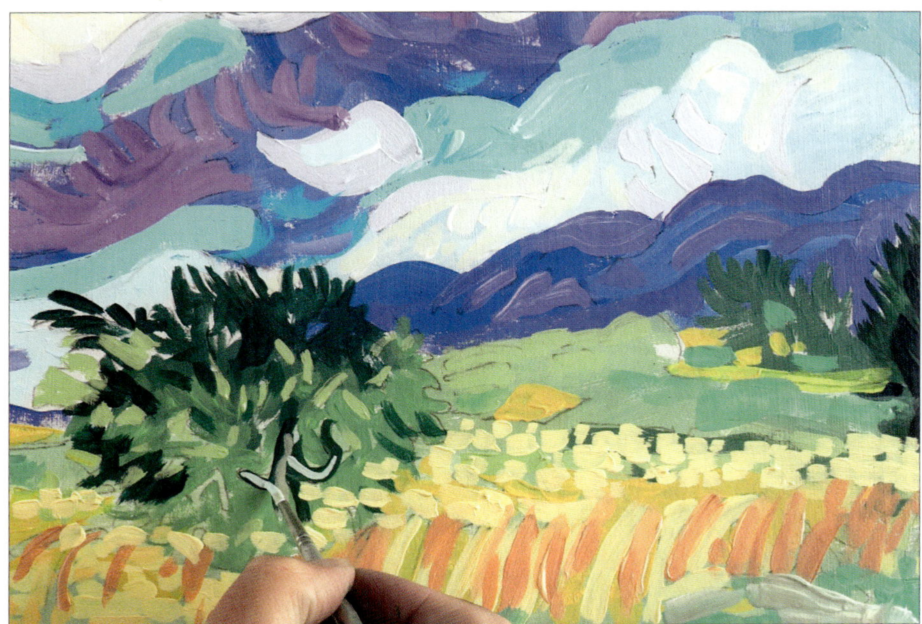

38 Change to the no. 2 round brush and paint the trunk of the left-hand bush, and some branches, with the same colour.

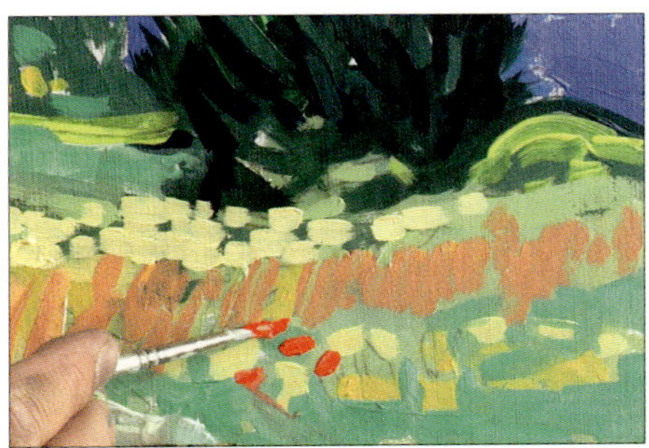

39 Paint poppies on the green in front of the cypresses with a mix of cadmium red light and a tiny bit of white.

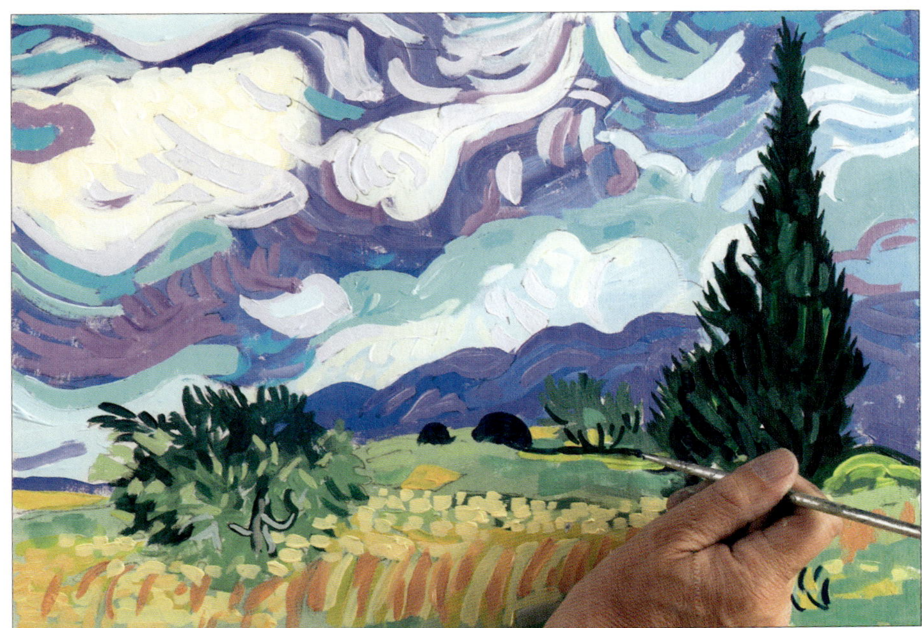

40 Make a dark mix of burnt sienna and phthalo blue to paint touches of detail in the foreground, and dark shapes and lines in the distance.

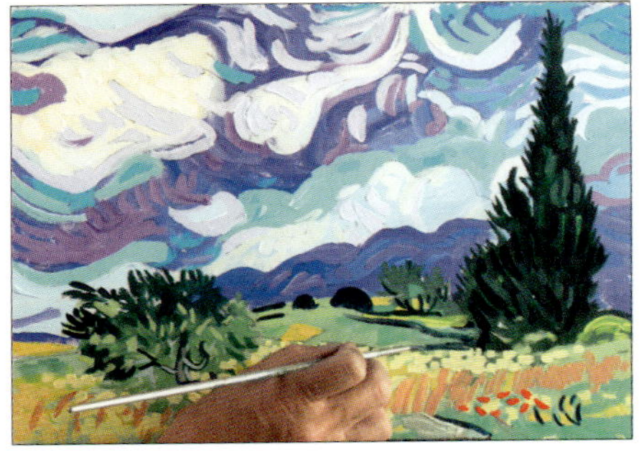

41 Add more darks on the left, and lines down towards the cypresses.

Overleaf

The finished painting.

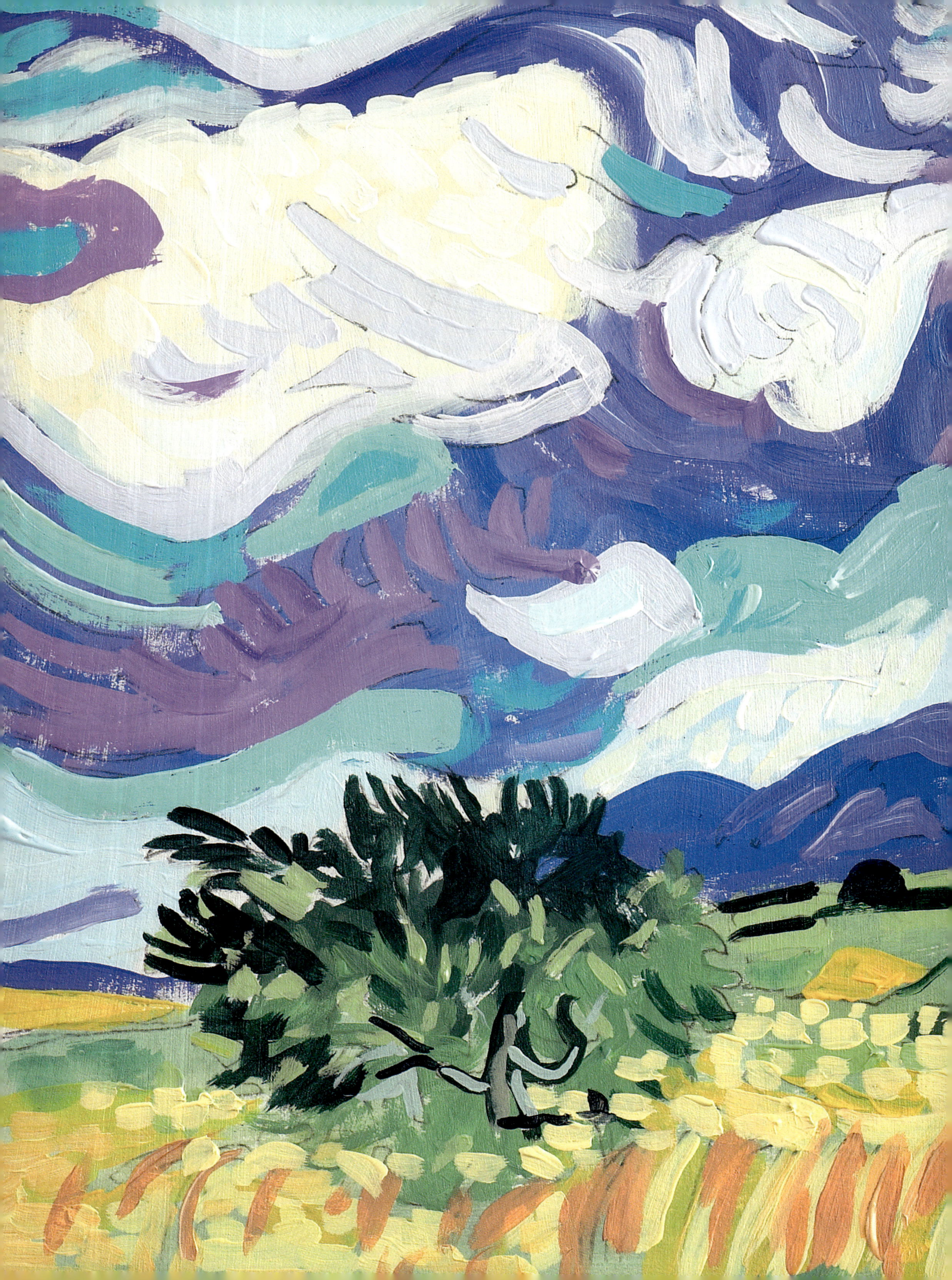

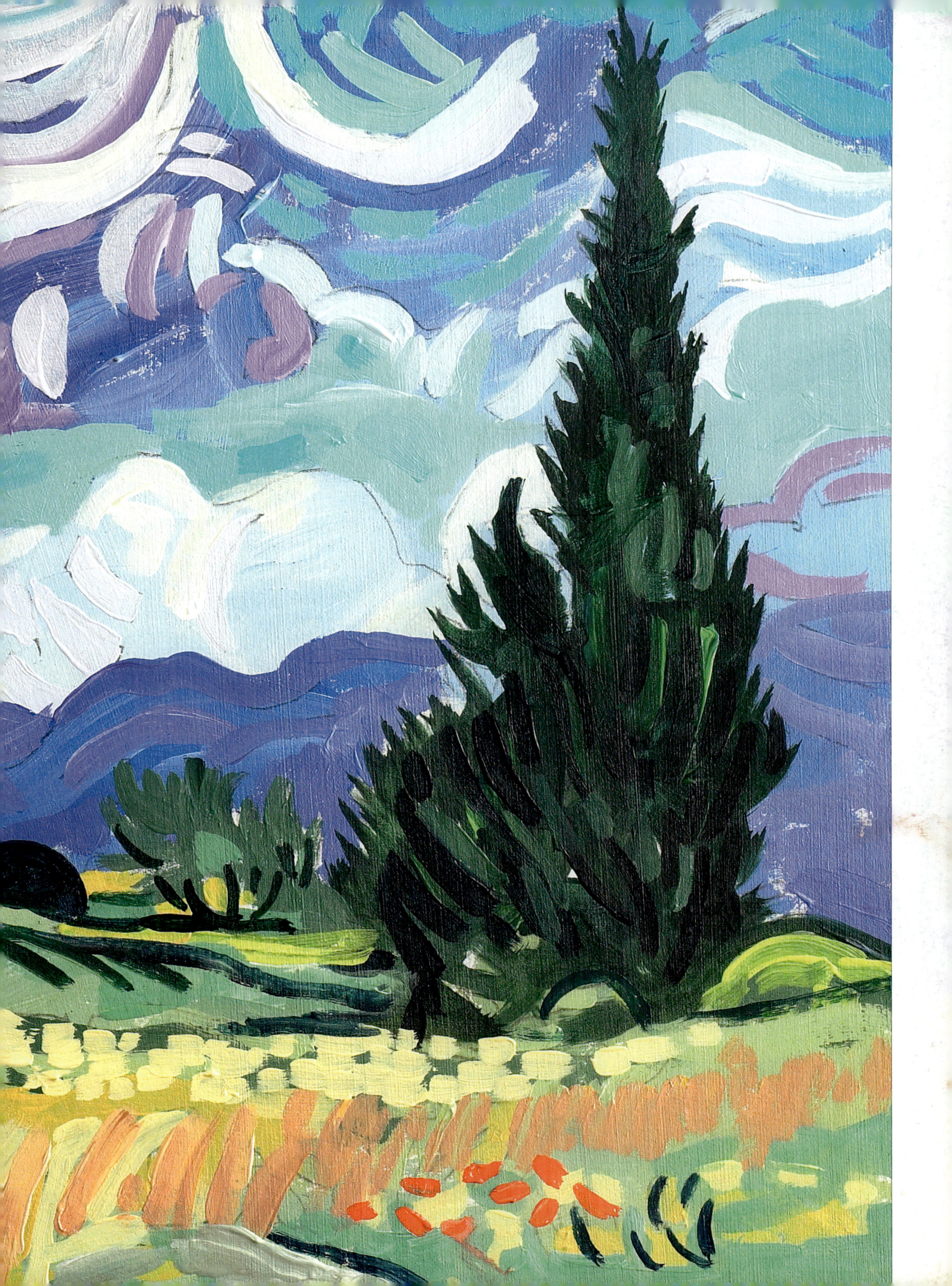

Provence Lavender

For this image I have taken several typical Van Gogh motifs, and incorporated them into an image from my memory of travelling through Provence. The shape of the sky was taken from Van Gogh's *Enclosed Field With Rising Sun*, the mountains are similar to those in *Field of Spring Wheat at Sunrise* and the lines of crops are to be found in *Landscape With Carriage and Train*. You might find that looking up these paintings helps to inspire your work.

I have kept to a predominantly orange and blue colour combination, as these are the Provençal colours described by Van Gogh in letters to his brother, Theo.

TRACING

5

You will need

Grey board primed with white gesso

Colours: lemon yellow, cadmium yellow deep, titanium white, cadmium orange, cadmium red light, phthalo blue (green shade), dioxazine purple, Naples yellow, sap green, burnt sienna, burnt umber, quinacridone magenta

Brushes: no. 12 flat bristle brush, no. 6 flat bristle brush, no. 2 round bristle brush

Masking tape and board

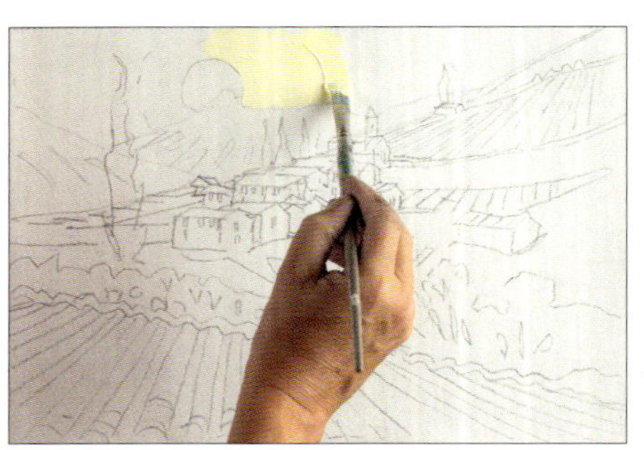

1 Use the no. 12 flat brush and a mix of lemon yellow, cadmium yellow deep and white to block in the sky. Work round the shape of the sun.

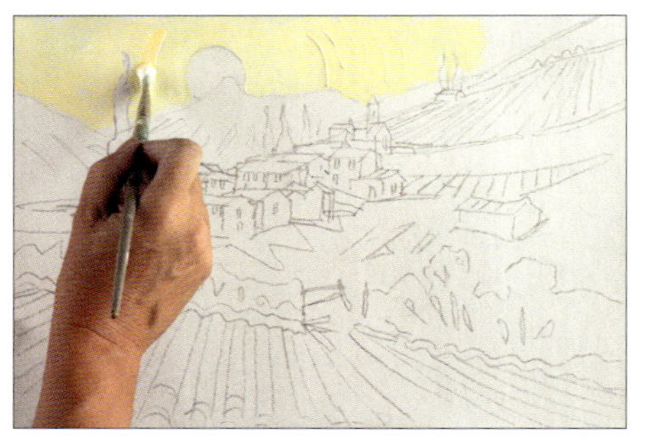

2 Add more cadmium yellow deep to the mix and paint in curves around the shape of the sun.

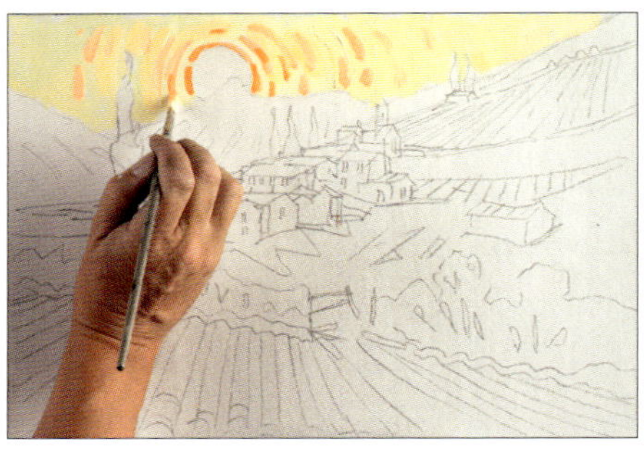

3 Change to the no. 6 flat brush and add cadmium orange to the mix. Paint curved lines round the sun.

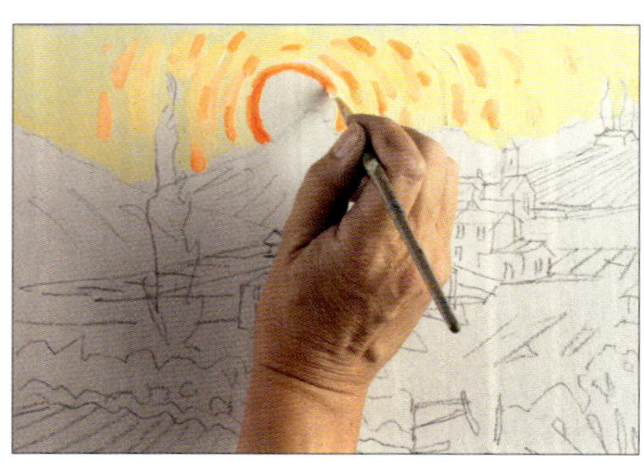

4 Add cadmium red light to the mix and paint a red-orange line round the sun.

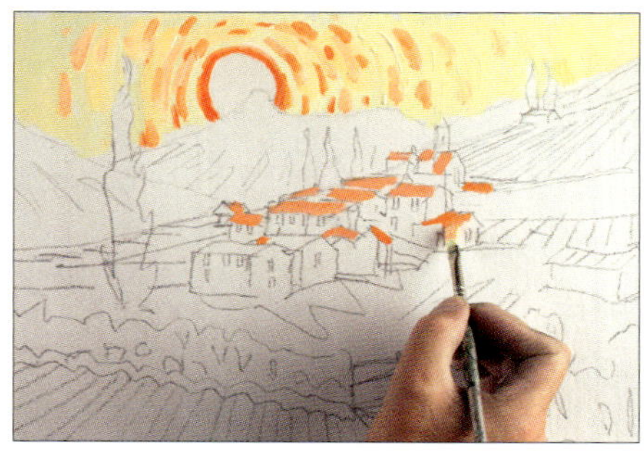

5 Add white to the mix and paint the roof tops.

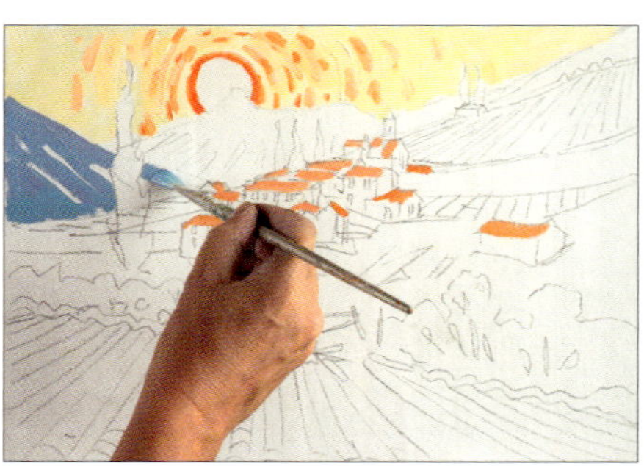

6 Block in the mountains with the no. 12 flat brush and a mix of phthalo blue (green shade), lots of white and a hint of dioxazine purple.

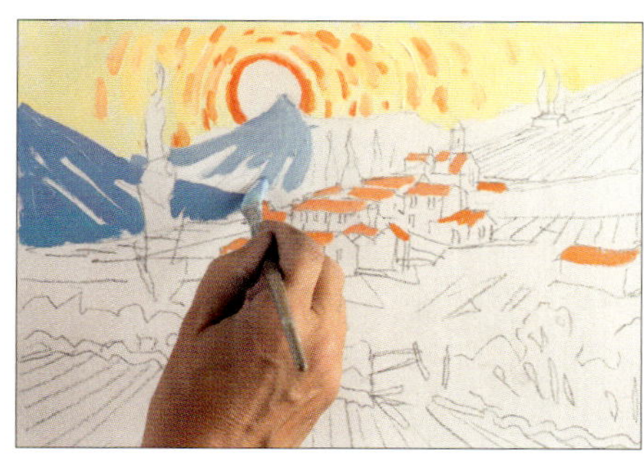 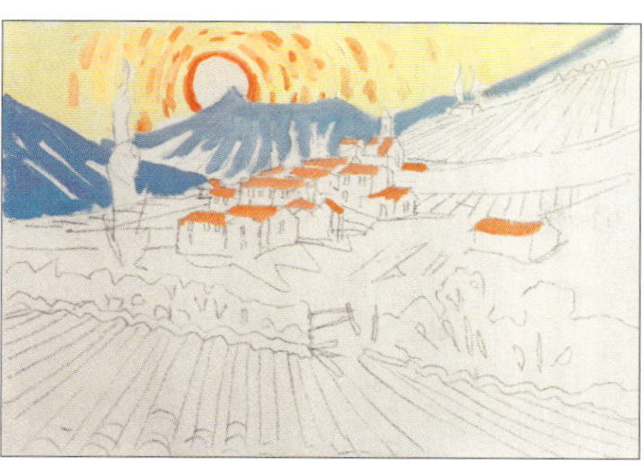 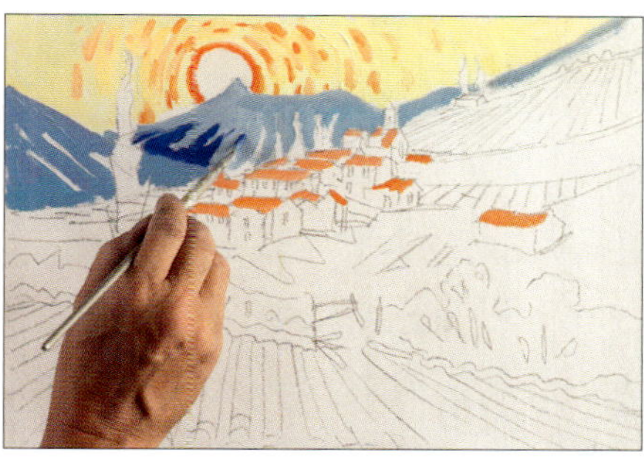

7 Add a little white to the mix to paint the next mountain to the right. Dip the corner of the brush in pure white to create streaks as you paint brush strokes down the mountain.

8 Continue in this way to the right of the painting.

9 Use the no. 6 flat brush with a darker mix of phthalo blue and dioxazine purple to paint shadows on the mountain.

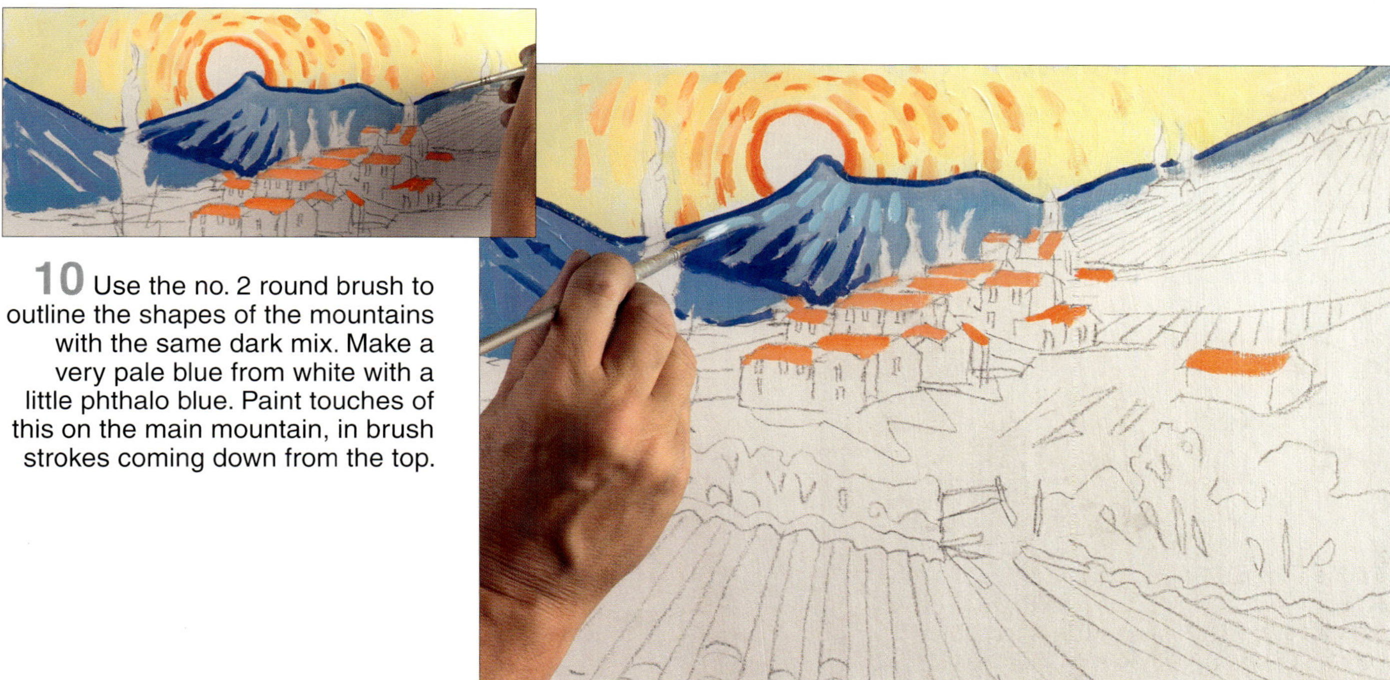

10 Use the no. 2 round brush to outline the shapes of the mountains with the same dark mix. Make a very pale blue from white with a little phthalo blue. Paint touches of this on the main mountain, in brush strokes coming down from the top.

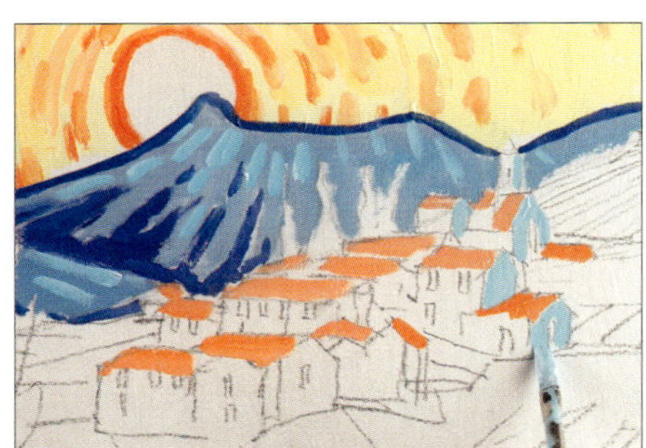 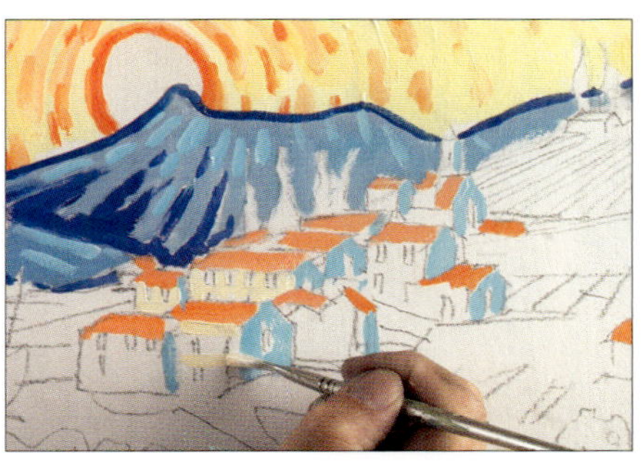 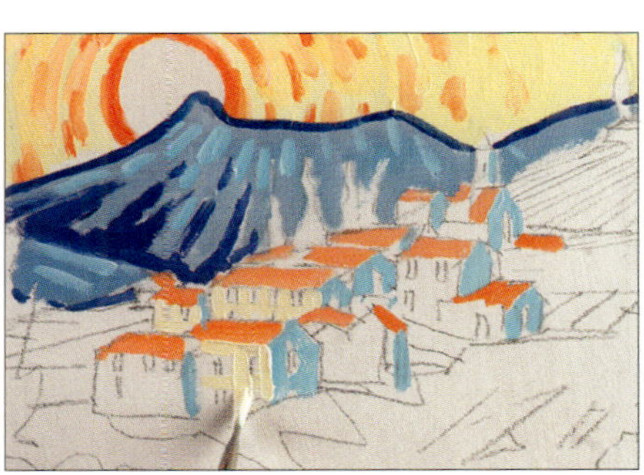

11 Paint the same light blue on the right-hand sides of the houses using the no. 6 flat brush.

12 Paint the fronts of the houses with Naples yellow and white. Paint round the windows and paint with horizontal strokes first.

13 Next paint vertical strokes.

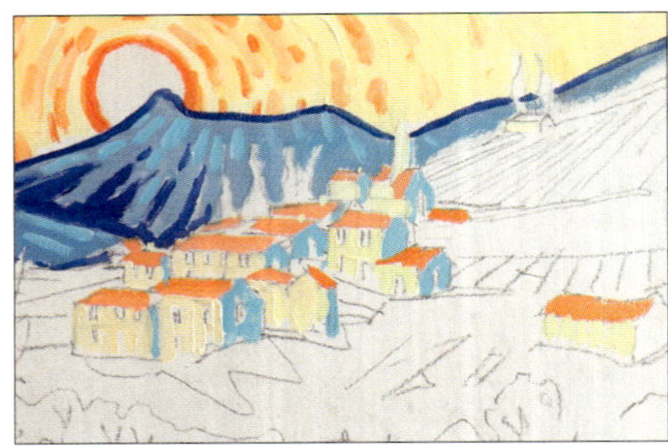
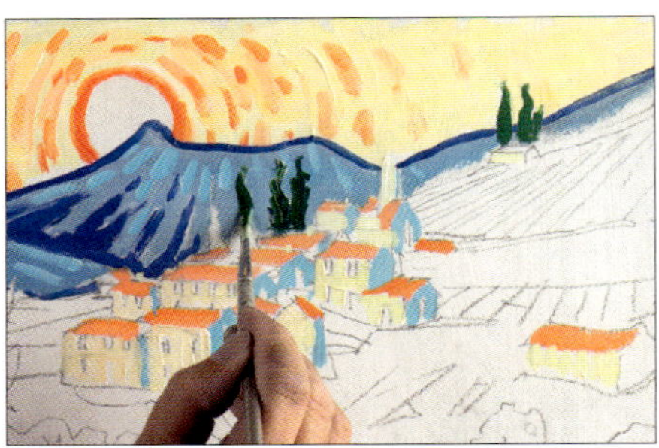
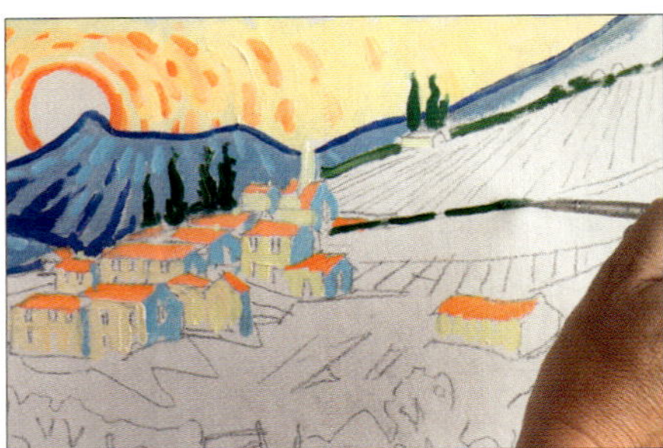

14 Add lemon yellow to the mix to brighten some of the houses and the barn on the right. Add white to make the distant buildings and the church very pale.

15 Mix sap green with white and a touch of phthalo blue and paint the distant cypress trees. Dip a corner of the brush in lemon yellow to create a streaked effect.

16 Use the same brush and colour to paint the hedges dividing the distant fields.

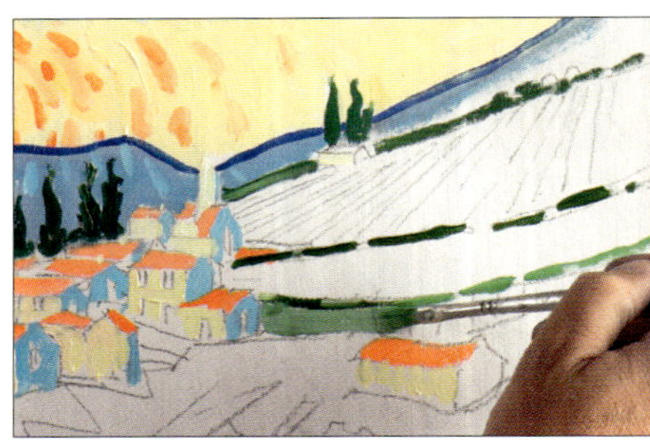
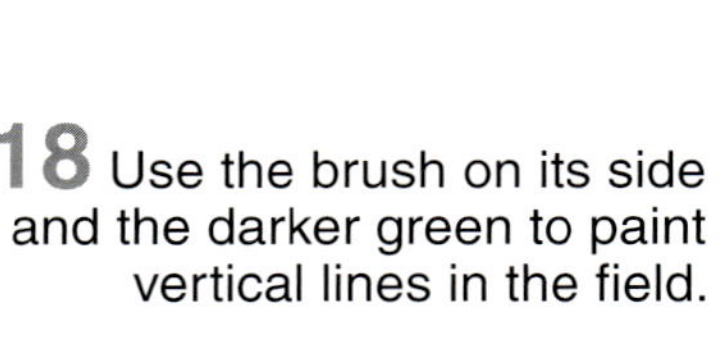
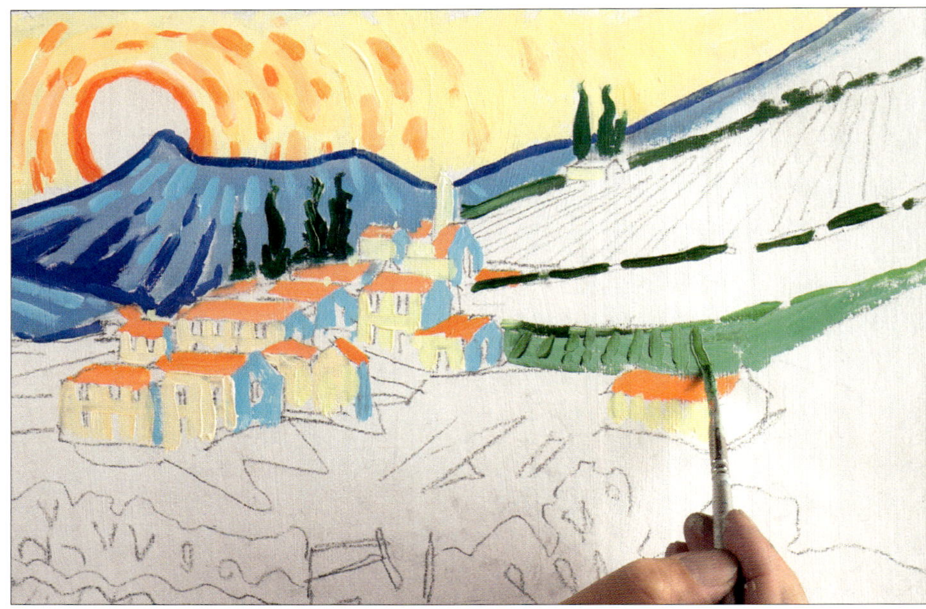

17 Add lots of white and some lemon yellow to the mix to paint the field in the middle distance.

18 Use the brush on its side and the darker green to paint vertical lines in the field.

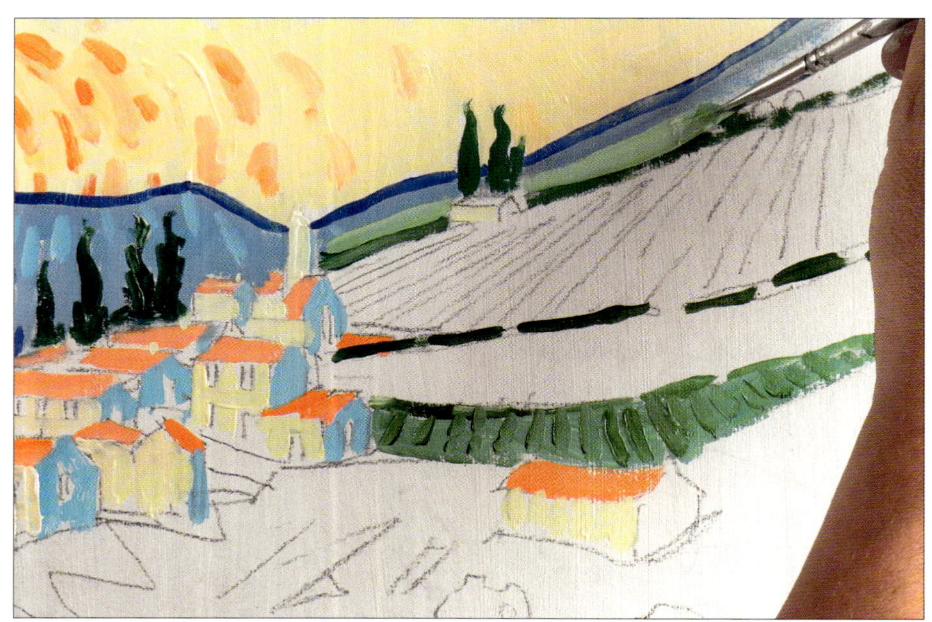

19 Add more white and lemon yellow to the paler green to make it paler still and paint the distant field.

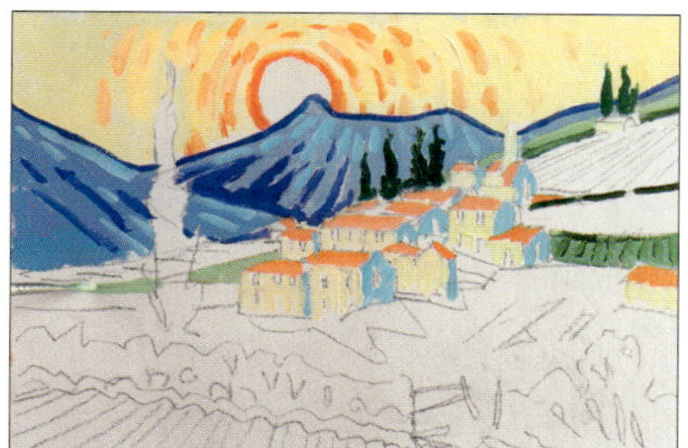

20 Use the same pale green to paint the triangular field on the left.

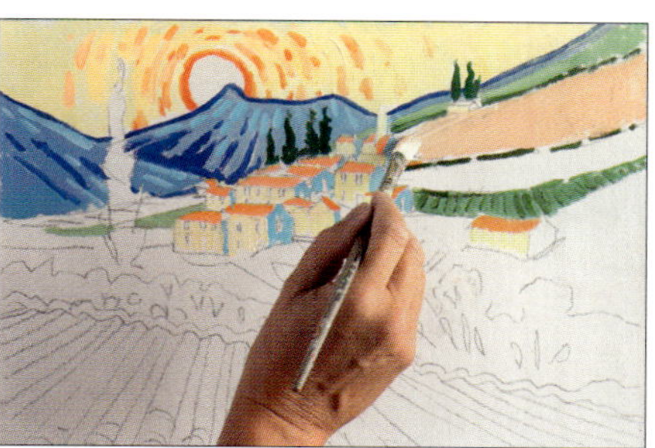

21 Make a fairly thin, dilute mix of cadmium orange, burnt sienna and white, and use the no. 12 flat brush to block in the soil colours in the distant fields.

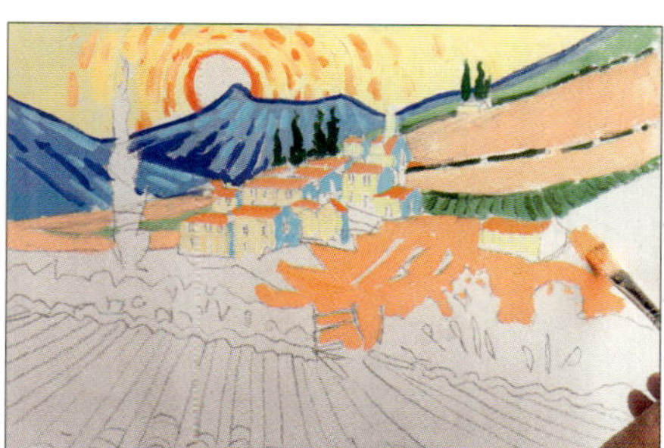

22 Continue painting the fields. Add more cadmium orange and burnt sienna as you come forwards.

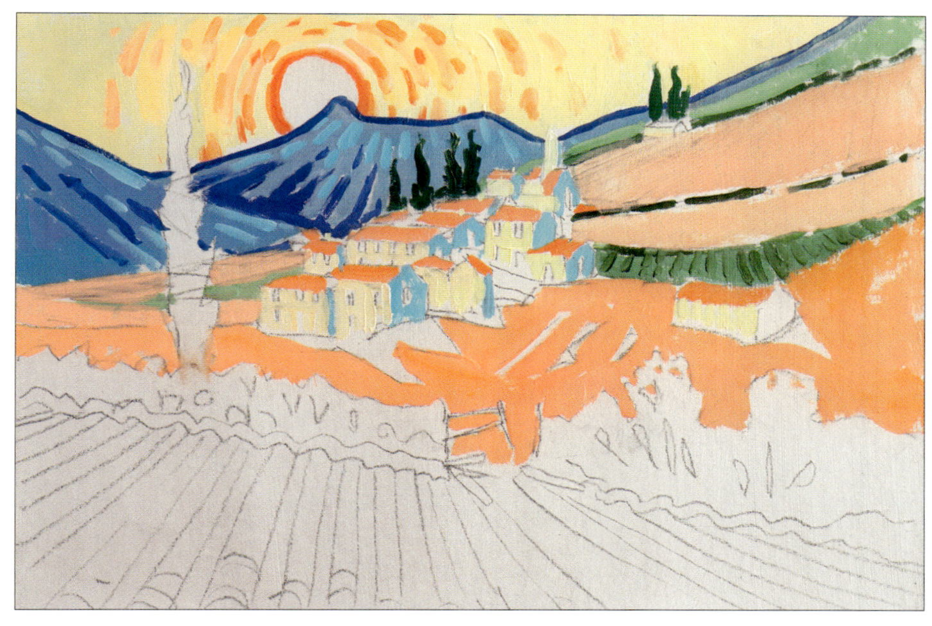

The painting so far.

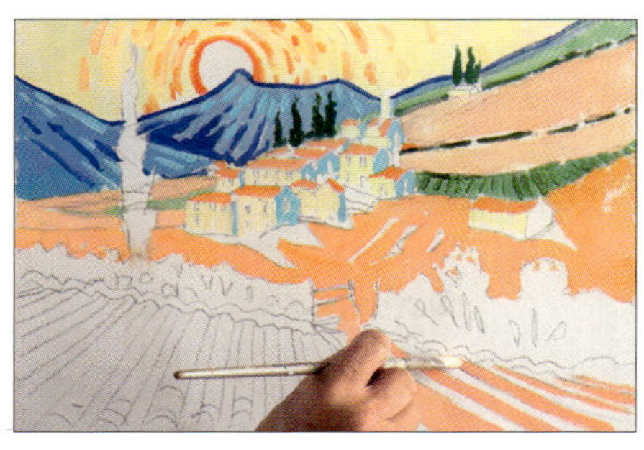

23 Add more cadmium orange and a hint of cadmium red light and use the no. 12 flat brush to paint the lines in the foreground. They should be thinner and closer together the further away they go.

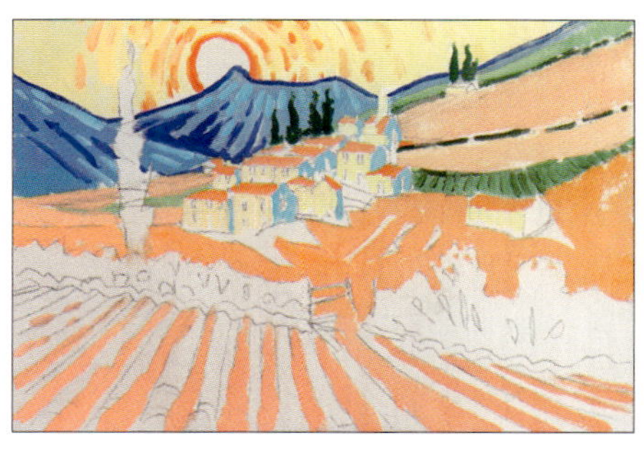

The painting with the lines completed.

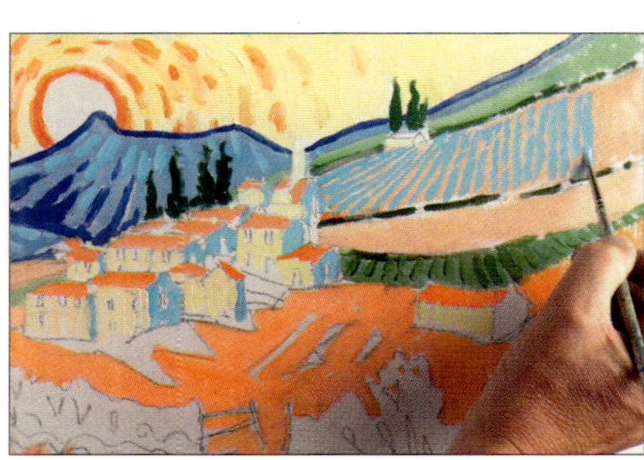

24 Change to the no. 2 round brush and use a mix of phthalo blue and white to paint the lines in the distant field.

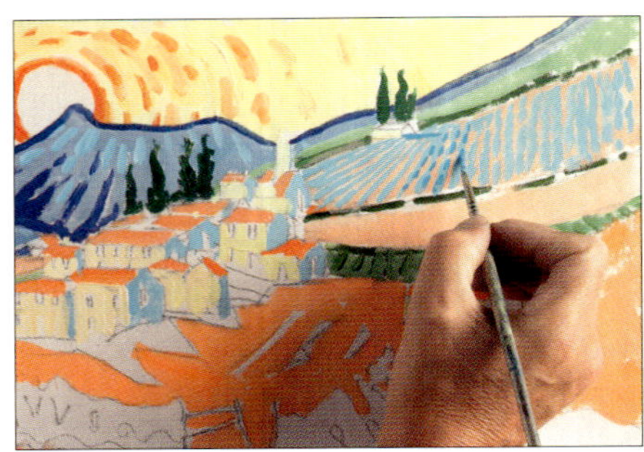 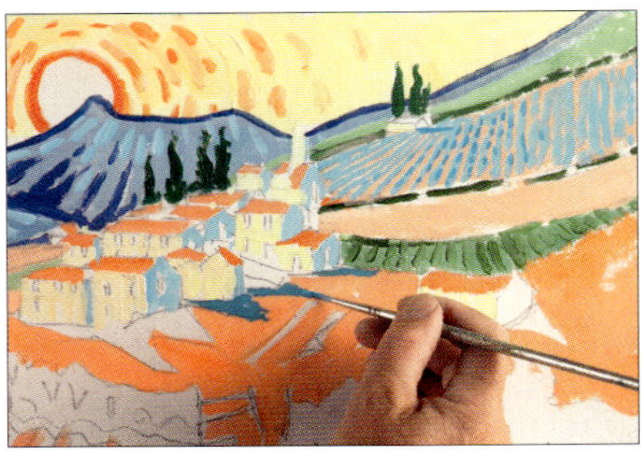 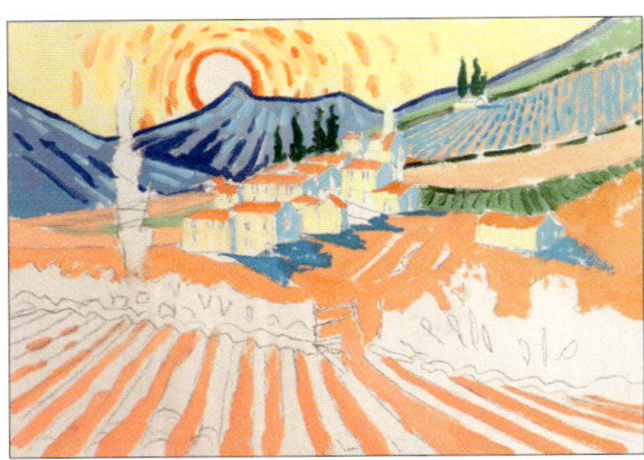

25 Add a little more phthalo blue to paint shadows on some of the lines.

26 Make a darker mix still by adding more pththalo blue and paint the cast shadows from the houses.

27 Add a cast shadow from the barn in the same way.

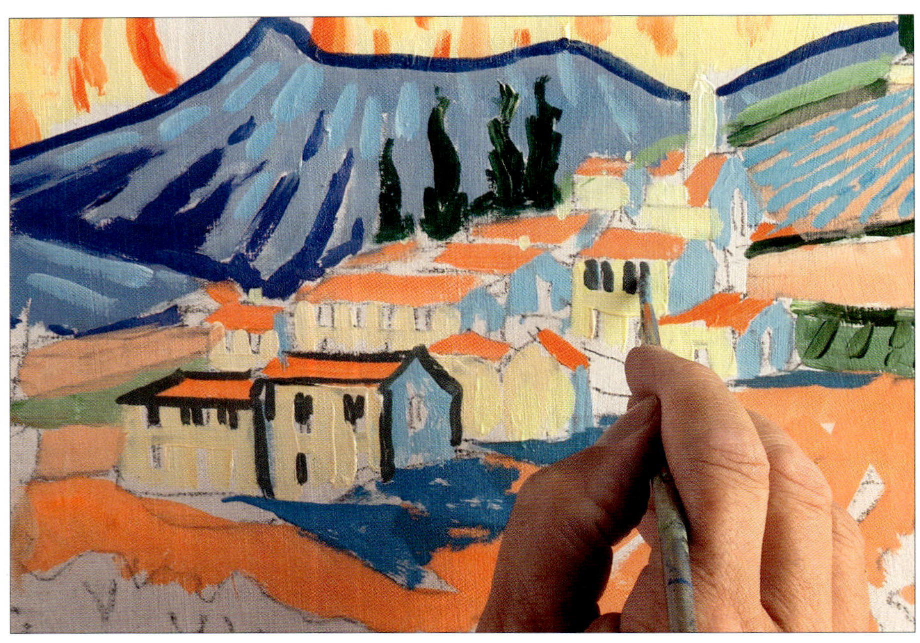

28 Add burnt umber to the blue shadow mix and use the no. 2 round brush to outline some of the houses and to paint windows with short vertical lines.

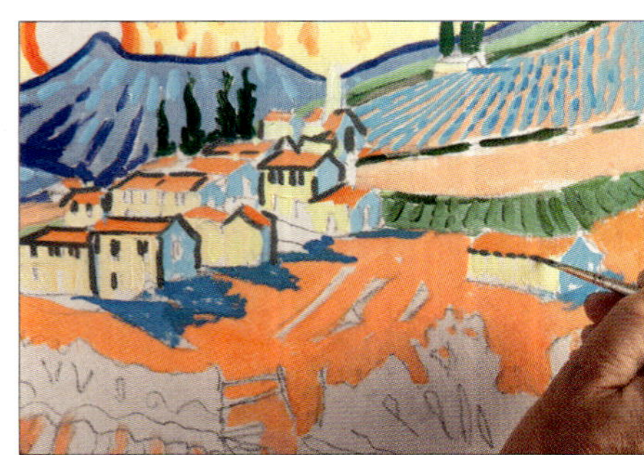 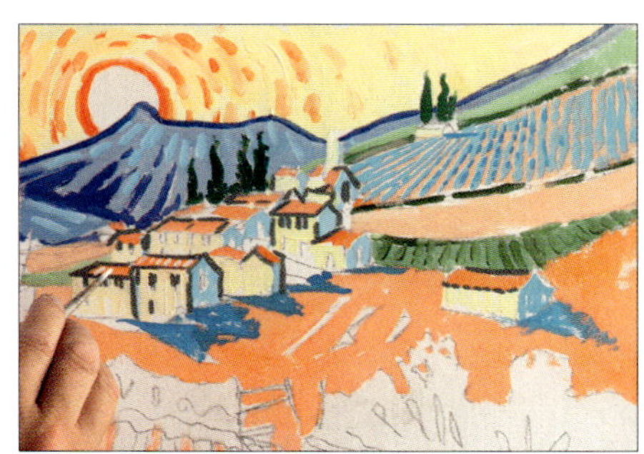 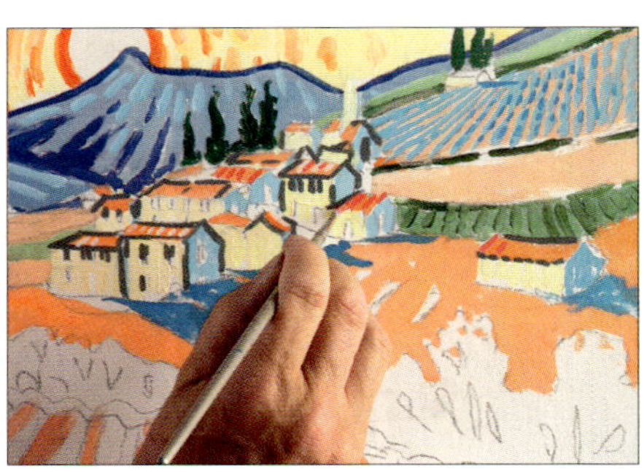

29 Paint the shadow under the barn roof with the same brush and mix, using short dashes to suggest the bottom of the roof tiles.

30 Mix white with a hint of the soil mix to paint the lines of tiles on the roofs of some of the houses.

31 Mix cadmium red light with a touch of quinacridone magenta to paint the lines on some of the other roofs.

44

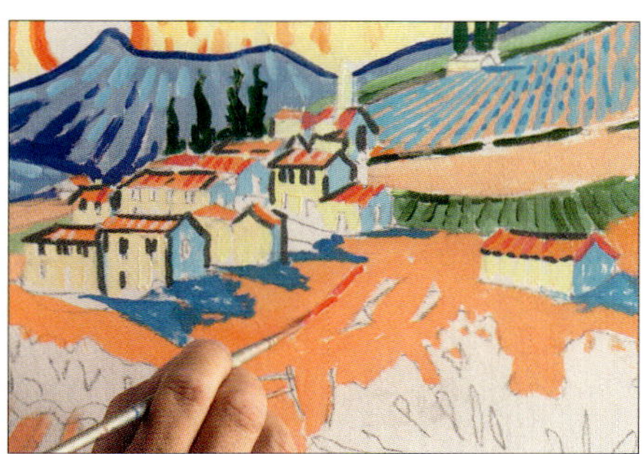

32 Paint lines and dashes on the ground with the same mix.

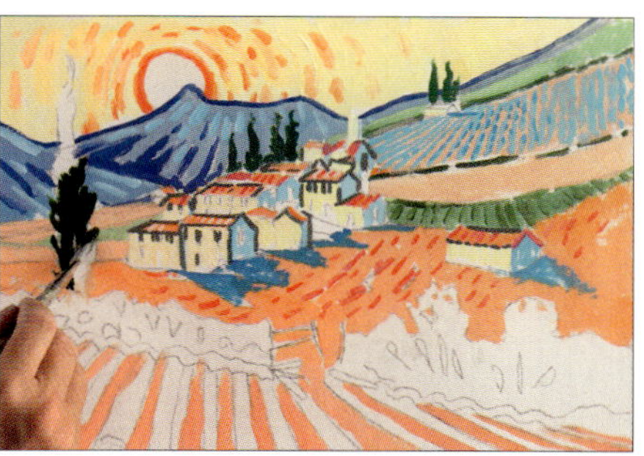

33 Paint the tree on the left with sap green and burnt umber and the no. 12 flat brush.

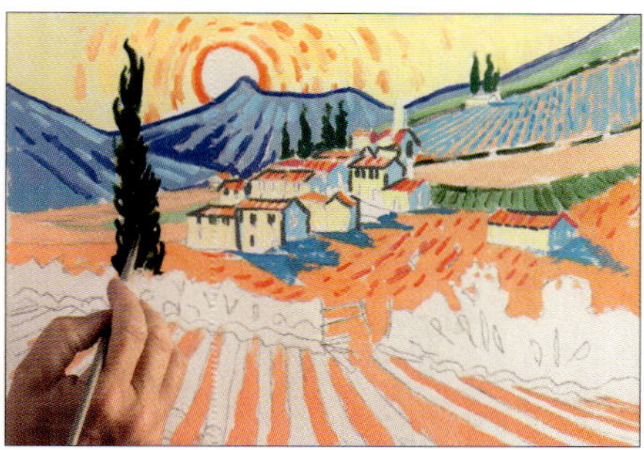

34 Mix phthalo blue, sap green and burnt umber and use the no. 2 round brush to paint dark lines at the edge of the tree for a wavy look.

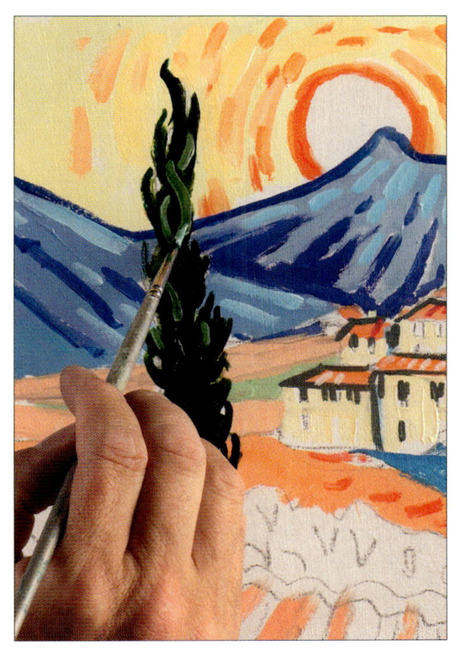

35 Add pale touches with a mix of white, sap green and a little burnt umber.

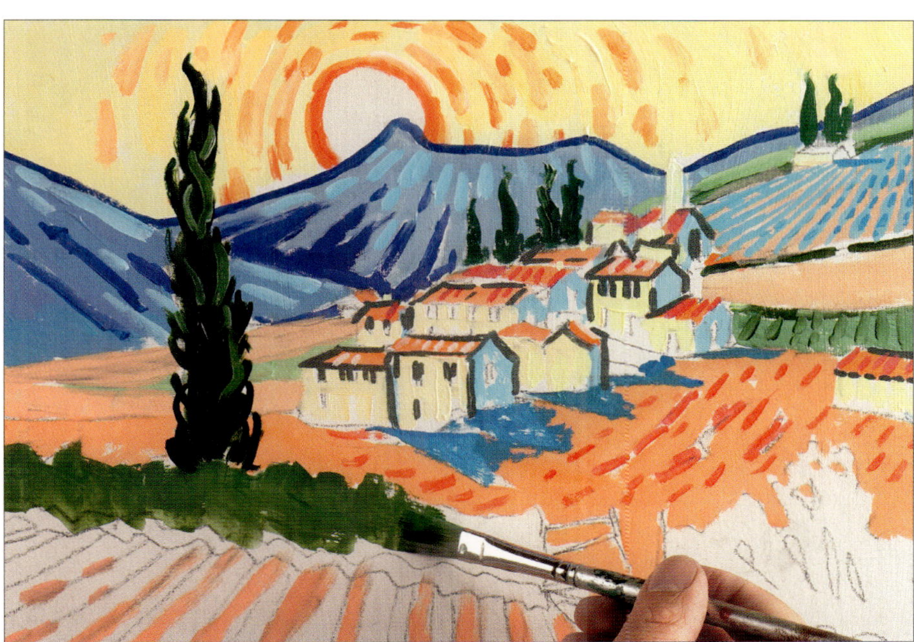

36 Use the same lighter green to paint the hedge in front of the tree, using the no. 12 flat brush.

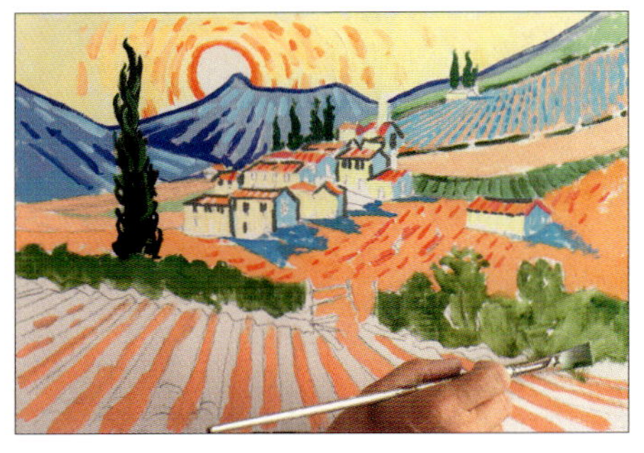

37 Continue painting the hedge on the right-hand side of the gate. Dot brush strokes around it to suggest foliage.

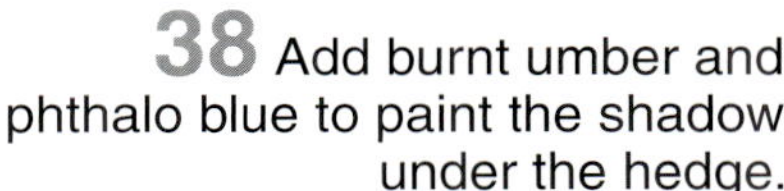

38 Add burnt umber and phthalo blue to paint the shadow under the hedge.

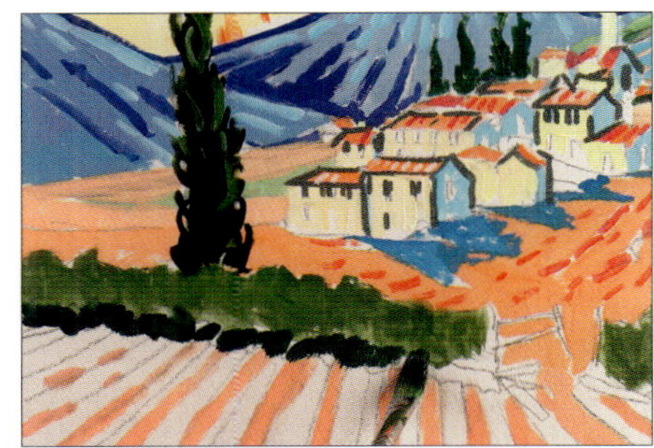

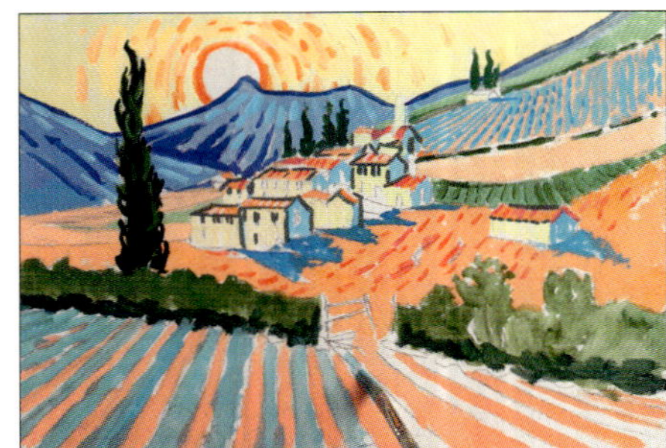

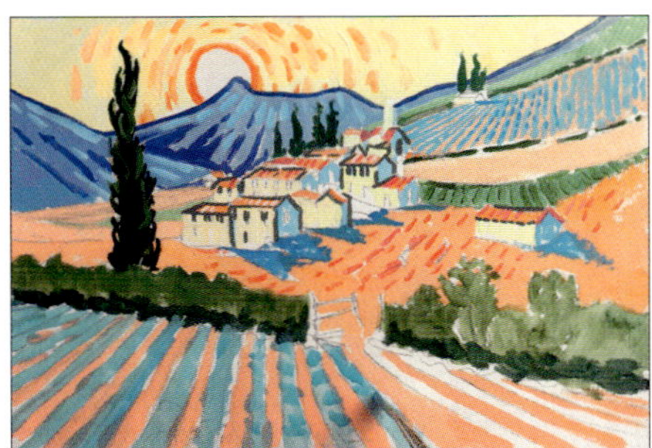

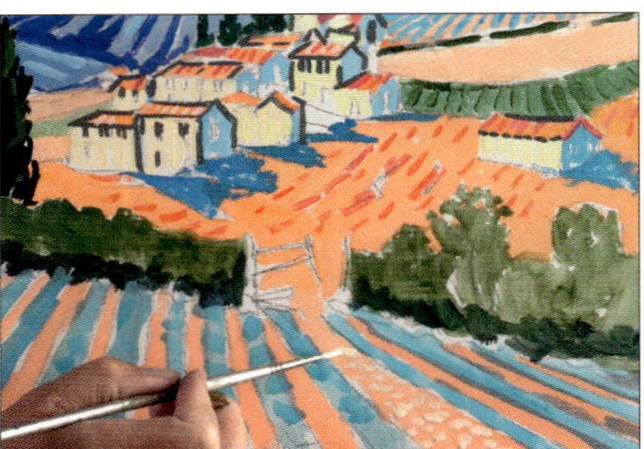

39 Using a mix of phthalo blue and white, block in the rows of lavender.

40 Make a slightly darker mix of the same colour and paint dashes of texture on top of the blocked in rows.

41 Mix white with a touch of cadmium orange and add horizontal dashes to break up the soil area.

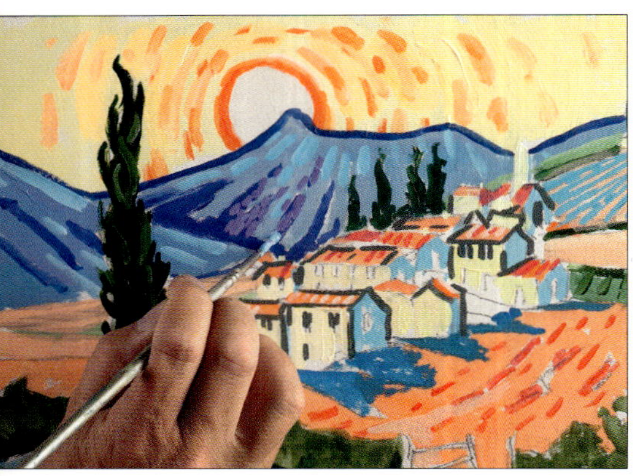

42 Now mix white with phthalo blue and dioxazine purple to lighten the shadow area on the mountain with dashes of colour. Use the no. 2 round. Acrylic paints dry darker so make sure the shade is much lighter than the background shadow.

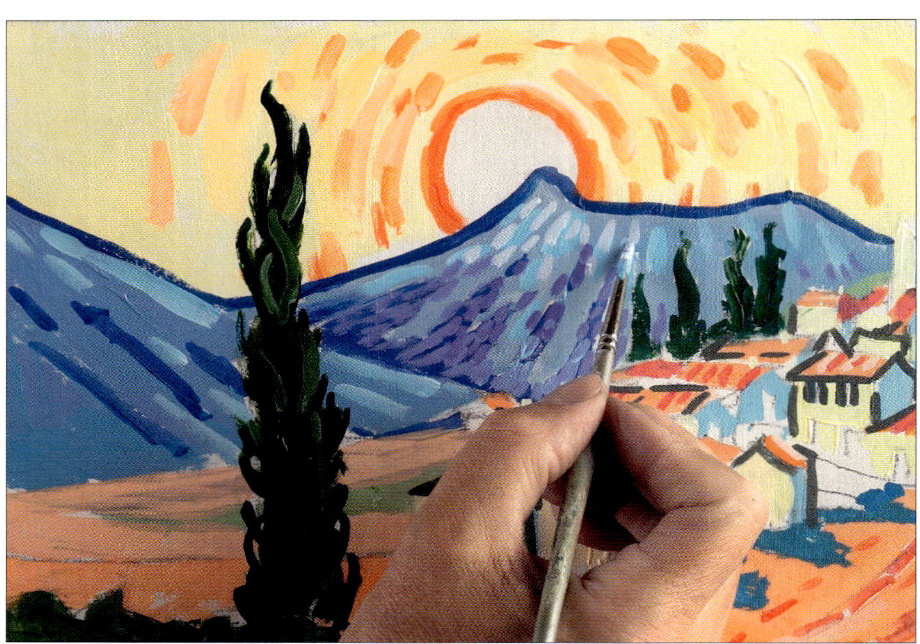

43 Add lots of white to the mix and paint very pale dashes going down the mountain.

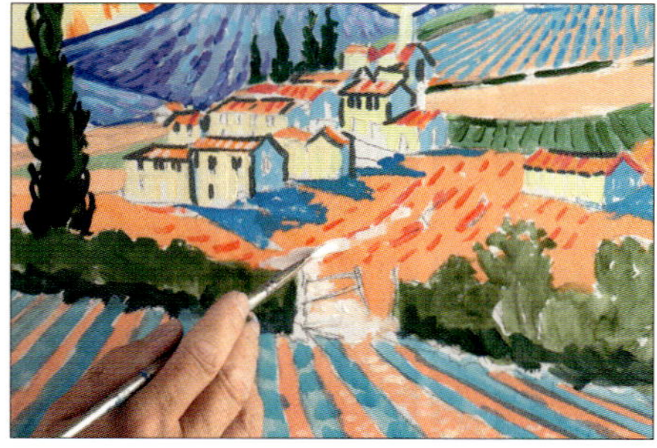

44 Change to the no. 6 flat brush and use the same colour to suggest the path.

45 Paint streaks of textured white on the buildings to lighten them.

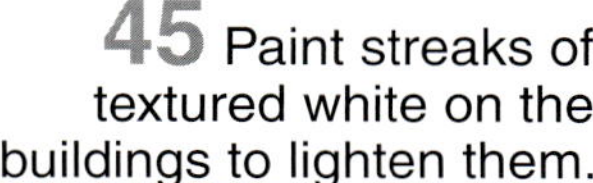

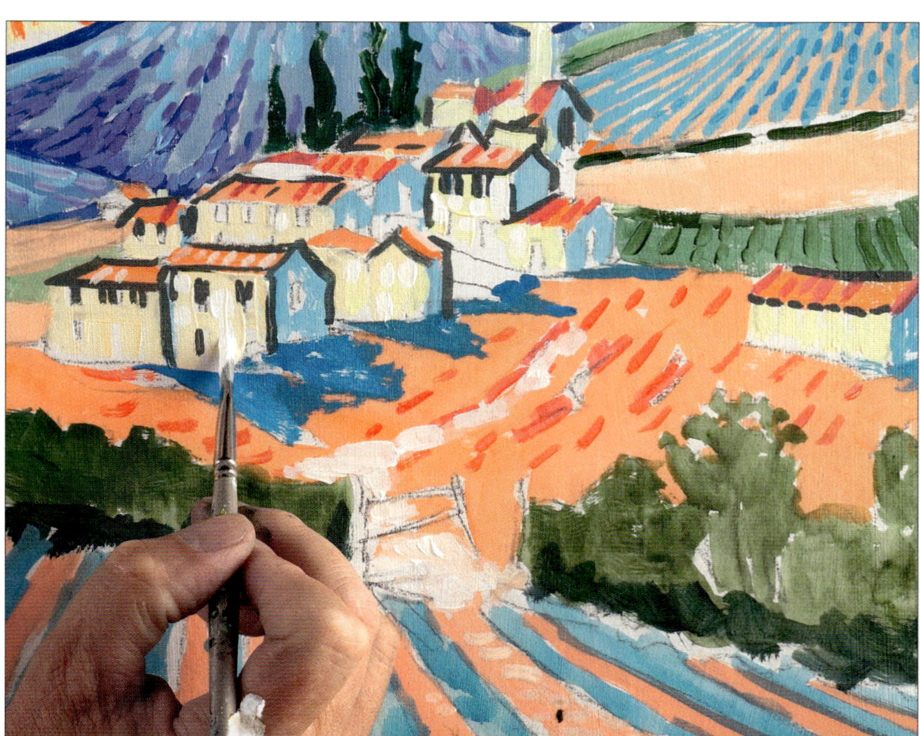

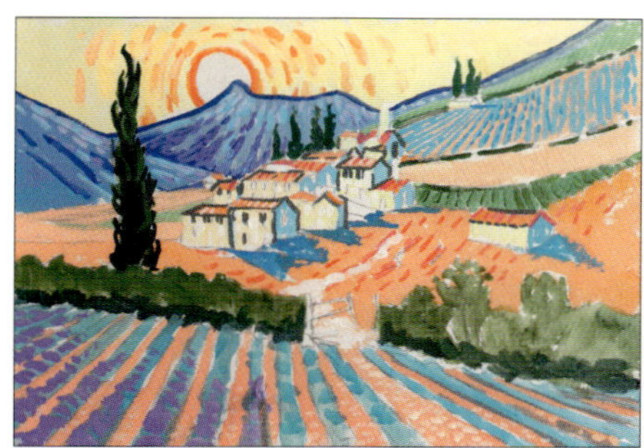

46 Mix dioxazine purple with a little phthalo blue and paint clumps of purple for the lavender, making sure the clumps are large in the foreground. Leave blue showing through. Leave the far ends of the rows blue as this will help make them recede.

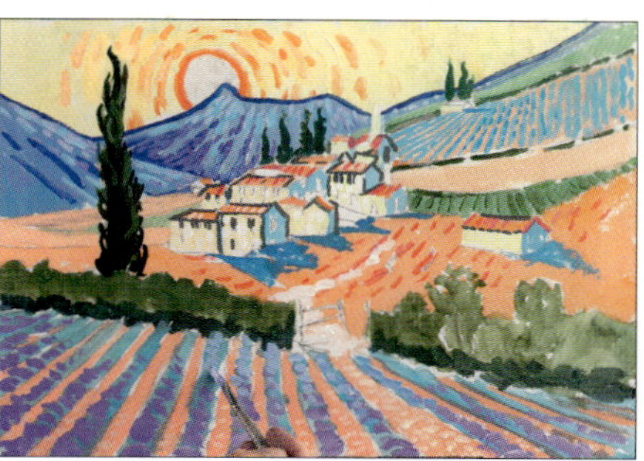

47 Add phthalo blue and white to the mix and paint touches on the furthest parts of the lavender rows.

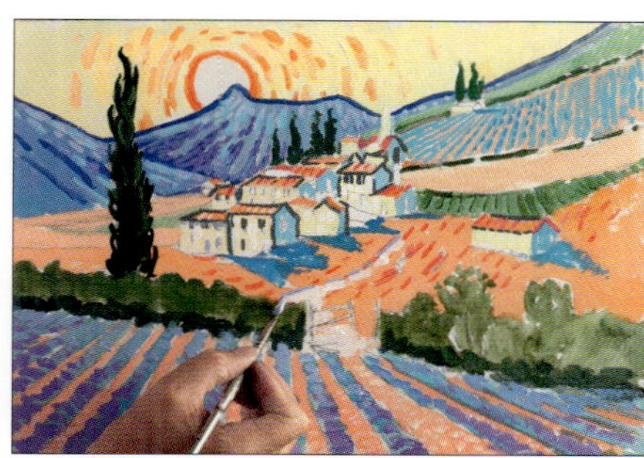

48 Define the edges of the path with the same colour.

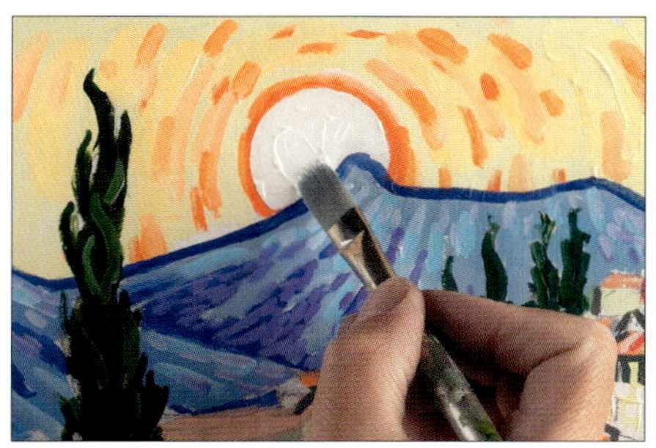

49 Use the no. 12 flat brush to paint the sun with white.

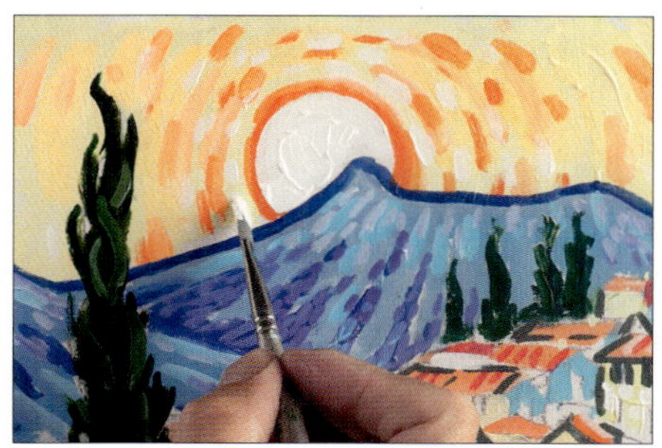

50 Paint white dashes in curves round the sun.

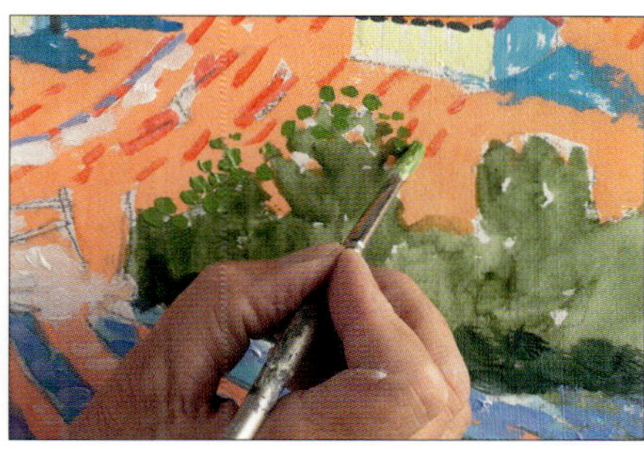

51 Mix sap green and lemon yellow with white and paint little dots and dashes around the bushes in the hedge.

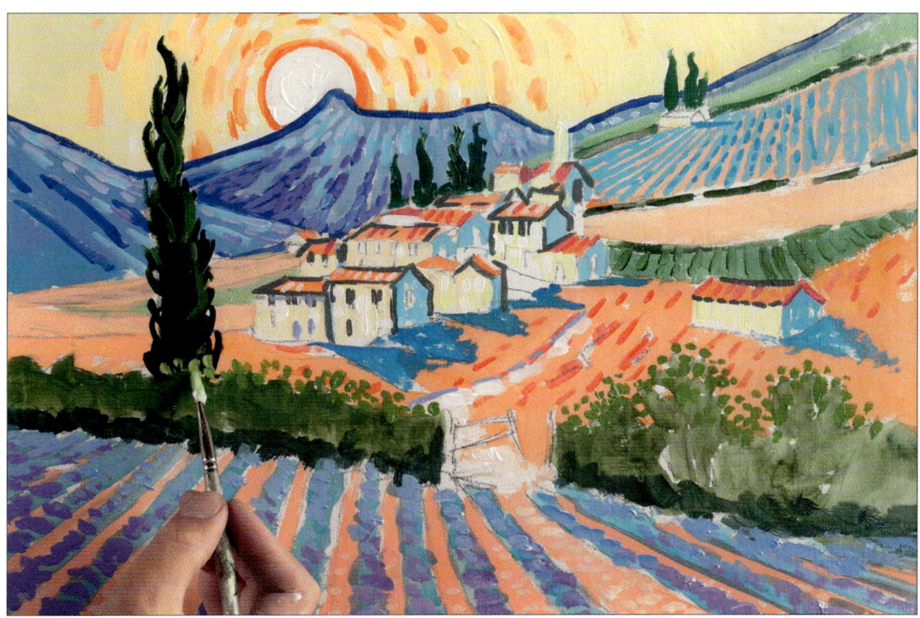

52 Make sure the hedge in front of the tree is paler than the tree, so that the hedge looks nearer.

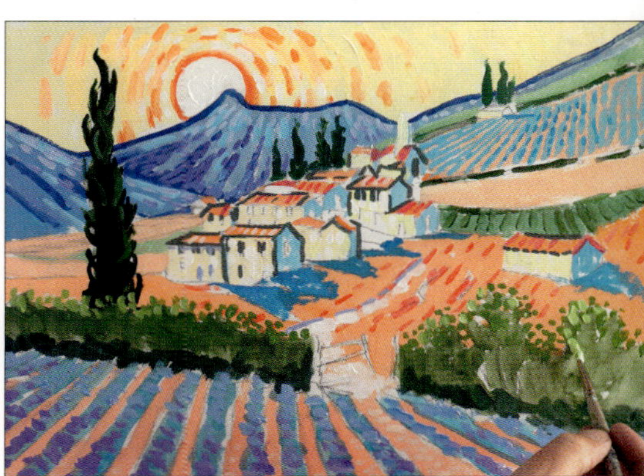

53 Add lemon yellow to the mix to further lighten the hedge.

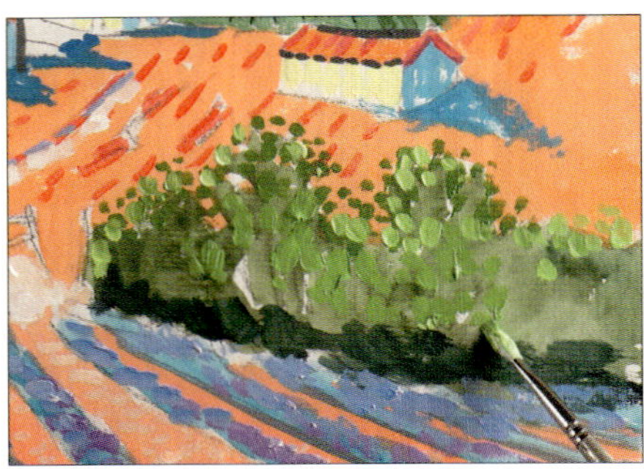

54 Make a darker mix by adding sap green and texture the hedge with dabs of colour.

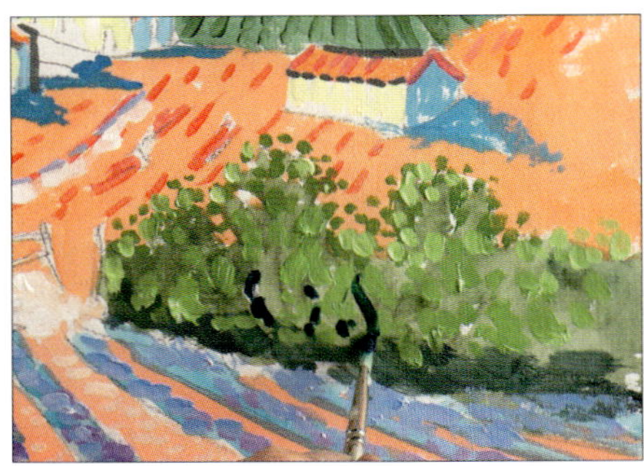

55 Mix sap green with phthalo blue to paint streaks of shadow in the hedge.

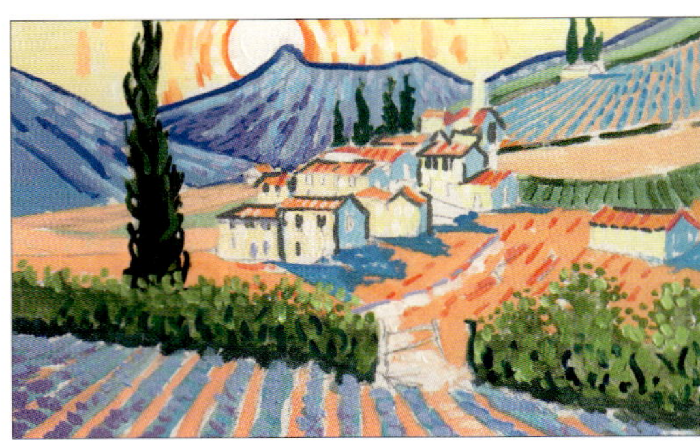

56 Paint little curved lines of the dark green all the way along the base of the hedge.

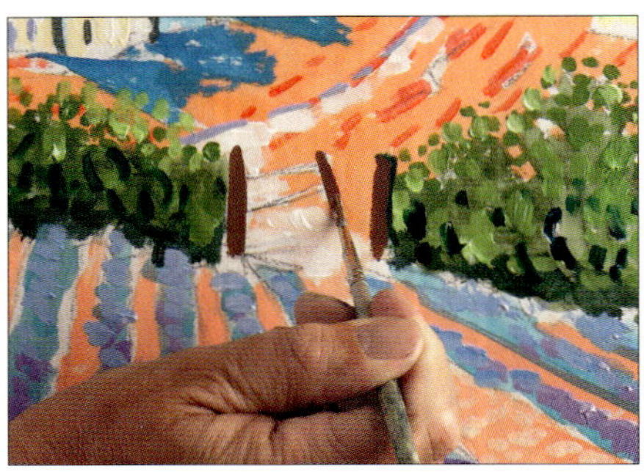

57 Paint the gate posts with the no. 6 flat brush and a mix of burnt umber and a little white, then change to the no. 2 round brush to paint the rest of the gate.

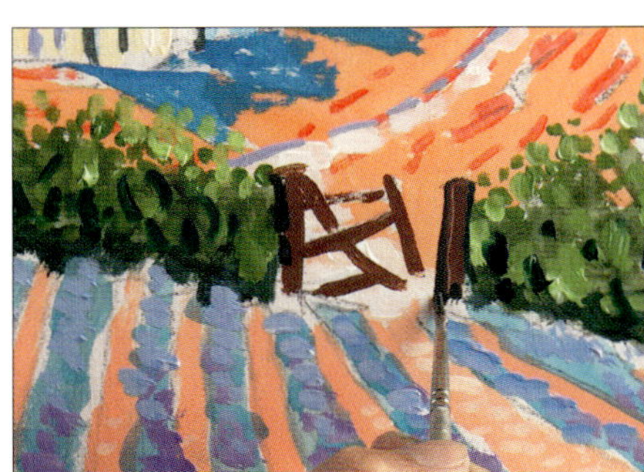

58 Outline the gate posts with phthalo blue.

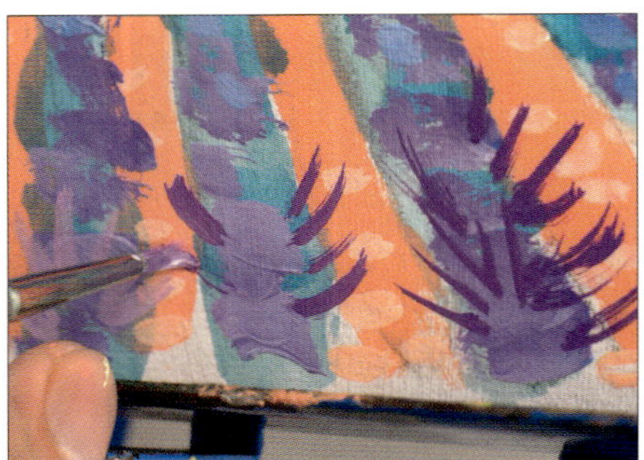

59 Mix dioxazine purple with quinacridone magenta and add this to white. Dilute with water so the paint flows well. Use the no. 2 round brush to flick up dashes to suggest the foreground lavender.

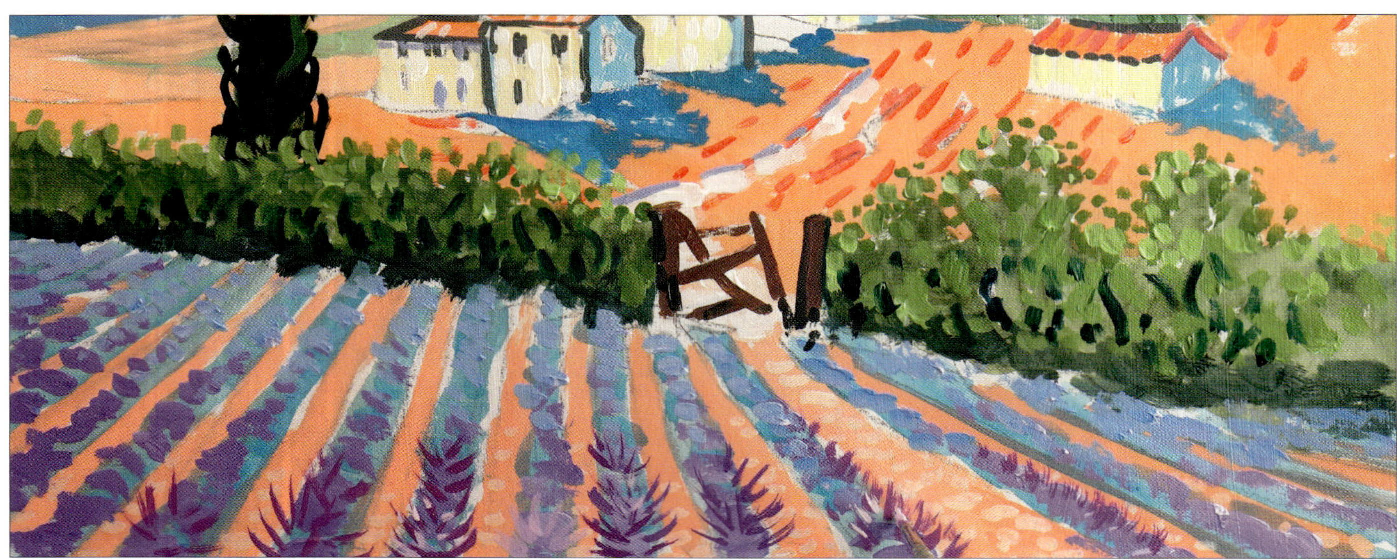

60 Continue adding lavender spikes in the same way in the foreground only. Mix white with a hint of quinacridone magenta and dioxazine purple and paint little dashes on the ends of the spikes.

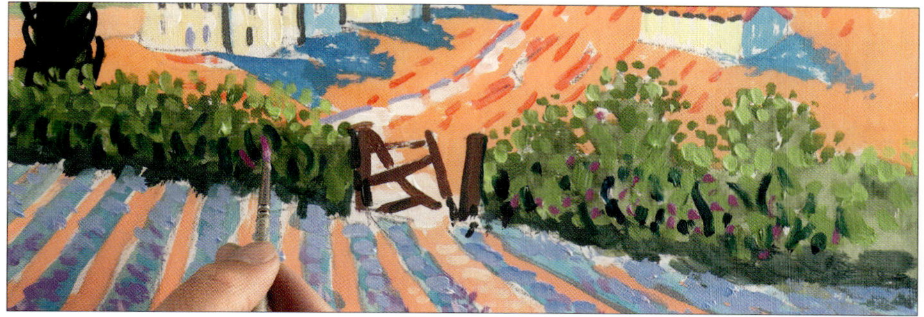

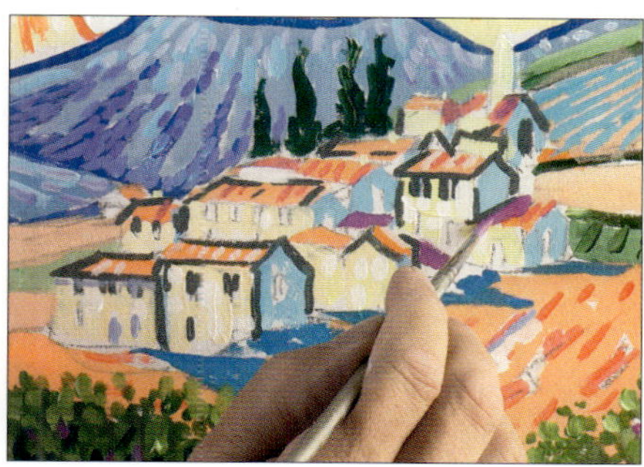

61 Paint dashes of neat quinacridone magenta among the greens of the hedge using the no. 2 round brush.

62 Paint cast shadows among the roofs of the buildings with the same colour.

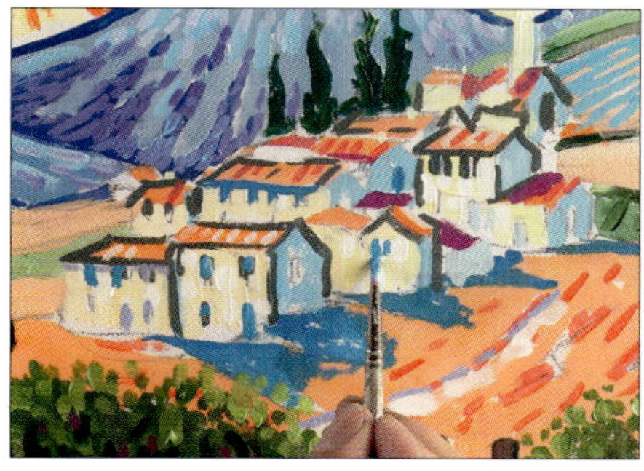

63 Mix phthalo blue with white to tone down the darks in some of the doors and windows.

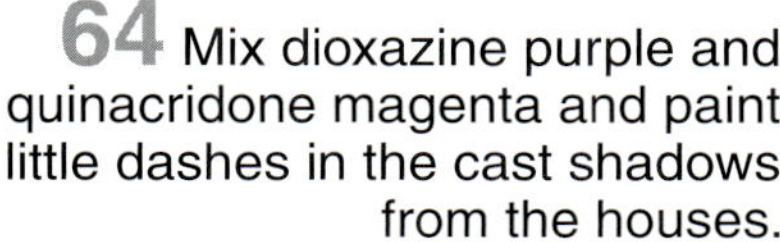

64 Mix dioxazine purple and quinacridone magenta and paint little dashes in the cast shadows from the houses.

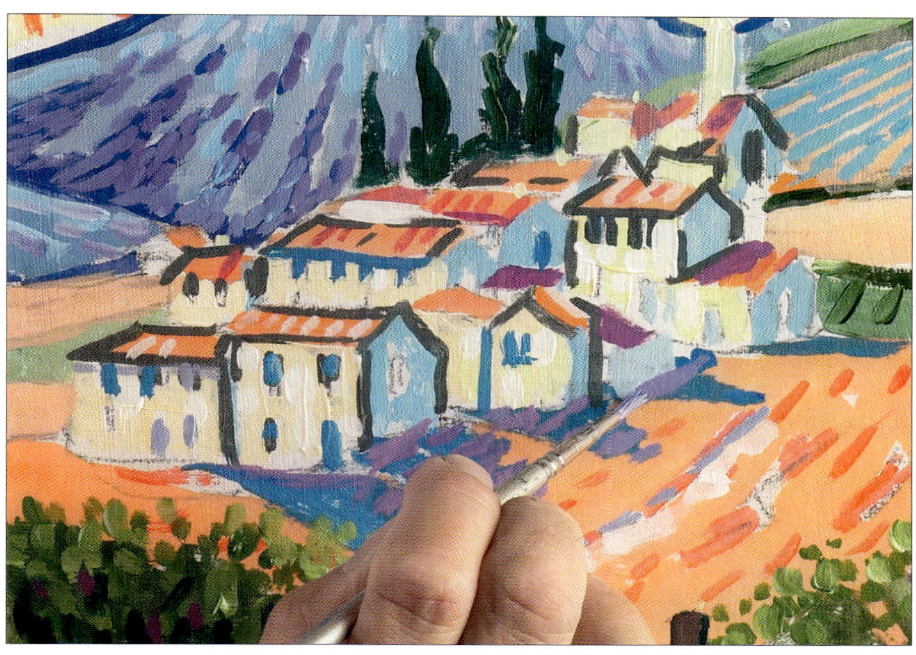

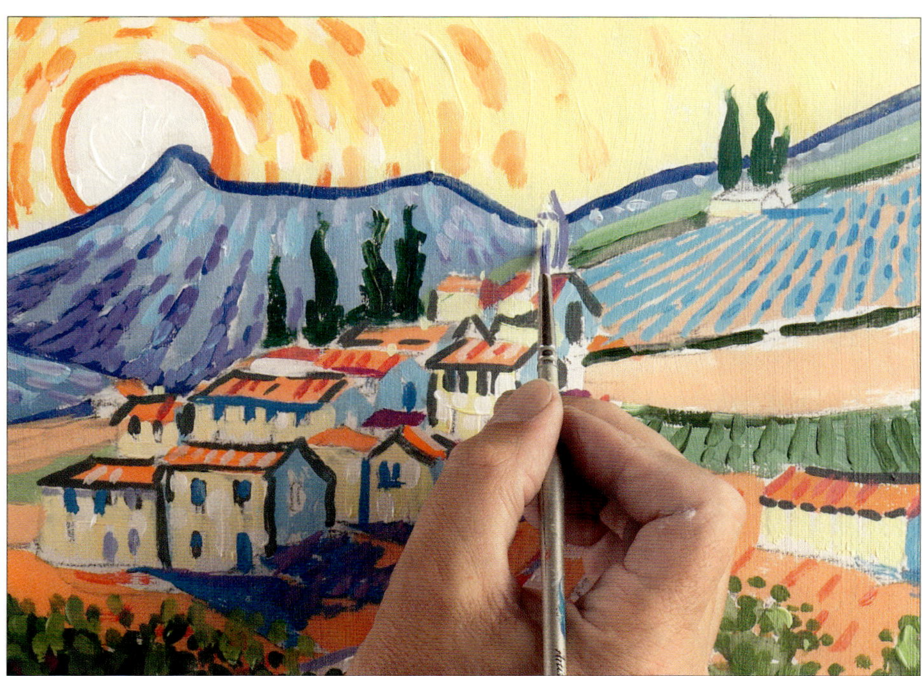

65 Finally, add white to the purple mix and define the shadows of the church.

Overleaf

The finished painting.

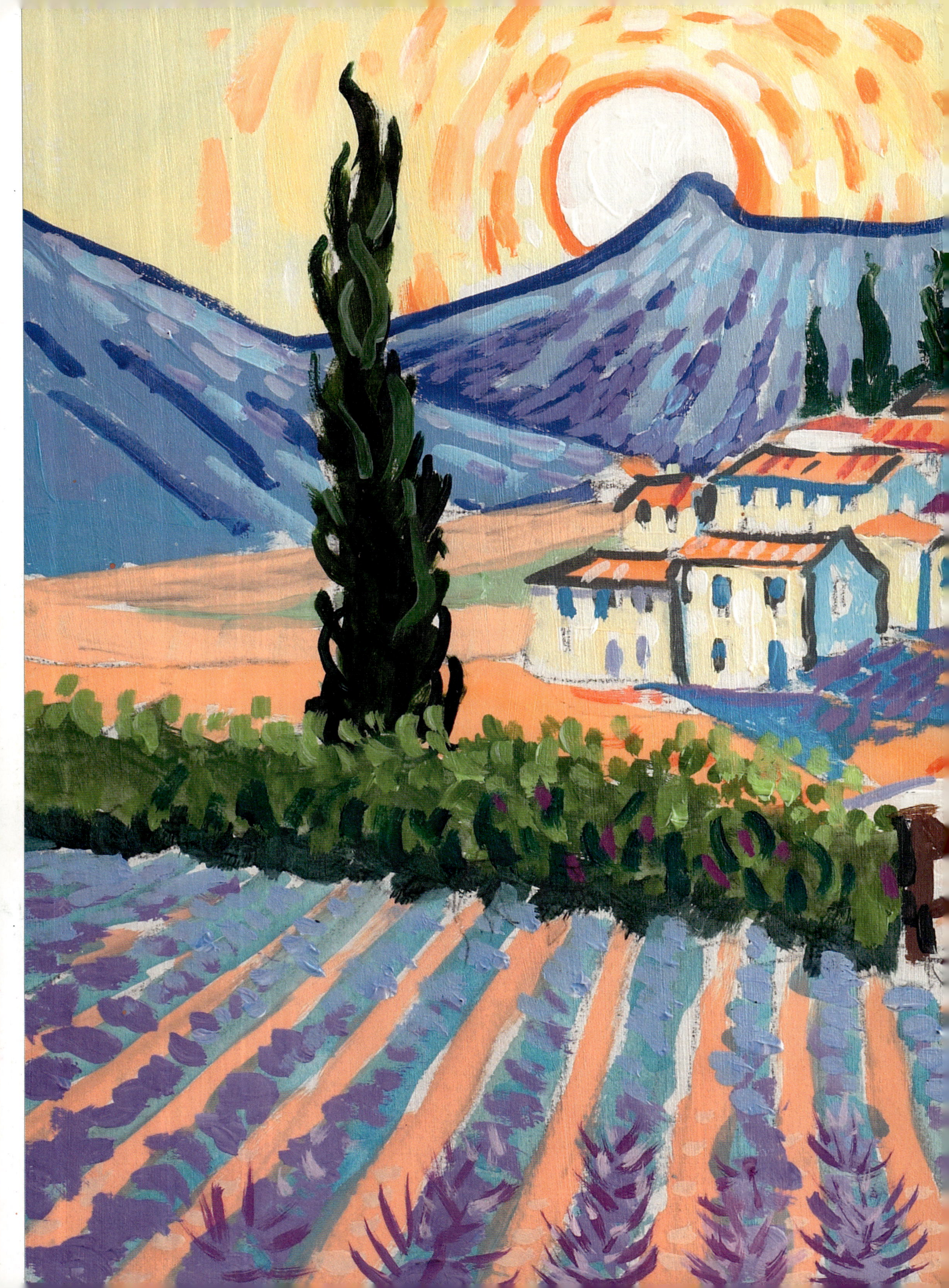

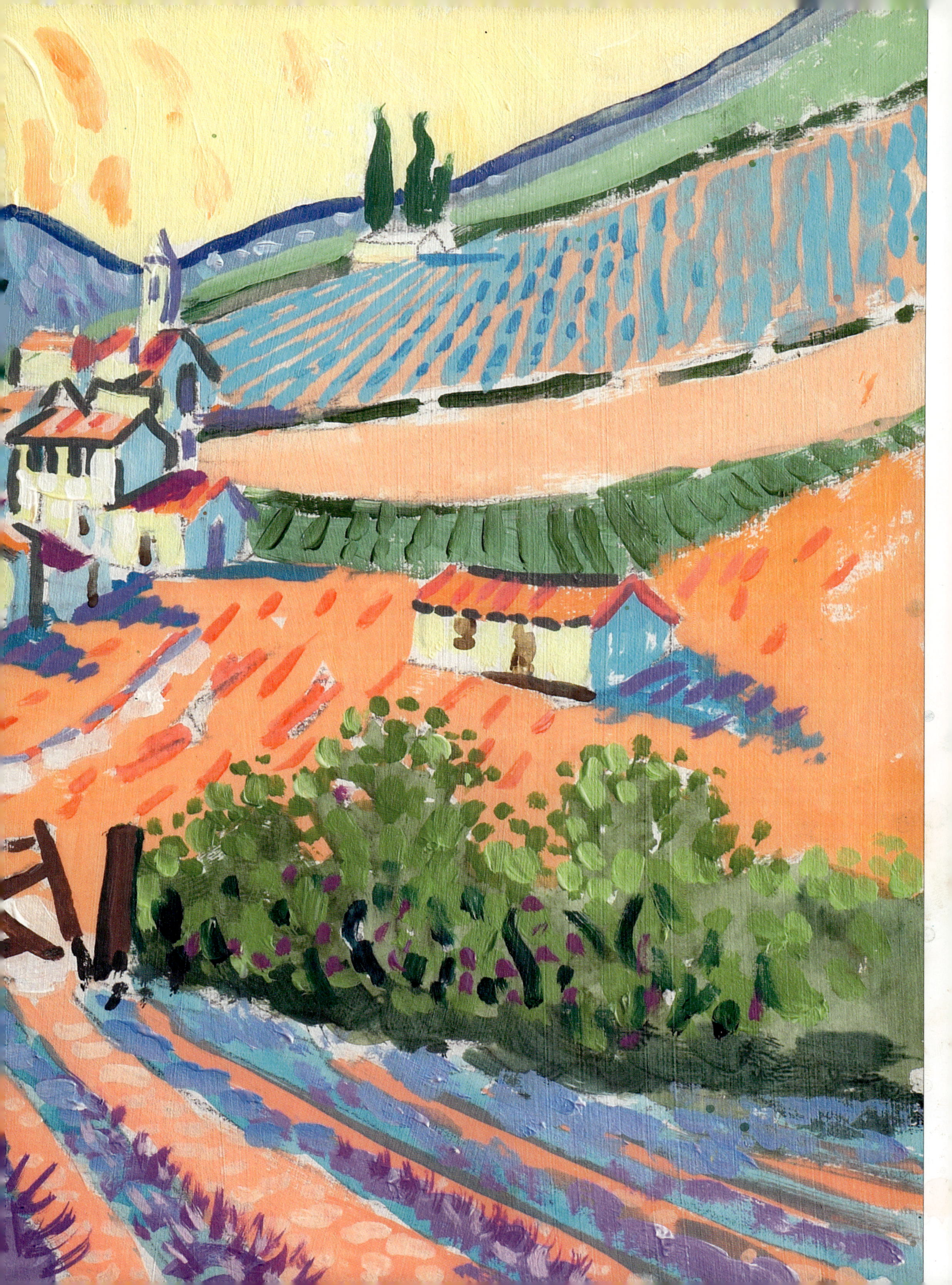

Working the Land

Van Gogh painted several of his works based on earlier paintings, elaborating or refining some of the details, or changing the colour scheme for an altered effect. I have done the same; this is based on a painting from another of my books, *Landscapes in Oils* and it has been changed to reflect the way that Vincent may have tackled the subject. I have incorporated short stabs of colour that imply the direction of the slope of the land, and included two figures: the man in drab colours and the woman with a dress that matches the roof of the barn. There is an impression of autumn-coloured trees in the background, with smoke coming from the distant cottage chimney. The blue cart is to be found in Van Gogh's painting *Harvest at La Crau*.

TRACING

6

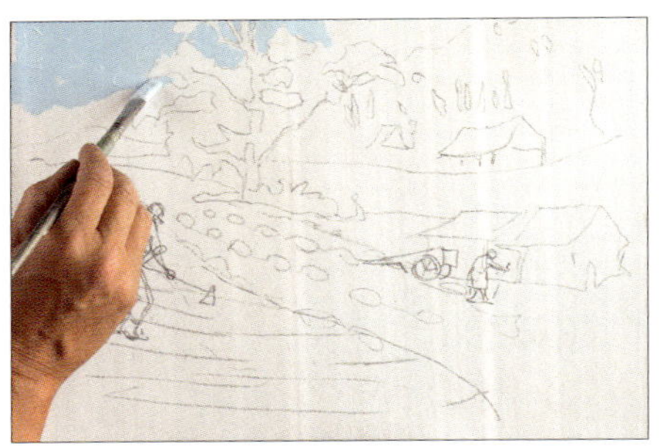

1 Block in the sky area with the no. 12 flat brush and white with cerulean blue. Make sure you leave plenty of texture.

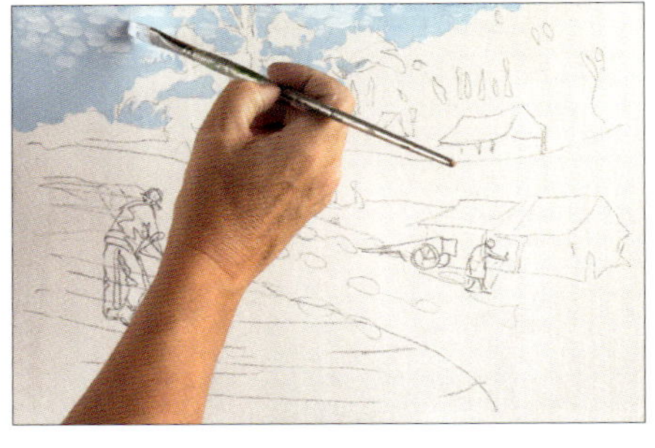

2 Add more white to the mix and paint little brush strokes in the sky.

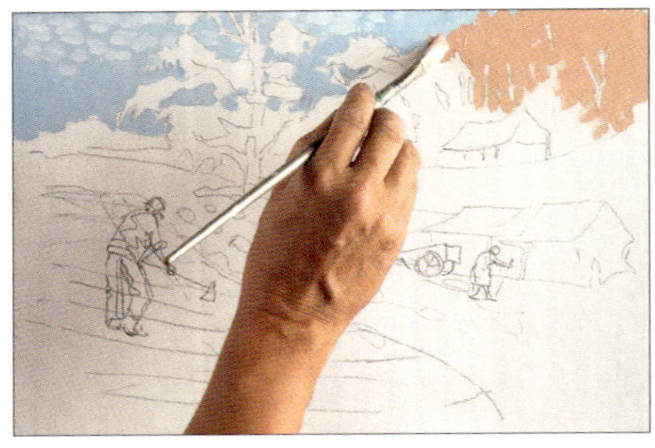

3 Add burnt sienna to the blue mix to make a brownish grey and block in the area of autumn trees on the right with short, stabbing brush strokes.

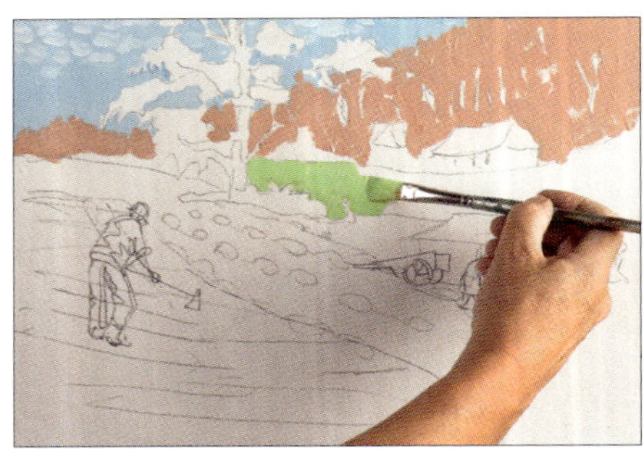

4 Make a vivid green from lemon yellow, a little cerulean blue and white, and block in the area of fields.

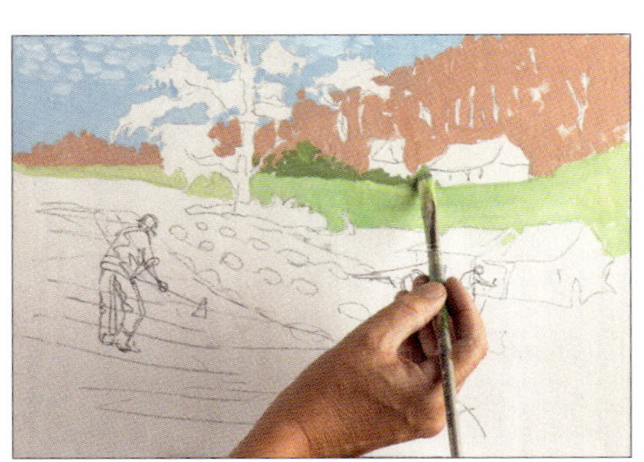

5 Add a little more cerulean blue and some burnt sienna to darken the green and use it to suggest trees and foliage in the distance.

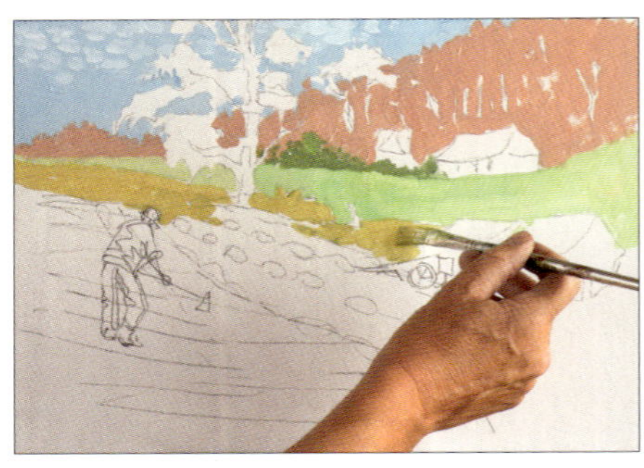

6 Mix burnt sienna, lemon yellow and white and block in the field coming forwards.

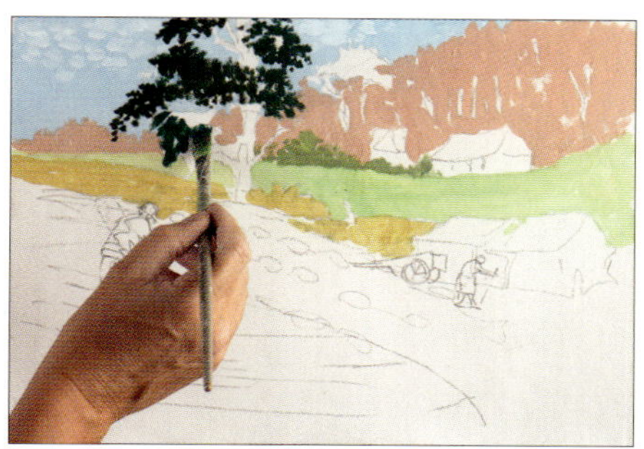

7 Mix a dark green from phthalo green and burnt sienna and paint the foliage of the main tree with a stabbing motion.

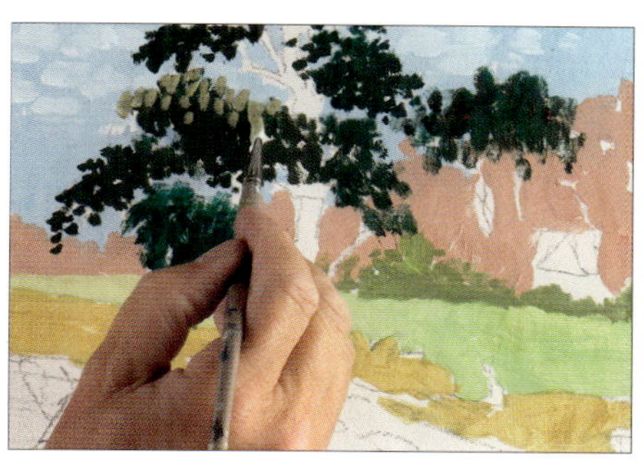

8 Change to the no. 6 flat brush and stipple on the lighter colour over the foliage.

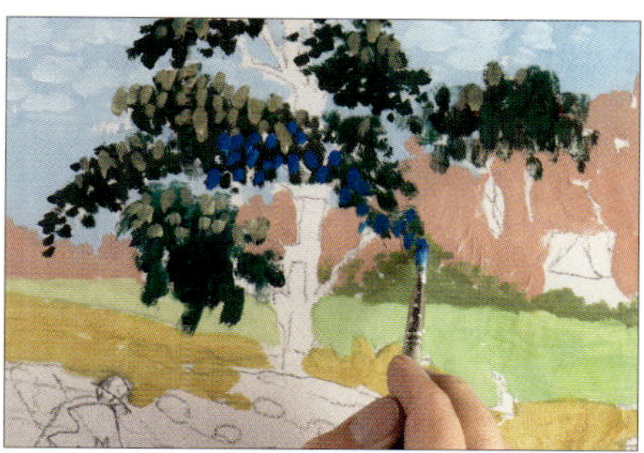

9 Mix phthalo blue (green shade) with a little white and stipple this on to the tree in dots, to break up the lower edges of the foliage.

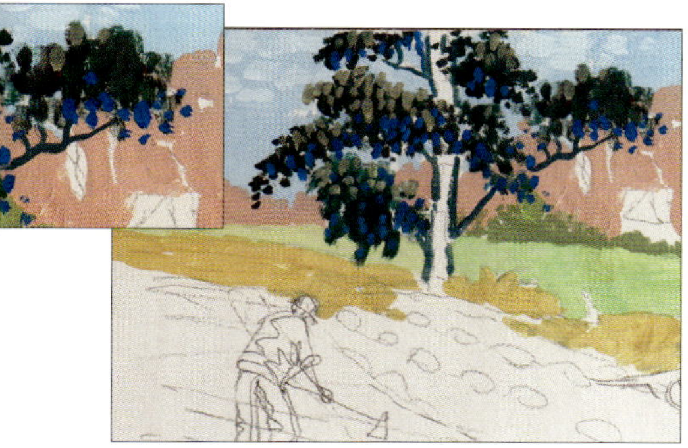

10 Add burnt sienna to the mix to make a dark grey. Use the no. 2 round brush to paint branches and to outline the trunk.

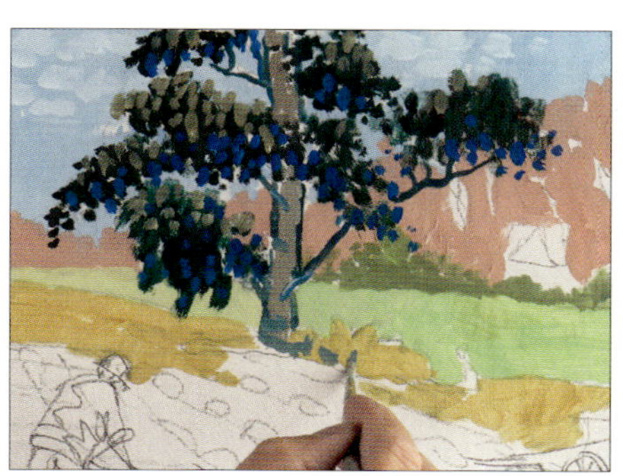

11 Add white to the mix and paint the trunk and the shadow below it.

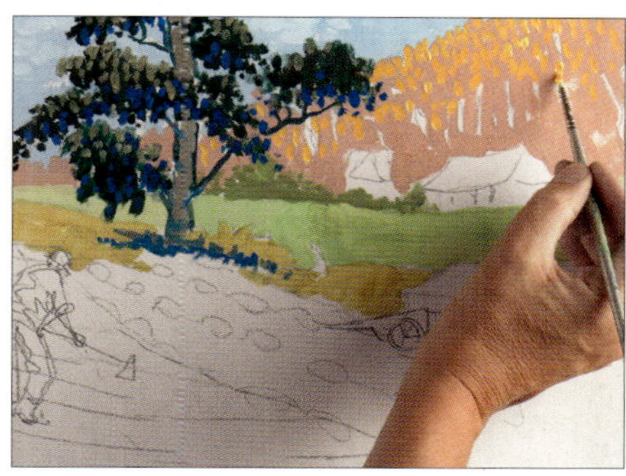

12 Paint dots of colour on to the autumn foliage on the right with a mix of lemon yellow, cadmium orange and white.

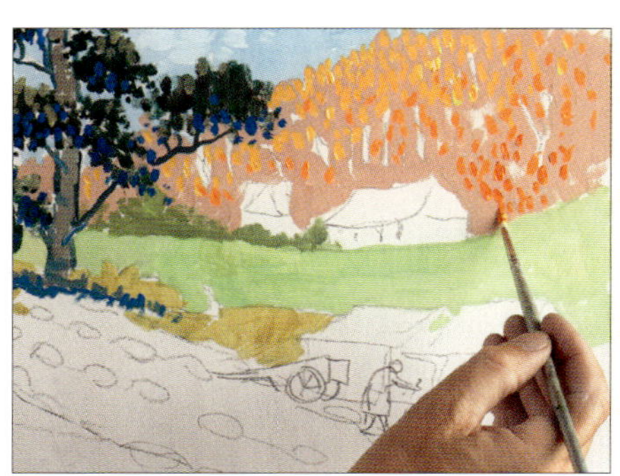

13 Paint dabs of neat cadmium orange, and then further forwards dab on a mix of cadmium orange and burnt sienna. Dip the edge of the brush in a different shade to create a streaky effect.

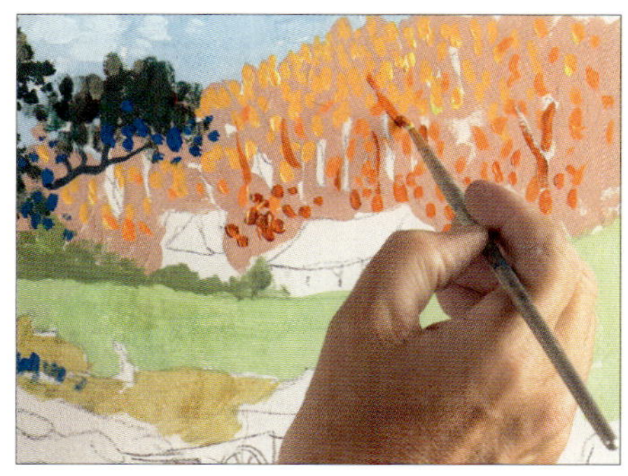

14 Paint longer brush strokes of the cadmium orange and burnt sienna mix to suggest branches.

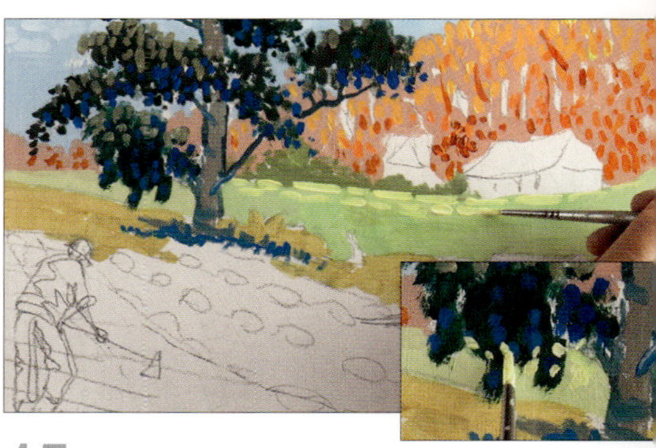

15 Add a touch of lemon yellow to white and paint horizontal strokes along the pale, distant field. Paint tiny dots on the bottom of the main tree's foliage to suggest light showing through the leaves.

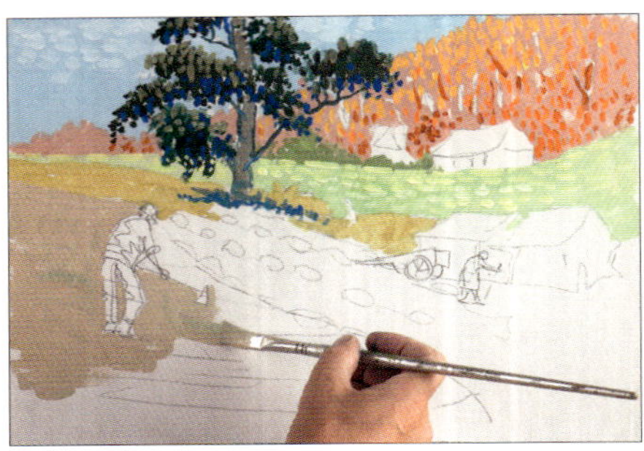

16 Change to the no. 12 flat brush and mix burnt sienna with white and a little cerulean blue for the underpainting of the foreground field. Paint carefully round the figure.

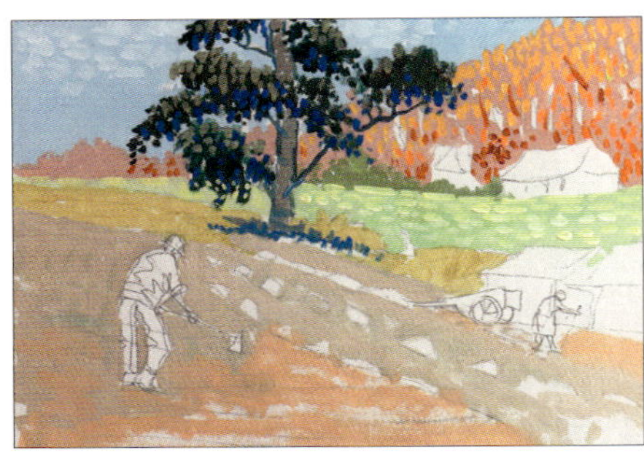

17 Paint round the cabbages in the field. Add a little cadmium orange to the mix and paint the warmer-coloured soil further forwards.

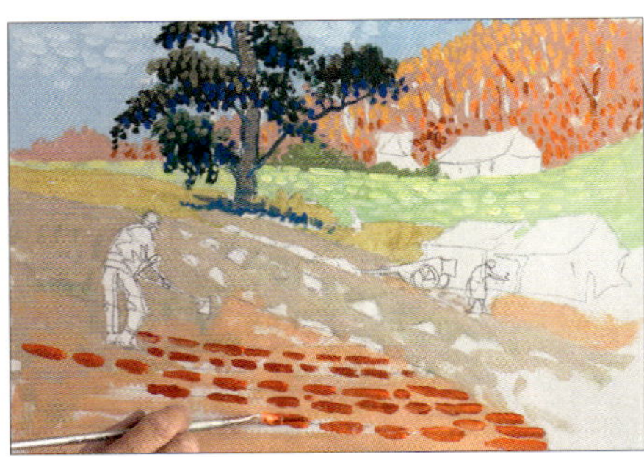

18 Mix cadmium orange and cadmium red with burnt sienna and use the no. 6 flat brush to paint the furrows in the foreground field.

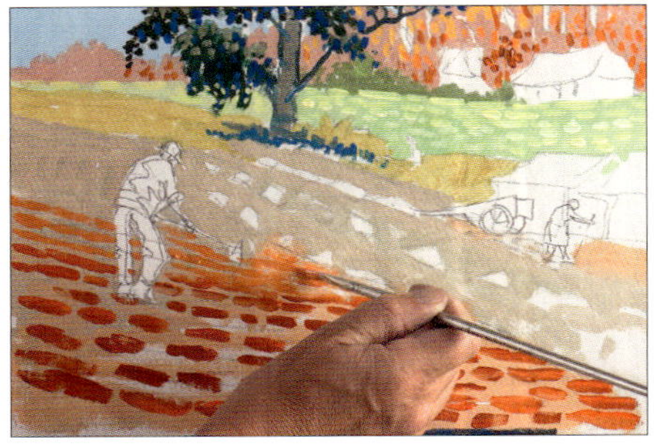

19 Add a little white and lemon yellow to the mix to paint the furthest furrows. The lines should be paler and less dotted than those in the foreground.

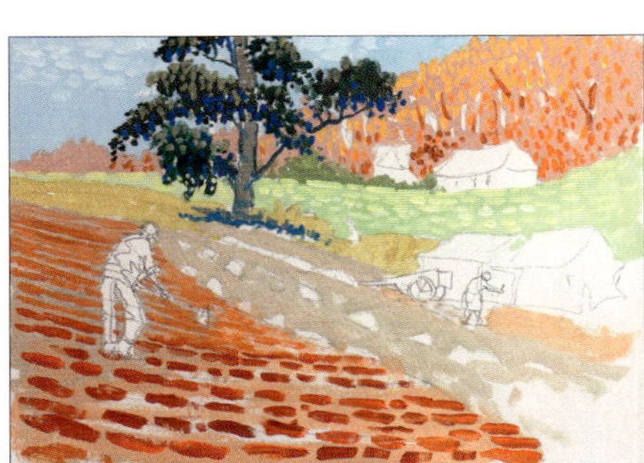

The painting so far.

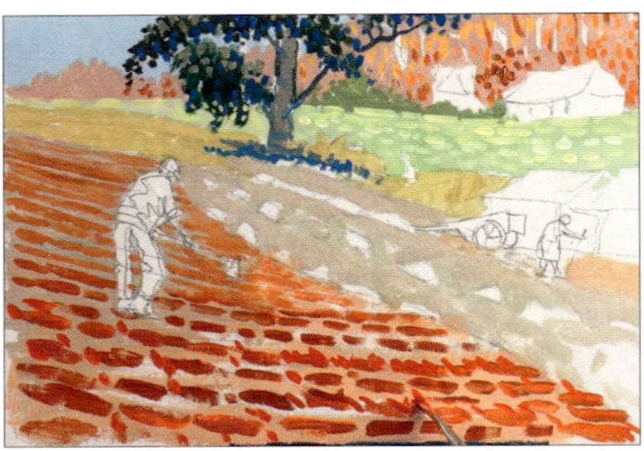

20 Use a mix of cadmium red and burnt sienna to paint lines going across the furrow lines, suggesting soil that has been turned over.

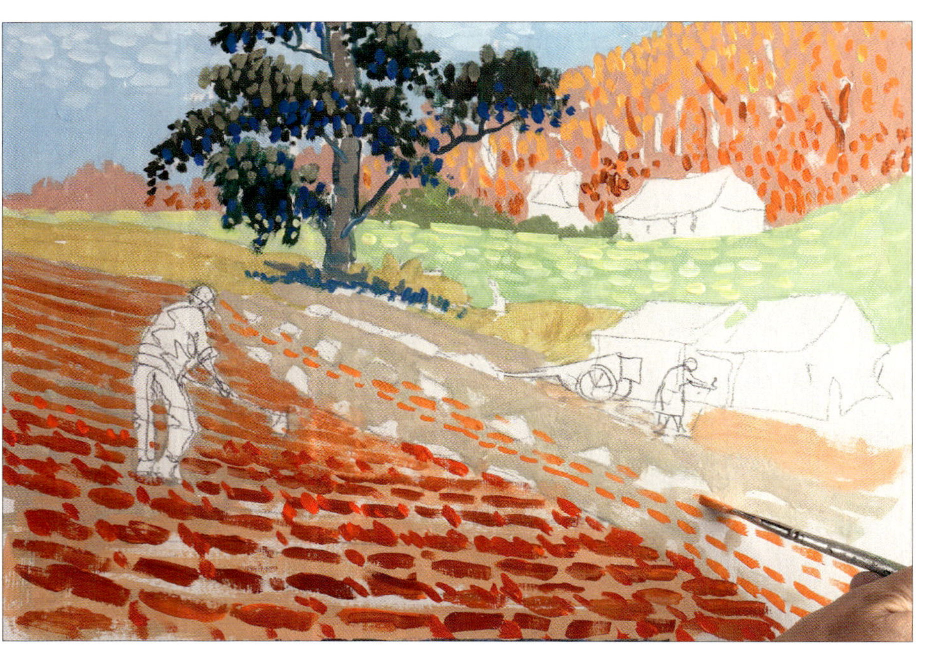

21 Add lemon yellow and white to the mix and paint thin dashes diagonally across the painting in the area of the crop.

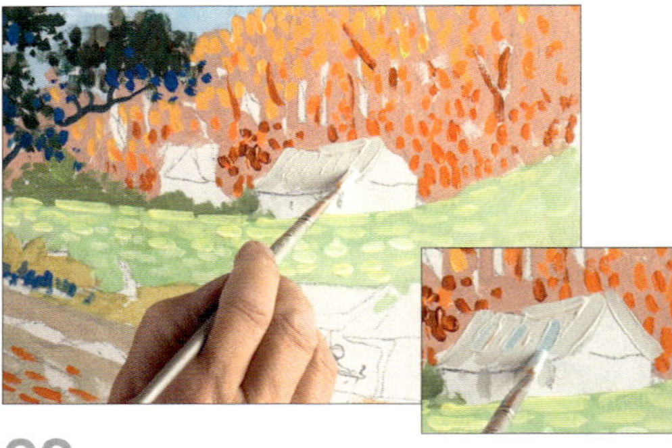

22 Use the no. 6 flat brush and a mix of cerulean blue, burnt sienna and white to paint the roof of one of the distant buildings. Add more cerulean to the mix and paint brush strokes to suggest tiles.

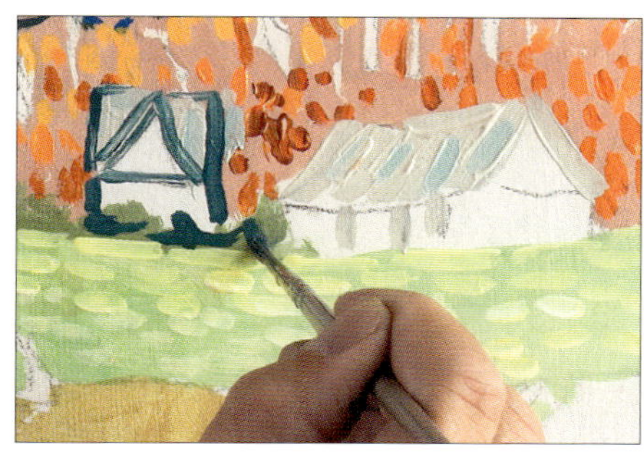

23 Change to the no. 2 round brush and outline the left-hand building with a mix of cerulean blue and burnt sienna.

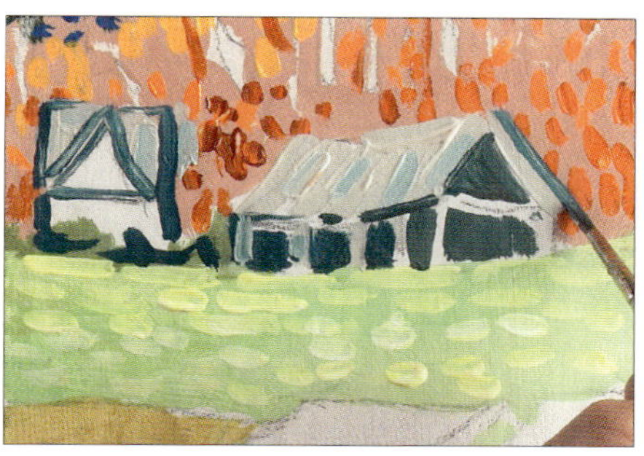

24 Use the same mix to paint the dark details of the right-hand barn.

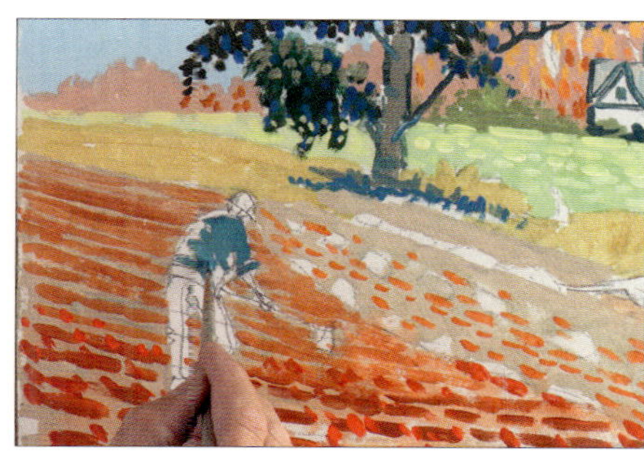

25 Paint the shaded right-hand side of the man's shirt with the same colour.

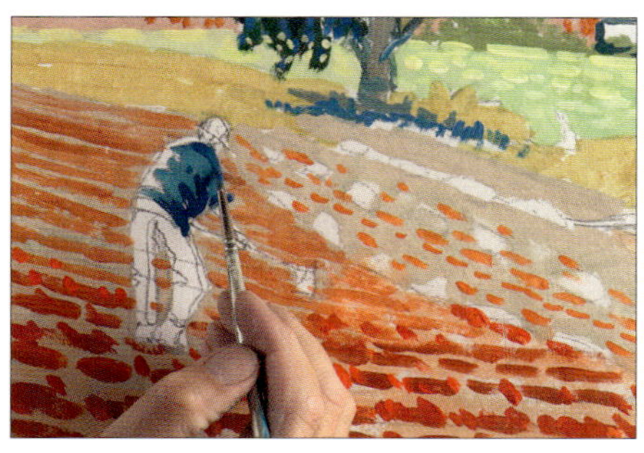

26 Add burnt sienna to the mix to darken it and paint shadow on the figure's jacket.

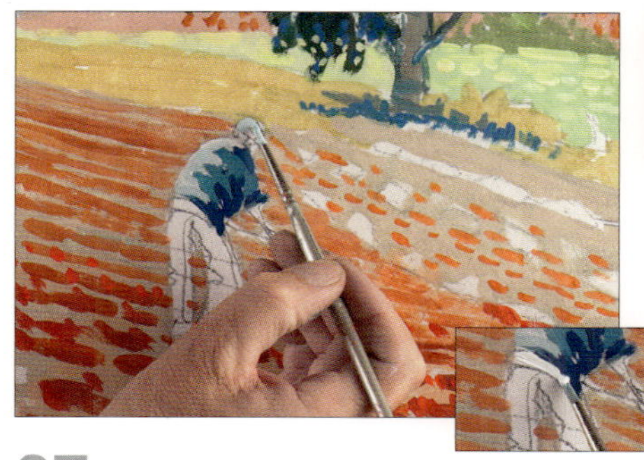

27 Add a touch of this colour to white and use it to paint the lighter side of the jacket, and the hat. Paint the shirt that is showing in white.

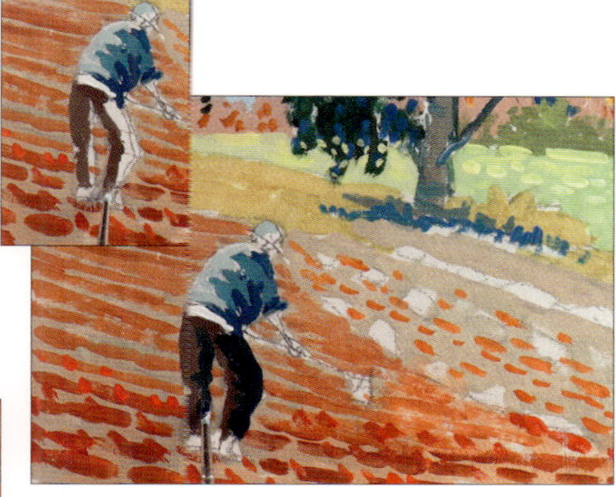

28 Mix burnt umber with a hint of cerulean blue for the left-hand side of the trousers. Add lots of cerulean blue for the shadowed side.

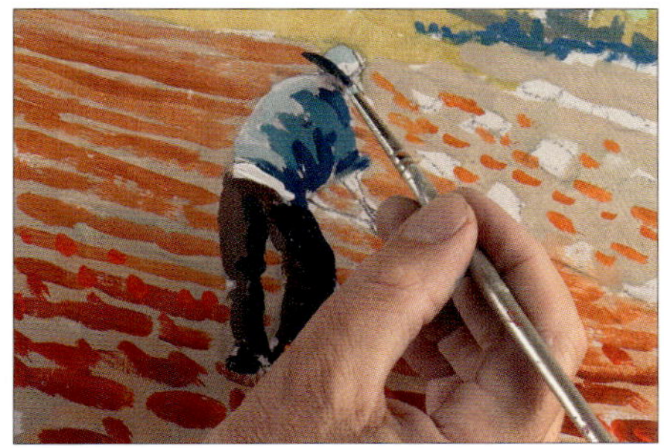

29 Use the same dark shade for the boots and under the brim of the hat.

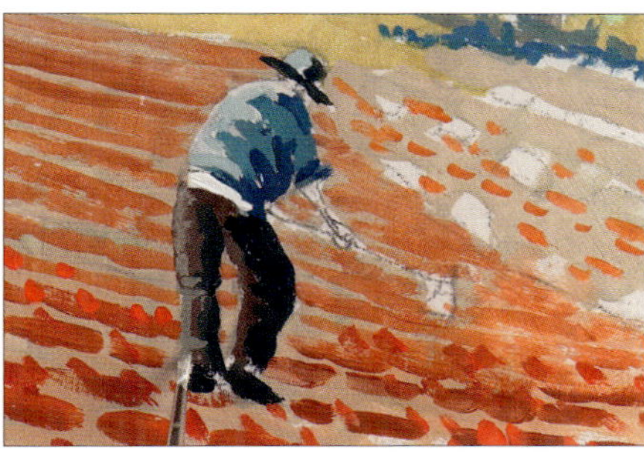

30 Mix burnt umber and white with a little cerulean blue to highlight the left-hand side of the trousers, to suggest creases.

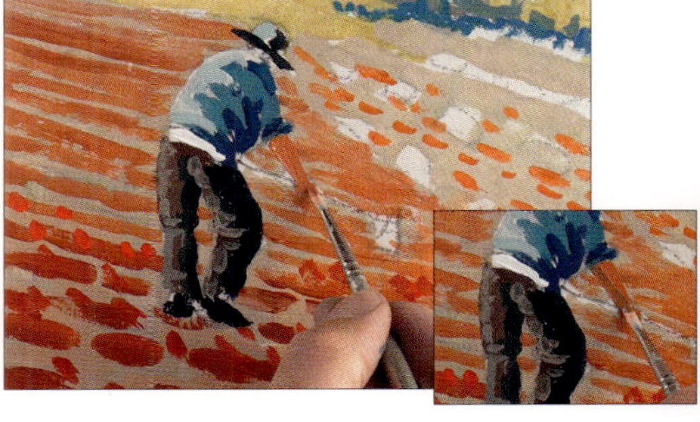

31 Mix burnt sienna and white to create a flesh tone for the arm, then shade this by adding burnt umber.

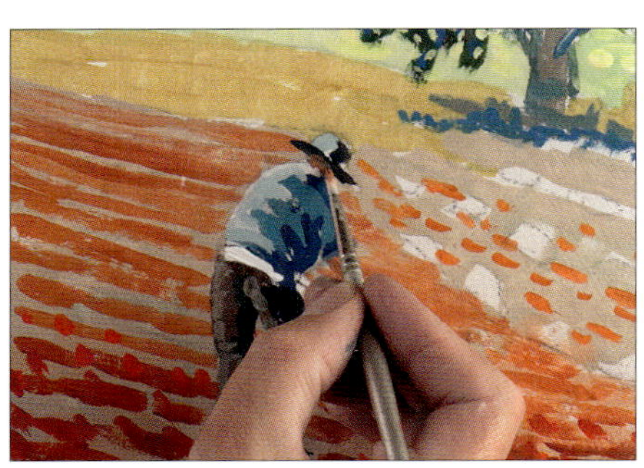

32 Paint the head with the same colour.

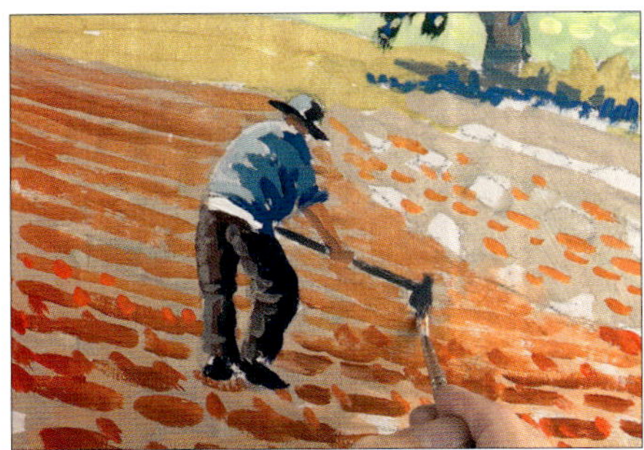

33 Add cerulean blue to the mix and paint the hoe.

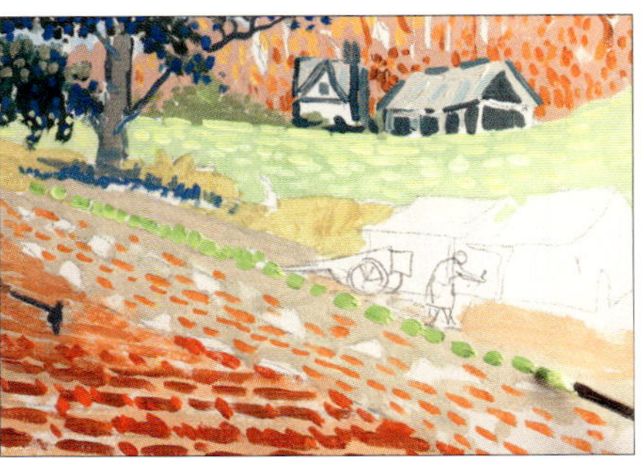

34 Mix lemon yellow with a little sap green and white and paint dots for the cabbages, making them larger as you come further forwards.

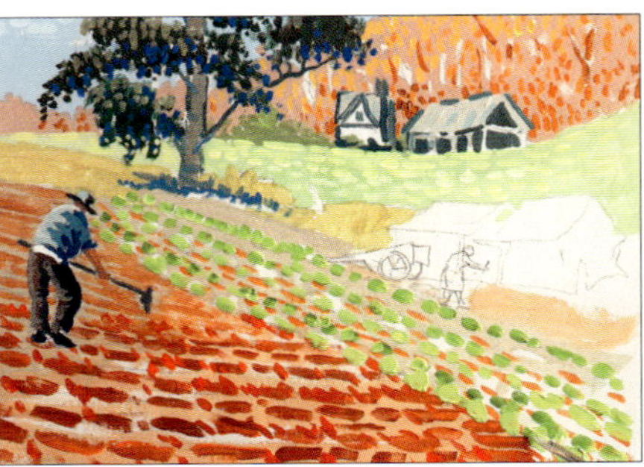

35 Continue adding more rows of cabbages. Pick up different shades of green on either side of the brush to create a streaky effect and make textured marks.

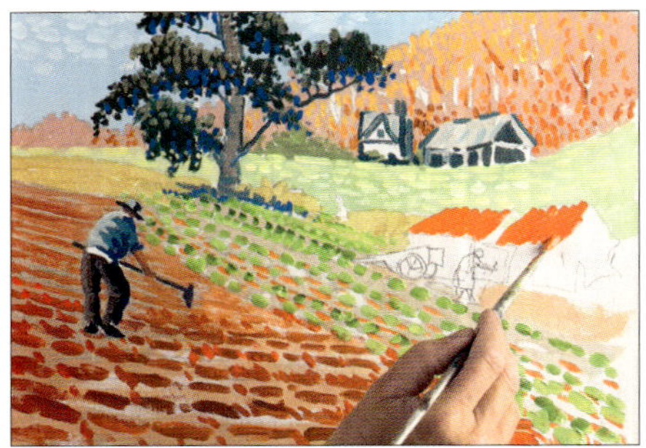

36 Paint the shed roof with burnt sienna and a little white, using the no. 6 flat brush.

37 Add more white and some cadmium orange, and paint strokes to suggest tiles.

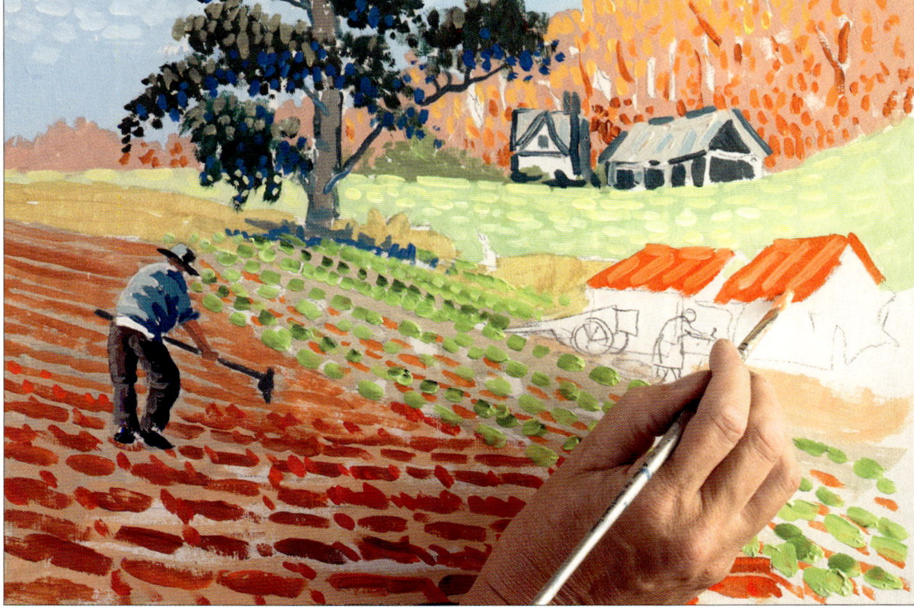

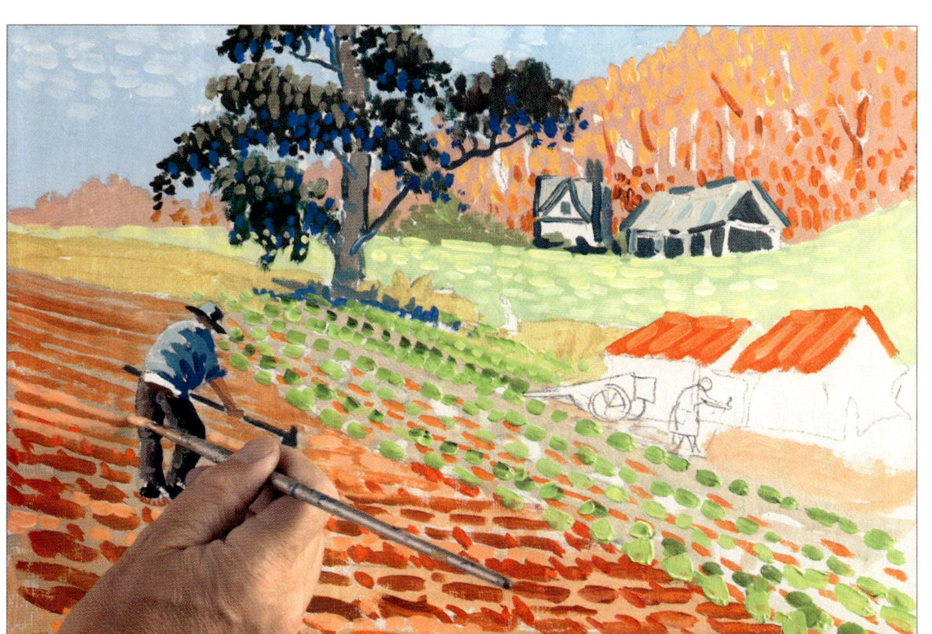

38 Use the same colour to paint dots and dashes in the soil, filling gaps and adding texture.

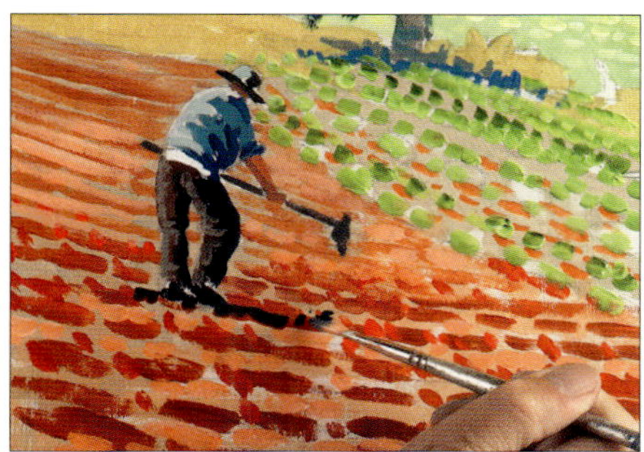

39 Paint the man's cast shadow with burnt sienna and cerulean blue.

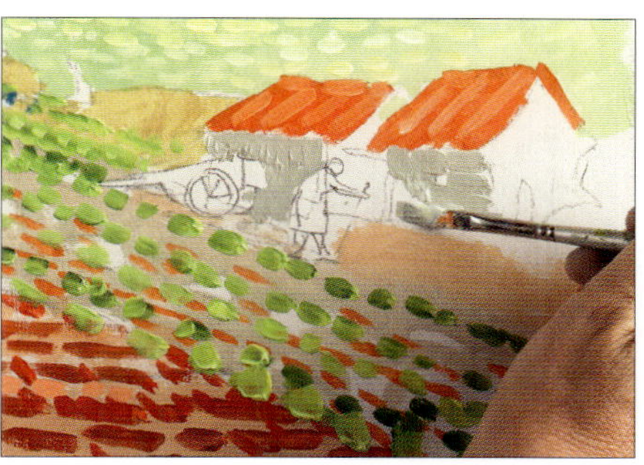

40 Add this mix to white and paint the front of the shed with thick paint for a streaky, textured effect.

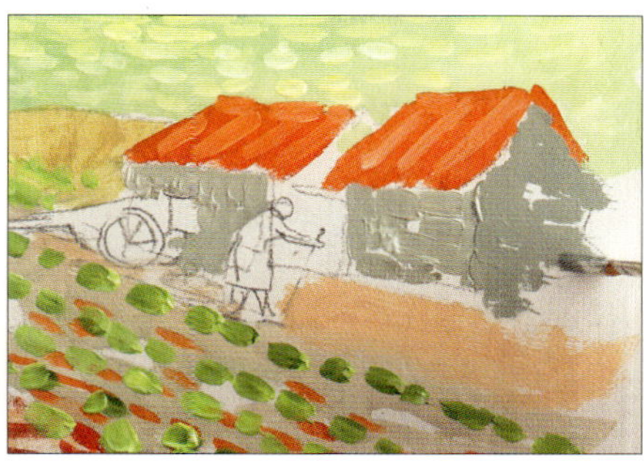

41 Add more cerulean blue to darken the mix a little and paint the shadowed side of the shed.

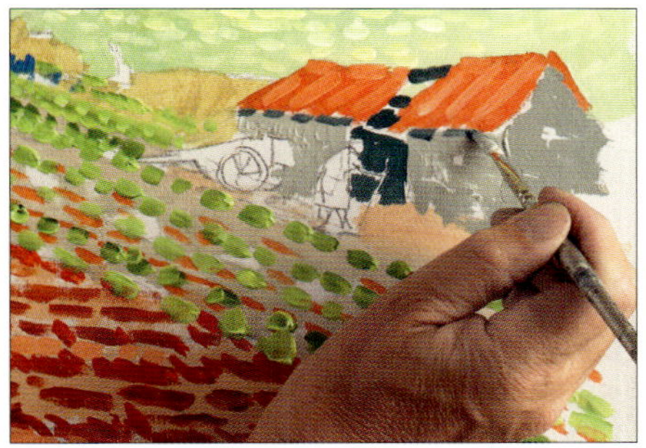

42 Add more cerulean blue and burnt sienna to paint the darks inside the shed. Paint carefully round the figure. Add shadow under the eaves.

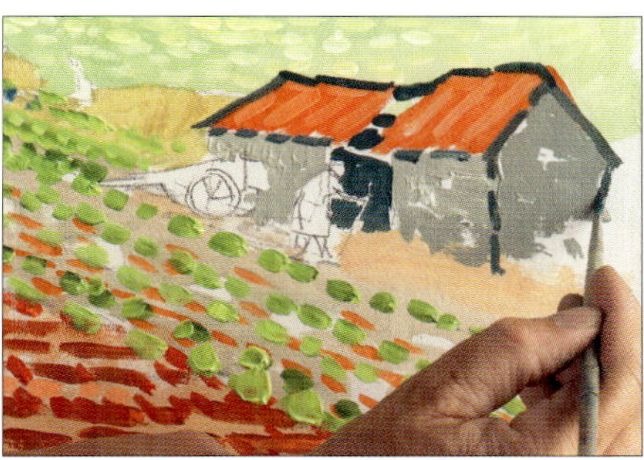

43 Change to the no. 2 round brush and paint an outline for the building using the same dark colour.

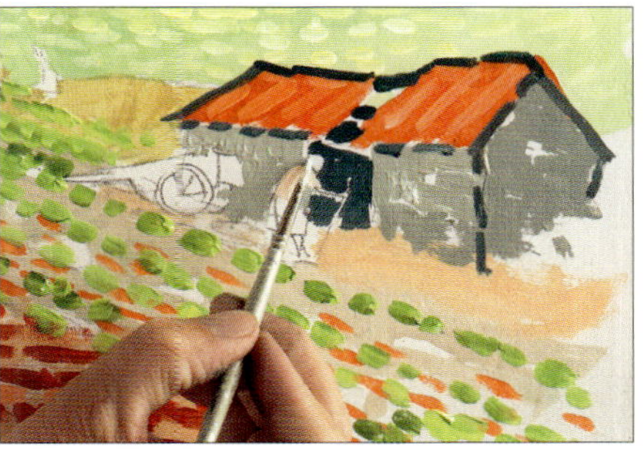

44 Mix white with a little Naples yellow to paint the top of the woman. Add a touch of cerulean blue to paint her right-hand side and her hair.

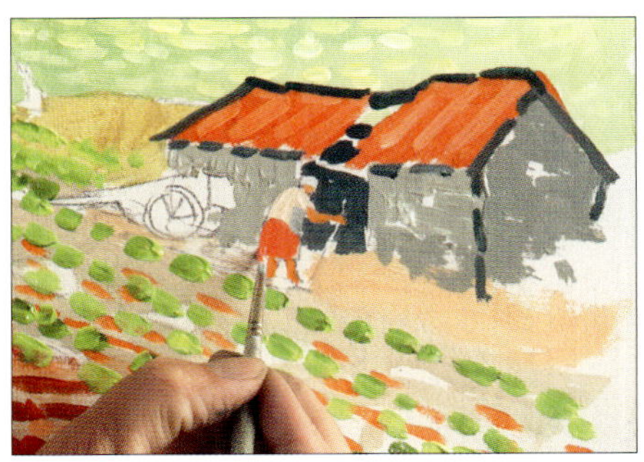

45 Mix burnt sienna and cadmium orange to paint the face, arm and legs, then paint the skirt in cadmium red light with a little white.

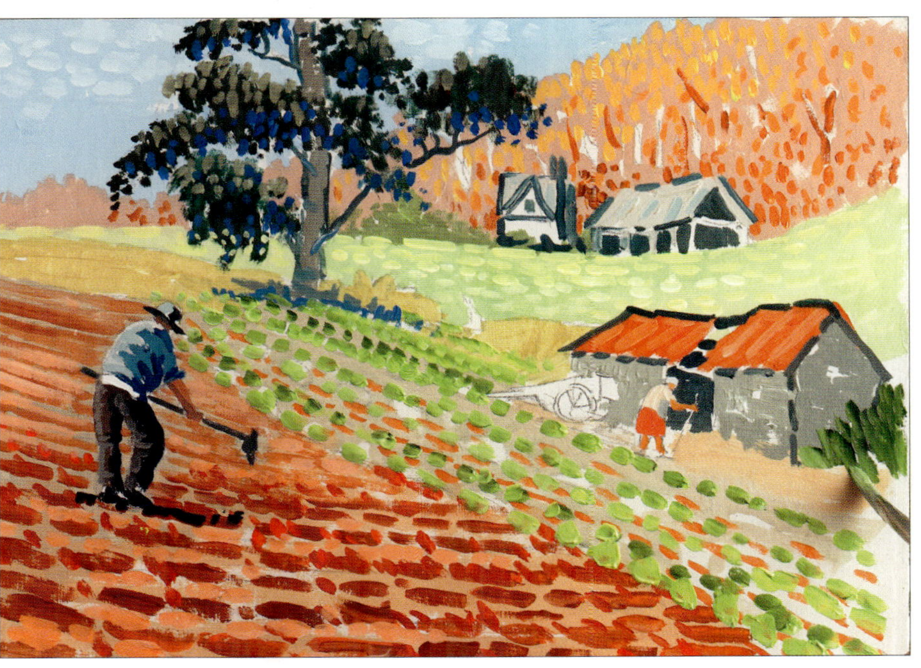

46 Paint the foliage on the right of the shed with sap green and a little white on the no. 12 flat brush.

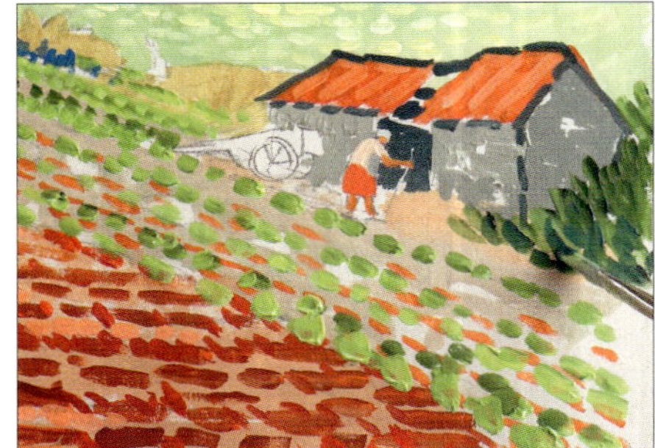

47 Add a little phthalo blue to the green mix and paint the darker parts of the foliage.

48 Shade the right-hand sides of some of the cabbages with the same mix.

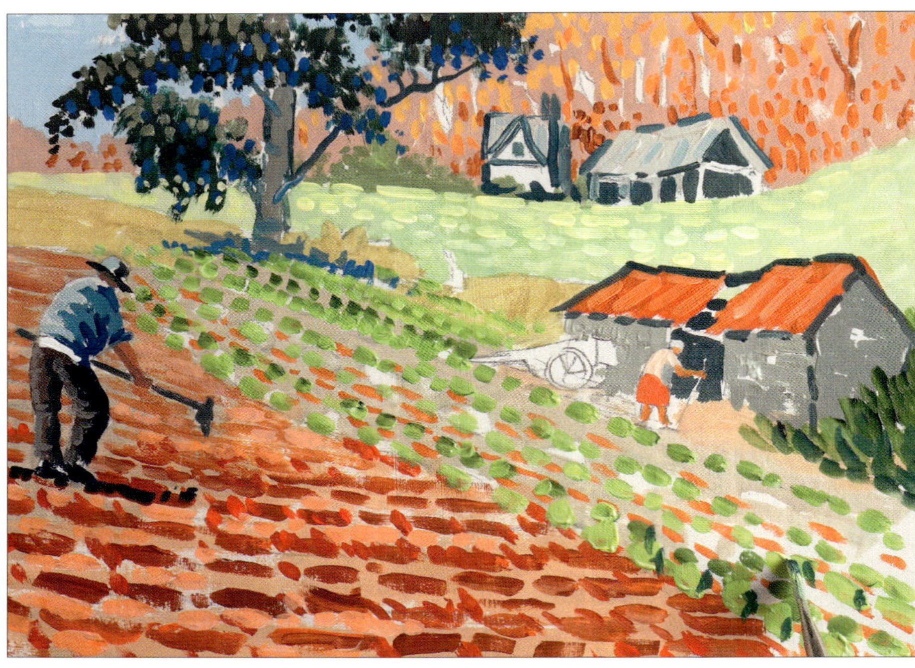

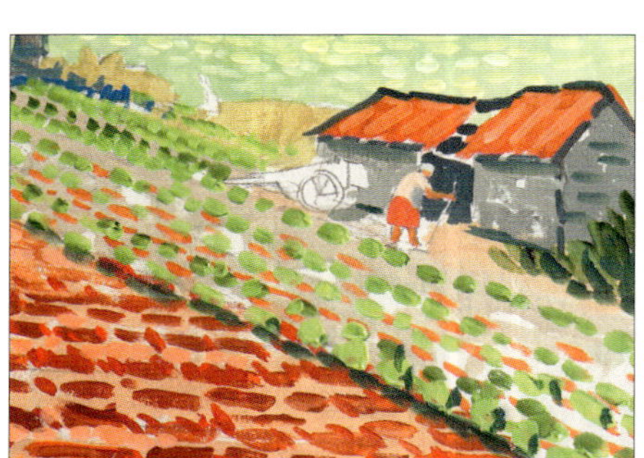

49 Paint shadow under the cart with a grey mixed from white, burnt sienna and cerulean blue. Paint dashes on the shed to suggest stones, using the dark green mix.

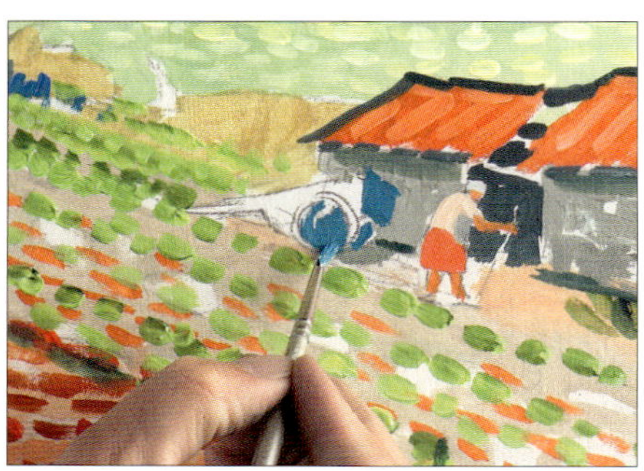

50 To paint the cart, mix phthalo blue, lemon yellow and white and use the no. 2 round to paint the shaded parts.

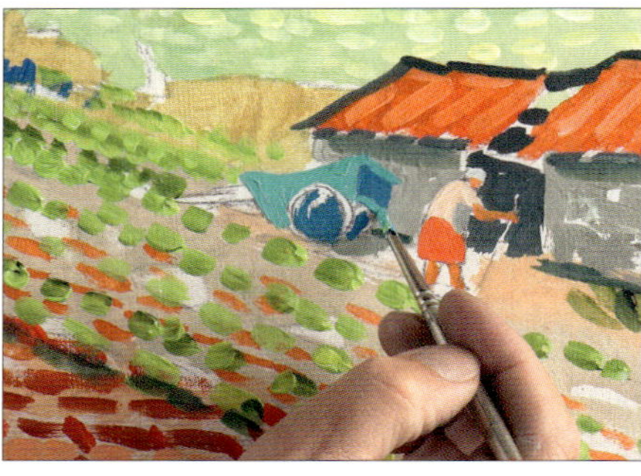

51 Add white to paint the lighter side of the cart.

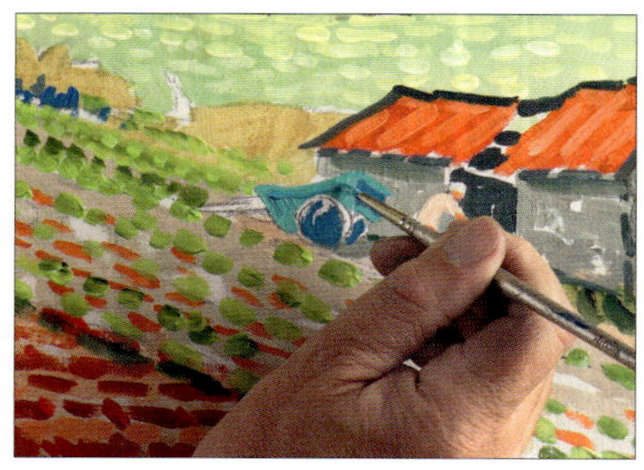

52 Use the darker mix again to suggest woodwork.

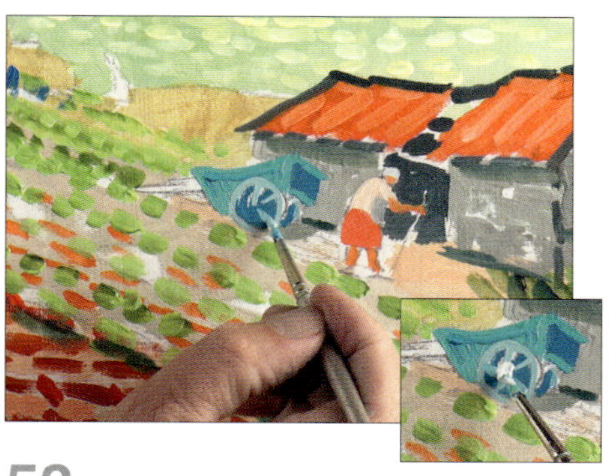

53 Mix phthalo blue, burnt sienna and white for a pale grey, and paint the wheel rim and spokes, then paint the hub in white.

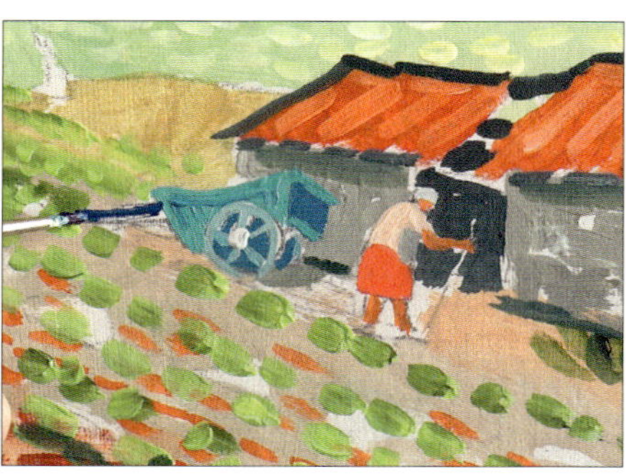

54 Return to the dark blue to paint the handles.

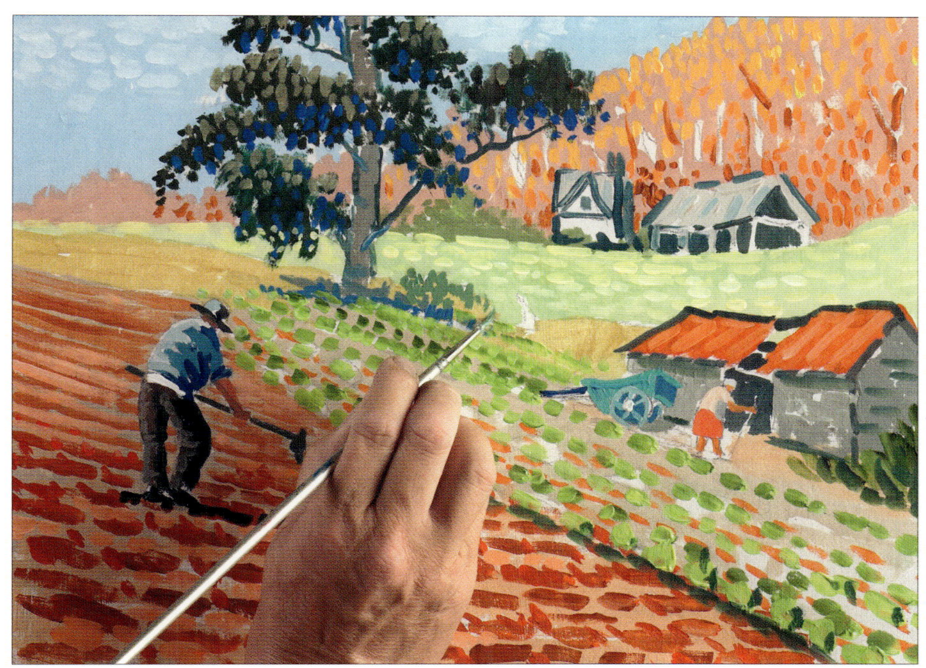

55 Add lemon yellow, burnt sienna and white to the dark blue mix to make a dark green and paint stabbing strokes under the tree.

56 Add a little more white to the mix and paint tiny dashes to the left of the tree, implying distant crops.

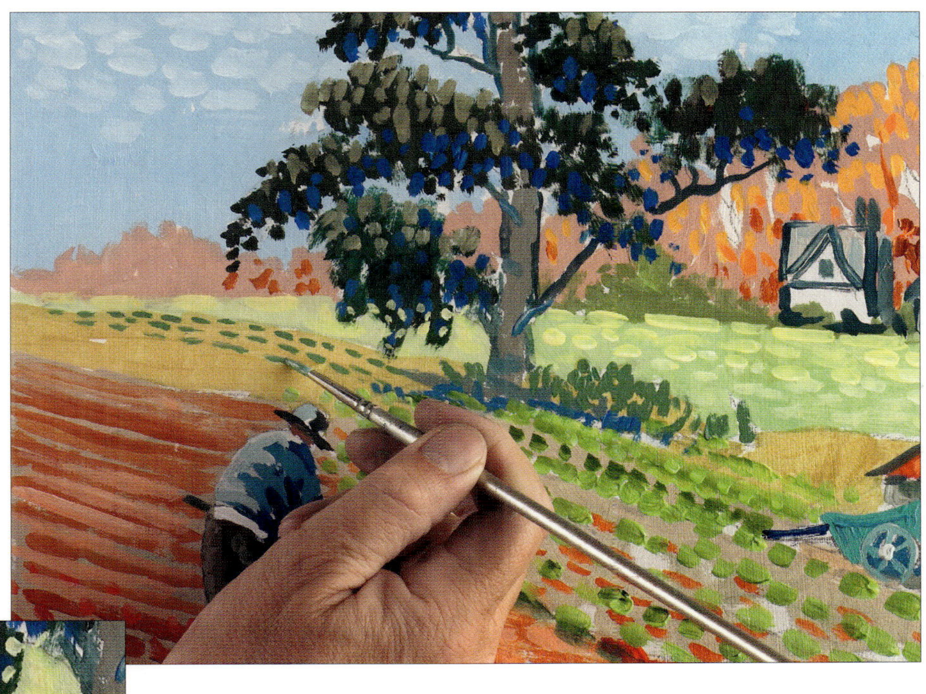

57 Paint white on the left-hand side and brim of the man's hat, add a collar to his shirt and white lines for highlights down his back.

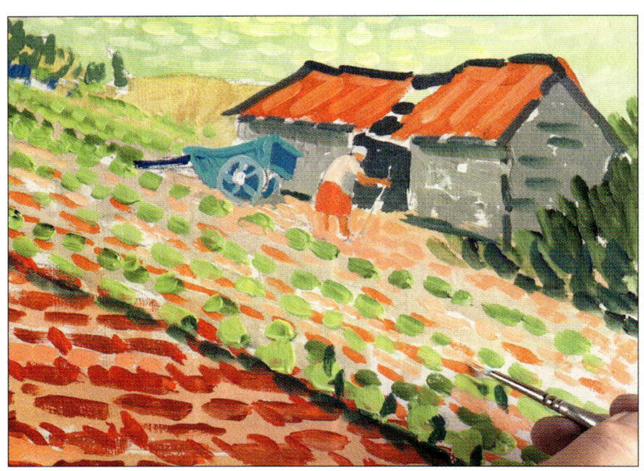

58 Mix burnt sienna and white to tidy around the woman, and to add light touches to the soil.

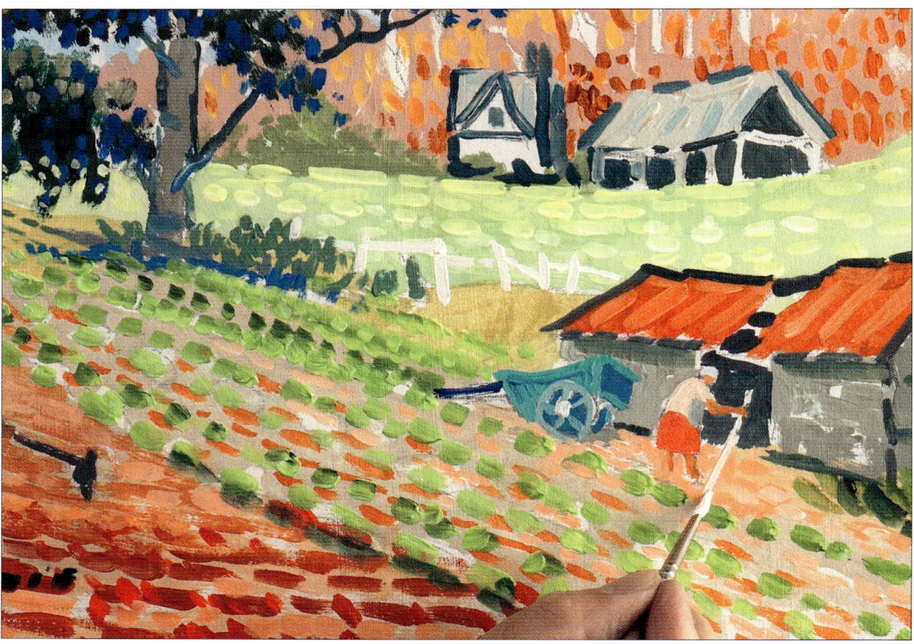

59 Paint the fence and the woman's stick in white.

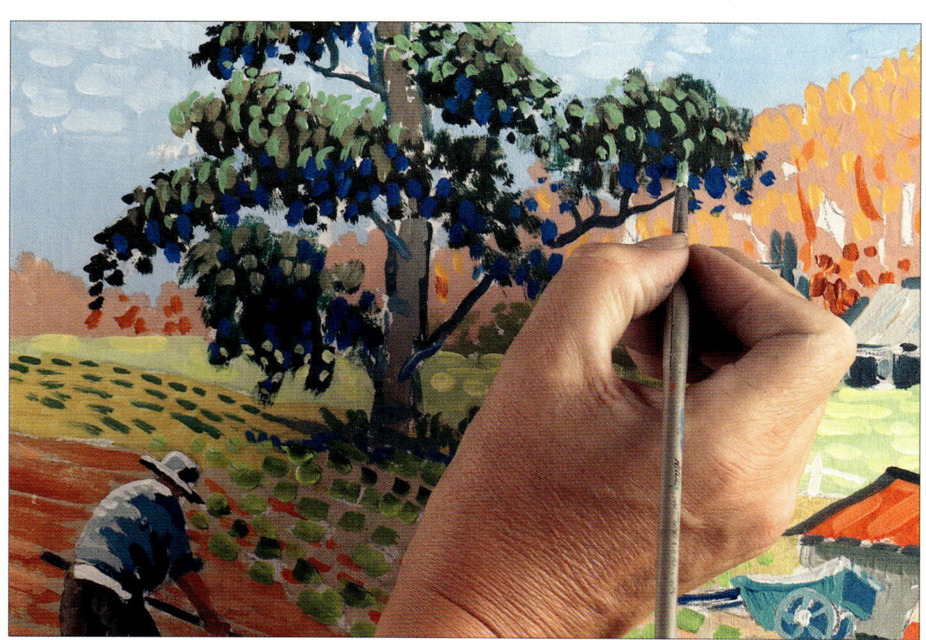

60 Stand back from the painting at this point and add any details you feel are necessary. I added white to the top of the cart and to the main figure's sock. I also mixed lemon yellow a hint of sap green and burnt sienna and painted dabs of this colour on the tree.

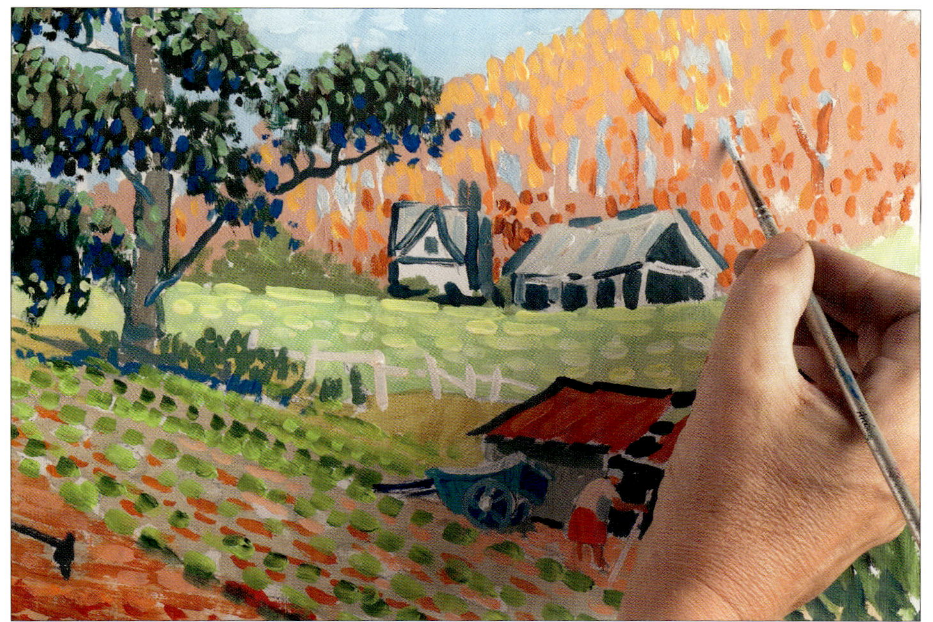

61 Mix white with a touch of cerulean blue to suggest gaps in the autumn trees where the low sky shows through. Paint long strokes and dabs.

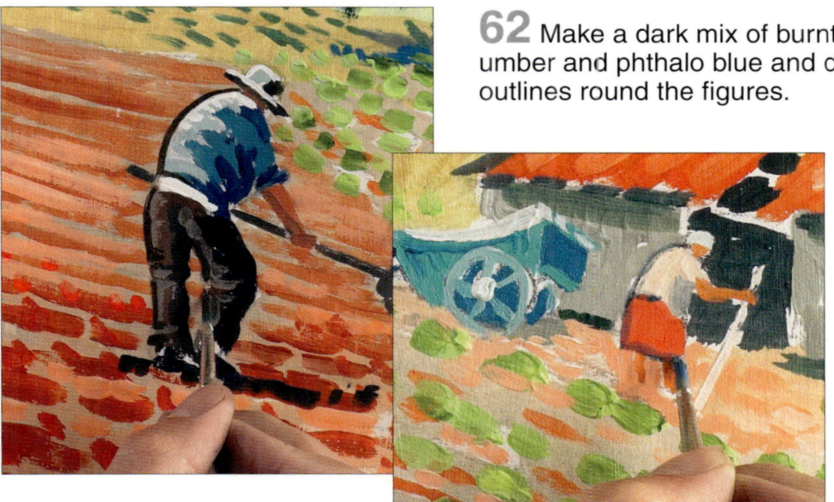

62 Make a dark mix of burnt umber and phthalo blue and draw outlines round the figures.

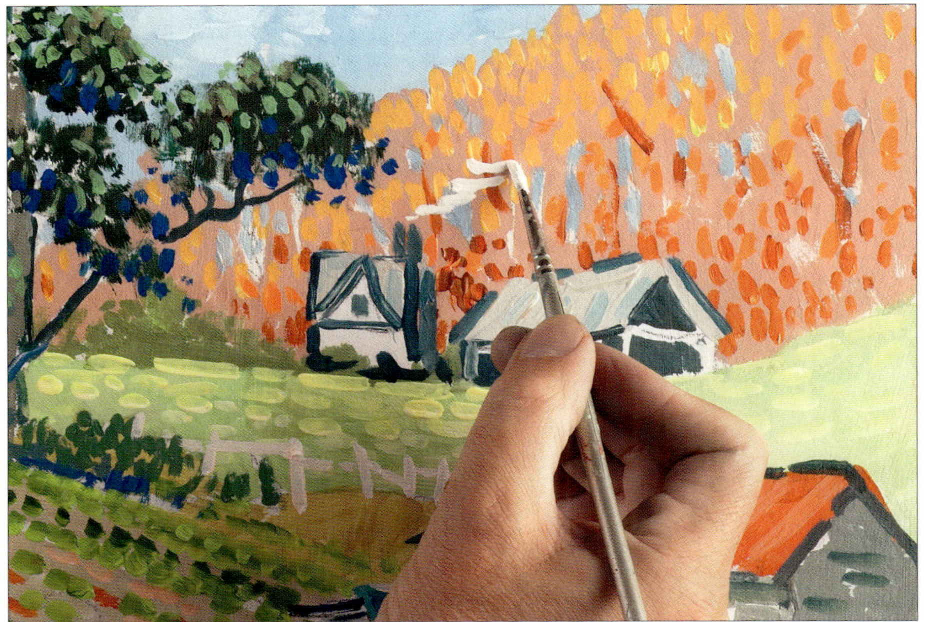

63 Finally, paint white smoke coming from the distant chimney with horizontal strokes of the no. 2 round brush.

Overleaf

The finished painting.

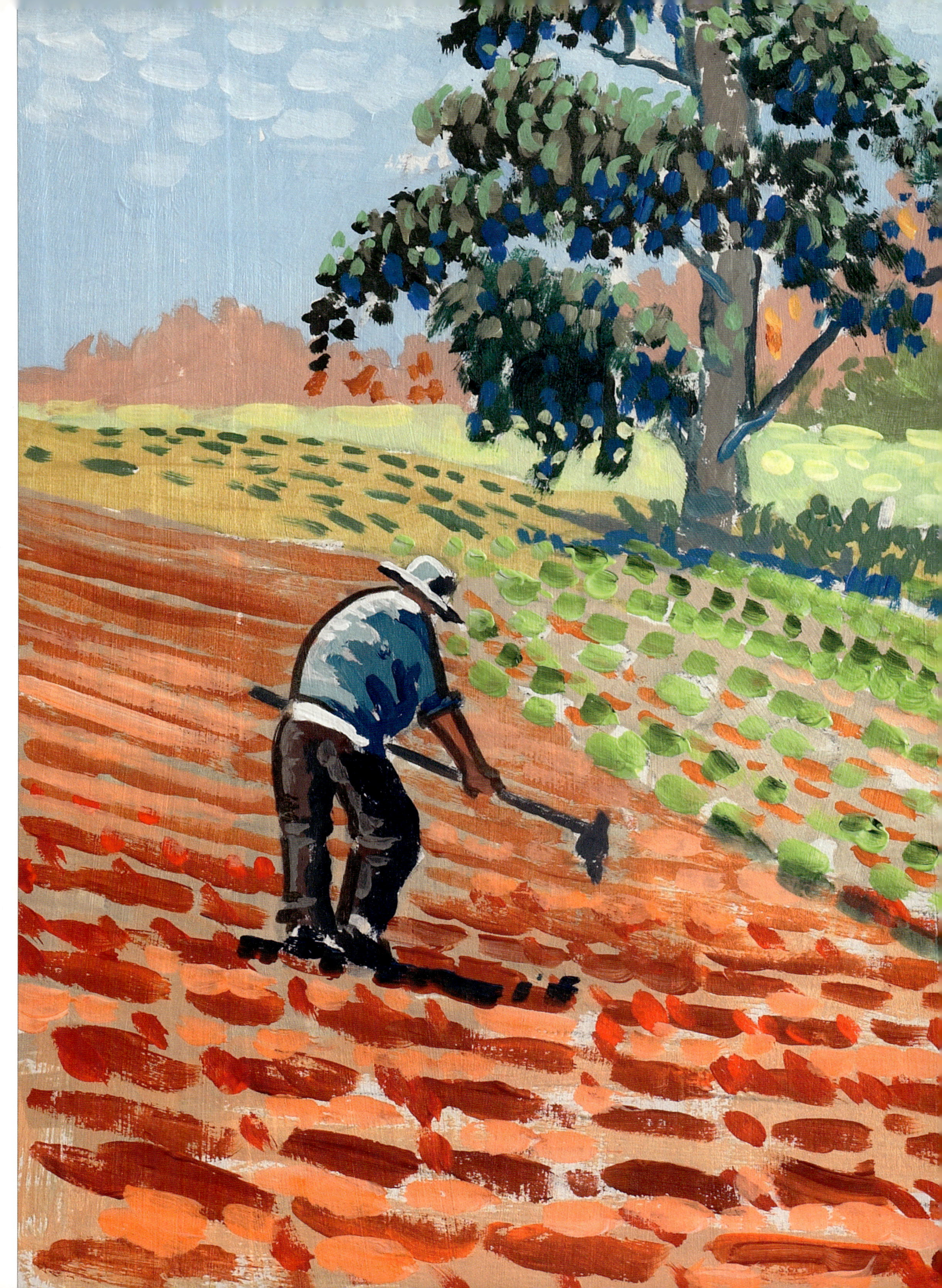